3/2019

WITHDRAWN

D003174·3

THURSDAY NIGHT LIGHTS

NUMBER FORTY-SEVEN

*Jack and Doris Smothers Series in
Texas History, Life, and Culture*

# Thursday Night Lights

*The Story of Black High School Football in Texas*

MICHAEL HURD

University of Texas Press
AUSTIN

Publication of this work was made possible in part by support
from the J. E. Smothers, Sr., Memorial Foundation and the
National Endowment for the Humanities.

Requests for permission to reproduce material from this work should be sent to:
    Permissions
    University of Texas Press
    P. O. Box 7819
    Austin, TX 78713–7819
    utpress.utexas.edu/rp-form

♾ The paper used in this book meets the minimum requirements
of ANSI/NISO Z39.48–1992 (R1997) (Permanence of Paper).

LIBRARY OF CONGRESS CATALOGING-IN-PUBLICATION DATA

Names: Hurd, Michael, 1949– author.
Title: Thursday night lights : the story of Black high school football in Texas /
    Michael Hurd.
Description: First edition. | Austin : University of Texas Press, 2017. | Includes
    bibliographical references and index.
Identifiers: LCCN 2017012988
    ISBN 978-1-4773-1830-0 (pbk : alk. paper)
    ISBN 978-1-4773-1484-5 (library e-book)
    ISBN 978-1-4773-1485-2 (non-library e-book)
Subjects: LCSH: Prairie View Interscholastic League (Tex.) | Football—Texas—
    History—20th century. | School sports—Texas—History—20th century. |
    Discrimination in sports—Texas—History—20th century. | African American
    football players—Texas—History—20th century. | African American football
    coaches—Texas—History—20th century.
Classification: LCC GV959.52.T4 H87 2017 | DDC 796.3309764—dc23
LC record available at https://lccn.loc.gov/2017012988

doi:10.7560/310342

# Contents

*For my late parents, James D. Hurd, Sr. (Pemberton High School, Marshall, TX, ca. 1937), and Emily Jean Baxter Hurd (Dunbar High School, Texarkana, TX, 1943).*

*For my running buddies—here's to the good times when we were young and attending PVIL athletic events— Claude Edwards, Lorenzo "The Hog" Houston, and Donald Ray Palmer.*

*For all of the coaches, players, administrators, students, and teachers who made the PVIL experience unique and successful.*

*To my good buddy, Terry Huffman, may he rest in peace.*

# Introduction

Immediately across the street from the Evan E. Worthing High School campus in south Houston, where Reed Road greets Scott Street, a roadside gauntlet of strategically spaced hitchhikers would line Scott headed north from Sunnyside to Third Ward in the late afternoon, shortly after school recessed for the day at three o'clock. Their destination was Jeppesen Stadium, Houston's public school football arena, which was nested on the corner of Scott and Wheeler on the eastern fringe of Third Ward, the cultural and entertainment hub for black Houstonians.

Raised thumbs jabbed the air as the hitchhikers stared down the occupants of every vehicle, hoping to recognize at least one friendly face that would surely offer a ride, though thuggish types gave more a threatening, menacing scowl as the would-be passengers shouted the question of the day, "Goin' Third Ward?!"

As a matter of fact, at that time of day, on a Wednesday or Thursday in the fall when the 1960s Worthing Colts had a Prairie View Interscholastic League (PVIL) football game scheduled, it seemed just about every able body in Sunnyside was Third Ward–bound, and most of the cars and their passengers—hitchhikers too—were adorned with some kind of green-and-gold clothing or trinket. Giggling teenage girls standing at bus stops shook pom-poms back and forth, their green-and-gold strands having survived the afternoon's pep rally, and similar strands knotted to car radio antennas flew freely in the breeze, creating a flickering green-and-gold stream as the vehicle accelerated. A nonfootball athlete making his way to the game might sport a bright green letterman's pullover sweater emblazoned with a centered yellow *H* with the word "Worthing" sewn in green across its bar.

My game-day road to Jeppesen began amid the mania of three

teenagers—my sister, brother, and me—scrambling to get ready for school, taking turns in the bathroom, and mother putting lunch bags together, though she also had to get ready for school, teaching second-graders at Kay Elementary, and dad having coffee as he read Mickey Herskowitz's column in the *Houston Post* sports section. From the kitchen, Clifton "King Bee" Smith's ever-cheerful voice from radio station KCOH blasted through the speakers of our General Electric clock radio, stationed on the kitchen sink's tiled counter and reverberating throughout our bandbox of a three-bedroom house. Houston had two major black radio stations, KCOH and KYOK, and we would go back and forth, listening to both, but on game-day mornings it was usually "King Bee," who agitated fans about that evening's game while alternately spinning the latest R&B tunes from Motown, Stax, and Don Robey's Peacock label. King Bee would take phone calls from listeners, but in between the rants of alumni and students defending their teams, he would sing a taunting tune (it sounded something like Duane Eddy's "Raunchy") about the outcome of the night's game, for example, "Yates gonna beat the devil outta Worthing, Yates gonna beat the devil outta Worthing." I would go off to school with that damned tune rattling around my brain, and it would still be there while I sat in math class trying to make sense of algebraic equations. After school, I would walk home with my transistor radio earplug in place, listening to KCOH's late-afternoon DJ, Skipper Lee Frazier, who was "bringing a mountain of soul to Houston," as he rapped in the show's intro from an audience-friendly studio walled with a semicircle of large vertical panes of tinted plate glass facing Almeda Road on Third Ward's western border. When you passed by and waved, Skipper Lee returned the favor with a deep, cackling laugh and responded on air, "Hey, hey, Chevrolet!"

My dad, a welder, had played football in Marshall, Texas, at Pemberton High School in the late 1930s. He was a huge sports fan. On nights when Worthing's games didn't conflict with his night shift at the Armco Steel Mill in Pasadena, he would gladly toss me the keys to the big Pontiac Grand Prix and away I would go, picking up my running buddies Donald Ray, Claude, and Lorenzo "the Hog," and maybe we would pack in a hitchhiker or three, all in the name of school pride. On game nights, south Houston high school football fans motored, thumbed, walked, or bused their way for five miles up Scott Street to Third Ward, bouncing and bumping across the railroad tracks at Holmes Road, through South Union, with its bustle of black businesses and middle-class homes, over Old Spanish Trail Road and through the heavily Jewish MacGregor neighborhood, with its stylish brick mansions, to Brays Bayou, before finally catching a glimpse of the stadium lights' halo glowing brightly against the early-evening sky.

And then you were inside. The game began, and what you saw, what you have heard about, what you will be talking about in homeroom the next day at school and maybe for years to come unfolded in a tapestry of athleticism, speed, power, and showmanship, all to the beats of thundering bass drums and blaring brass sections from dueling school bands seated in the stands on diagonally opposite sides of the field. The faces were black—players, coaches, officials, the great majority of fans—and represented Houston's black communities, which descended on Jeppesen to cheer their neighborhood teams: Third Ward had the Yates Lions, Fifth Ward was for the Phillis Wheatley Wildcats, North Houston had the Kashmere Gardens Rams, Independence Heights was Booker T. Washington Eagles territory, Sunnyside had Worthing, and from the Gulf Coast came visitors like Charlton-Pollard and Hebert from Beaumont, Port Arthur Lincoln, and Galveston Central.

Jeppesen was the Houston Independent School District's public school football facility, a dirty, beige-colored concrete edifice named as a nod to Holger Jeppesen, the district's former board president and a failed mayoral candidate who vigorously lobbied for the structure's 1941 development adjacent to the newly opened University of Houston campus. The school district teamed with FDR's Works Progress Administration to build the $650,000 stadium, and Jeppesen was all for that, though he had been "ornery", as one board member recalled, when arguing against the board spending money to establish the nation's first PBS station, KUHT, on the UH campus. (In its earliest days, the University of Houston was affiliated with Houston ISD.) Another board member described Jeppesen as "a man of no education" who was "only interested in athletics." Jeppesen may have given credence to that description in 1952 when he lobbied against KUHT, which went on the air the next year. Jeppesen was certainly gung ho about the stadium, a 22,000-seat facility that opened on September 18, 1942. In the first game, Houston Lamar beat Dallas Adamson 26–7. Over the next thirty years, Jeppesen was home for high school football in Houston, including the annual Thanksgiving showdown between Wheatley and Yates, which drew an estimated forty thousand fans in 1961, then a national record for a high school football game. The stadium was known as the Houston Public School Athletic Field until 1958, when the school board voted to rename it after Jeppesen.

The stadium sat on a sixty-acre tract bordered by Holman Street to the north, Cullen to the east, Wheeler to the south, and Scott to the east. Scott was a major artery of asphalt potholes connecting the growing black communities from Third Ward south to Sunnyside. The stadium and its field house were one block east of the all-black high school named after the minister, community leader, and former slave John Henry "Jack" Yates, the first pastor of Antioch Baptist Church, established in 1866, the first black Baptist church in Houston. The crimson-and-gold Jack Yates High School Lions had a perfect home-field advantage, and a walking commute to observe competing PVIL teams and even Friday-night action.

Alphonse Dotson, a lineman for Yates, talked about those gatherings: "We would go over to Jeppesen and watch the [white] schools play on Friday nights. Hell, we could play with them and play well, hold our own. We would have done well against them, but that they kept us separate was for a different reason. We'd also have some camaraderie with guys from [PVIL schools] across town, might have a fight. But, as long as you weren't courting a girl from somebody else's neighborhood you were fine. You wanted to win when you played against them, but you wanted them to do well afterwards."

The stadium stood as a buffer between the Houston College for Negroes, just getting its start by holding night classes at Yates, to the southwest on Wheeler, and segregated UH immediately to the northeast on Cullen. By 1947, the College for Negroes had begun developing its own campus, and Wheeler ran through the center of what would become Texas Southern University.

The Wednesday- and Thursday-night games I saw at Jeppesen, the players and coaches, were what I knew about high school football. So I was puzzled the first time I heard the phrase "Friday night lights." And as I researched this book, I found that I was not alone in that reaction, since most of the former PVIL players and coaches I spoke with around the state agreed the term had little to no meaning for them. Most black high schools in Texas played on nights other than Fridays unless they had their own facility, but only a few did, such as Texarkana Dunbar. Its Buffalo Stadium was located behind Theron Jones Elementary School, and during lunchtime my classmates and I chased one another around the field. On game nights, I would wander through the gravel-and-red-clay parking lot, look for my parents, and pass visiting players in dirty, sweaty togs kissing their cheerleader girlfriends before boarding buses for the trip home. (I thought that was pretty cool.) White schools had priority for the Friday-night use of public stadiums shared with black schools. Asked about Jeppesen Stadium's use, a stunned former PVIL football player responded as though the place was the PVIL schools' private domain: "You mean they used that stadium on Friday nights?"

I remember a cold, drizzly December night in 1961 at Jeppesen. I was twelve, and sat bundled up next to my dad in the stands as Orsby Crenshaw and the Austin L. C. Anderson Yellow Jackets won a 20–13 contest against Yates for the PVIL Class 4A state championship. Anderson was coached by Raymond Timmons, who that night bested the great Andrew "Pat" Patterson, whose team had come into the game undefeated. It would be the last of four state titles for the Yellow Jackets, and the only state championship game I ever witnessed.

That was my high school football experience growing up, attending segregated schools in the 1960s.

It had nothing to do with Friday night lights.

More to the point, as one PVIL alum put it, "Friday night lights? That's white folks."

This book is about "black folks" who coached and played high school football behind the veil of segregation in Texas for half a century, 1920–1970, as members of the all-black Prairie View Interscholastic League, whose games were played primarily on Wednesday and Thursday nights in most towns, Tuesdays in others, some on Saturdays, but rarely on prime-time Friday nights, when games for white schools were played. The book's title, *Thursday Night Lights*, is not just a riff on "Friday night lights," but also identifies a defining reality of high school football games played in racially charged times when even the midweek scheduling of games for black teams carried a "less than" feel. The PVIL's genesis was as the Texas Interscholastic League of Colored Schools, organized three years after white policemen and citizens' mistreatment of black soldiers from the Twenty-Fourth US Infantry led to the horror—seventeen people shot and killed—of the Camp Logan mutiny and Houston riot of 1917, and folded in 1970, one year after the University of Texas fielded its last all-white football team.

Emotionally, I have been writing this book since adolescence, and the first time I saw PVIL greatness up close and personal in David Lattin and Otis Taylor, Worthing and Sunnyside heroes. I remember a profusely sweating "Big Daddy D" jogging coolly in his own world around the school track on a hot spring day to whatever groovy tunes were streaming through his transistor radio earplug, and Taylor, back in the 'hood, sitting at the wheel of his brand-new candy-apple-red Thunderbird convertible as the fellas in Reedwood took a break from playing basketball to crowd around and admire the vehicle after he signed his rookie contract with the Kansas City Chiefs. Both guys would show up on the big stage. Lattin threw down a monster dunk to set the tone for Texas Western's destruction of Adolph Rupp's Kentucky Wildcats in the 1966 NCAA championship game, an upset for the ages that is credited with ushering in the recruitment of more blacks by previously all-white programs. Taylor, a strong but graceful receiver, was among the cadre of players from historically black colleges who helped bring the American Football League to life. In Super Bowl IV, Otis, a prototypical big, fast receiver, caught a short pass from Len Dawson, broke tackles by cornerback Earsell Mackbee and safety Karl Kassulke, and high-stepped down the right sideline to the end zone, securing the Chiefs' 23–7 upset win over Minnesota.

David and Otis were local heroes, and I followed their careers, but I had a vested interest in following other PVIL football players from the Houston area, too, as a fan and then as a sportswriter. I read team depth charts and player bios, noted high school affiliations, and had flashbacks of sitting in the stands at Jeppesen while watching some of those teams play. *Thursday Night Lights* reveals the PVIL quilt that was a patchwork of athletic, academic, and social achievements pieced together for a black community striving to succeed, to take care of its own despite the era's racism. For me, its history became a simmering narrative bred in familiarity, born from segregation.

I had to tell this story.

In spite of the times and conditions during the PVIL's tenure, when it closed shop in 1970, it could look back on a wealth of success stories and a football legacy that remains one of the most important—and unheralded—in the evolution of the black community in Texas. Many of its leaders and heroes participated in league events—athletics, academics, and music—representing schools that paid homage to national, state, and local black history figures: Booker T. Washington, Phillis Wheatley, H. B. Pemberton, Carter G. Woodson, John Henry "Jack" Yates, George Washington Carver, Paul Laurence Dunbar, L. C. Anderson. The PVIL produced students who became historic figures: the legislators Barbara Jordan and Mickey Leland, both from Wheatley High School in Houston; the Pearl Harbor hero Doris "Dorie" Miller, from Waco Moore; Heman Sweatt, from Yates, who successfully challenged the University of Texas Law School's separate-but-equal policy in 1950, leading to the school's integration; and General Marcelite Harris, from Kashmere Gardens, the first black female general in the air force, to name a few. Aspects of the PVIL experience are briefly mentioned in several books, but in high-school-football-mad Texas, the league has been tragically overlooked and undervalued, its coaches severely underrated, in part because of racist beliefs that black men lacked the intelligence necessary for competent leadership, discipline, and strategic thinking. There has never been an in-depth examination of the league's history or of the men who made the PVIL such a vibrant force in high school football. This neglect has occurred despite dozens of its players being among the most prominent in all of football history.

This book is meant to both remember and introduce the PVIL: what it was, why and how it came to be, why and how it came to an end. But mostly it presents some of the African American men and boys who coached and played high school football in Texas during an era of well-defined racial divisiveness, and shows how they went about the business of building successful careers that should have earned them widespread acclaim and respect, but did not. The work is hardly exhaustive—a rather thick encyclopedia would be required for that. Much of the PVIL's history has gone undocumented, even by the league.

Statistics for the league are few, since neither the PVIL nor its member schools emphasized the need to capture and maintain game, season, or career statistics. The league's official documentation doesn't go much deeper than yearly results of state championship games. This lack of data left me at the mercy of aging memories and myths. For example, Houston Washington's Eldridge Dickey is considered perhaps the best quarterback the PVIL produced, yet there is no official documentation of his stats, only stories about his abilities. That pattern is repeated throughout the book. Bubba Smith, another example, was an incredible defender, yet there are no official numbers about tackles made, just plenty of stories about his dominance. It is the same with coaches, though some newspaper accounts provide career wins and losses in feature stories celebrating a coach's retirement or in his obituary. But there are no official lists of most coaching wins, all-time leading rushers or passers, and so forth.

The late coach Walter Day's work *Remembering the Past with Pride: Organized High School Football for Blacks in Texas* was a godsend, with its newspaper clippings of PVIL playoff games. He had gone to Corsicana Jackson High School and Samuel Huston College (now Huston-Tillotson) in Austin, and then, after graduating in 1950, returned to Jackson to teach biology and begin a coaching career that included stops at Worthing and Fort Worth Terrell, where he retired from coaching in 1968. Day won three PVIL 2A state championships (1953, 1956, 1957) and eight district titles while at Jackson, and led Terrell to the 4A championship game in 1965, but the team was defeated 18–0 by Yates. He went on to serve as vice principal and later as principal at Terrell, assistant director of secondary education, and then director of pupil personnel for the Fort Worth Independent School District. He was principal of O. D. Wyatt High School until his retirement in 1986. Retirement meant that Day could devote full time to researching and writing a history of the PVIL, which he did for almost ten years. His resulting books included *Texas Black High School Champions before 1940: Football / Basketball / Track & Field* and *Championship Football for Blacks in Texas, 1940–1969: 4A, 3A, 2A, A.* In 2005, Day's work and persistence paid off when the University Interscholastic League for the first time officially included records from the PVIL competitions, by using Day's compilations. The coach took great pride: "It's about time. We wanted to be recognized and I wanted this information out there. I was inspired to do all that work, to make a contribution and I feel good knowing that without me, no one would have all this information."

We met only once before his death in 2011, and he was very supportive of my research, building on what he had accomplished. I was well aware of Coach Day's relentless drive to document the PVIL's history. He was outraged that much of that history had been destroyed when black schools closed in the transition to integration, and that many of the schools, as well as the PVIL itself, never consistently kept records, statistics, or histories. He crisscrossed the state, driving from library to library and copying newspaper clippings, which he bound and self-published in 1993.

In the introduction to *Remembering the Past with Pride,* he wrote: "Those who coached under the PVIL may be surprised to know that records of their achievements and those of outstanding young athletes have been misplaced and possibly lost. I consider this a historical atrocity. This may explain why many sports writers of today seem to ignore accomplishments of coaches under the PVIL."

The lack of official stats and in-depth coverage was a huge hindrance to researching this work, but listening to people's stories was not, and it is those voices that carry the book. There were many men with whom I was unable to connect, but the accounts included here give a good overview of, and insight into, the PVIL experience. The few speak for the many. In group meetings, former teammates and coaches gathered to tell me their stories, and through one-on-one telephone interviews, I was constantly impressed with their spirits—not just team camaraderie, but also a solid sense of family that has remained intact through several passing decades.

———

I first met the men of the PVIL Coaches Association in Austin at their 2007 Hall of Honor and Hall of Fame Banquet, an event that I have continued to attend annually. The organization diligently works to maintain and promote the league's history and to honor the men and women who excelled as athletes and coaches at all-black high schools. They were the prime references for me, guiding me toward information and connecting me with interview subjects. The banquets still inspire me, since I have the chance to meet the honorees and discover new stories. It is like sitting down at a family dinner because of the similar histories and relationships of the folks in attendance, who are from the same schools, towns, and competitions. It doesn't matter that no one outside of the cavernous hotel ballroom knows about the luminaries being lauded inside. It is humbling to see in one place so many men you have heard about and admired. Former teammates are reunited, and former foes embrace, laugh, and reminisce: "Hey, man, yeah, of course I remember you! Remember that game . . .?" For a couple of minutes, each gets to stand before his peers, family, and friends, accept a plaque noting his induction, and express gratitude to a higher power, to family, and to the

PVILCA for understanding, for someone finally saying, "We know what you went through, how you excelled, how you earned this moment." For most of them, it is the first time they have been publicly acknowledged to this extent, and their heartfelt and at times tearful words of thanks are incredibly moving, because everyone also knows the social struggles they survived in a racist system that denied and denigrated their hopes yet clearly did not douse their spirits.

Whatever the fiscal and social inequities, the PVIL created passionate, enthusiastic football rivalries. Underfunded schools overcame tremendous odds to succeed. The stories told here have historical value that will resonate around the state—and the nation. Records and trophies from the PVIL era may have been lost or discarded, but not so the voices and images, and I feel honored to present their stories here.

# CHAPTER 1

# The PVIL

## Emerging from the Shadows

*I was walking in downtown Conroe one day, and I was wearing my letterman's jacket. I passed a couple of white guys and heard one of them say, "They need to take that nigger coach Brown and let him coach the white team, 'cause these white boys ain't doin' nothin' and these niggers don't never lose."*

FRANK MOANING, Conroe Washington, 1960

### Montgomery County's Champions

Friday, September 5, 2014, was an evening of remembrance, recognition, and healing facilitated by high school football. The elderly black men clad in shimmering purple jerseys with gold numerals who proudly marched onto the field at Buddy Moorhead Stadium between the first and second quarters of the home opener for Conroe High School had been waiting, hoping for such a moment—their moment—for more than half a century. Earlier in the day, which the city had officially proclaimed "Booker T. Washington Bulldog Championship Day," Ellis Hubbard, Frank Moaning, head coach Charles Brown, and the other surviving members of two undefeated state-championship teams had been given rings at ceremonies honoring their teams' successes in 1960 and 1965. Those teams won a combined twenty-six games while losing none, but not for Conroe High School and not in this stadium, where, during that era, Friday-night high school football was an all-white affair.

If you wanted to see Brown and his Booker T. Washington High School Bulldogs of the Prairie View Interscholastic League back then, you had to travel three miles southeast of Moorhead, across US 75 to the other side of the Great Northern Railroad tracks, where Brown and his charges put together dynastic championship seasons at Conroe's high school for black kids and made Thursday nights winning time in Conroe. In a six-year span, no school in the Montgomery County area was better than the purple-and-gold Bulldogs, who from 1960 to 1965 were the dominant Class 2A team in the PVIL, the organization that governed athletic, academic, and music competitions for black high schools in Texas. Conroe played for the state championship in five out of six years, and in '60 and '65 crushed everybody unfortunate enough to line up against them on the way to the only state football championships in Conroe history, feats that were seen by many but heard about by few. White fans flocked to Bulldogs' games in standing-room-only numbers several layers deep, circling the field to experience the best show in a town that hadn't had that much to get excited about since the wildcatter George Strake hit a gusher that set off an oil boom in 1931 and a public frenzy worthy of a high school football state-championship celebration.

That was exactly the kind of reaction that you would expect after winning state in high-school-football-crazed Texas. Two state championships? Fast lane to immortality, team photos lining the walls of every Dairy Queen in the vicinity and maybe beyond, and players who would never have to pay for another chicken-fried steak dinner. The Conroe High School Tigers first fielded a football team in 1911. They still haven't won a state championship, and in the 1960s suffered the social indignity of taking a decided backseat to the black boys across the tracks, who won with regularity and won big, then sat back and waited for a fete . . . and waited . . . and waited. The Bulldogs had white fans, but even the power of high school football could not overcome ingrained racist practices. Brown and his players understood that fact in the sixties, but still couldn't avoid thinking of what should have been as they paraded in front of older and newer generations of appreciative, even if not idolizing, Conroe fans, black and white, seated together in a transformative scene.

"Back then," Hubbard reflected on segregation, "you knew what was going on."

———

Ellis Hubbard first picked up the game as a twelve-year-old. Conroe's black kids played whatever sport was in season—baseball in the summer, football in the fall, basketball whenever the weather was good. All the Conroe Bulldog football players could be found at the baseball diamond in the summer for Sunday-afternoon Little League games. In an age well before computers and television addiction, they never lacked for outside activities. For football, there was always encouragement from the big kids, the veterans, who mentored the up-and-coming, soon-to-be Bulldogs.

Hubbard described the expectations and sense of cohesion: "They'd played, and it was almost inevitable that I was going to play—same with the other guys. We knew we'd end up playing football. You didn't find kids getting in trouble that much. We knew each other, had summer jobs together, worked pretty hard hauling pulpwood, cutting wood, everything we could to be physical, get bigger and stronger. That was part of the challenge we put to ourselves, to get back there the next year."

Getting back "there" meant a return to the Class 2A playoffs and exacting revenge, perhaps, on Livingston Dunbar, which had bested Conroe in the 1959 quarterfinals, ending another run toward the state-championship game, which the Bulldogs had never reached. The 1960 team had many players returning, and they were single-minded in the quest for a breakthrough season. They had pledged as they walked off the field at Livingston, "We're going to win it all next year." It is a sentiment, in moments of defeat, with adrenaline raising levels of frustration, that has been and will be echoed by athletes ad infinitum, but it is a task always easier said than done. Yet few retreat from the challenge.

Hubbard laid it out: "It might have seemed like boasting, but we weren't going to accept defeat. We lost about eight players, but everyone coming back next year from that team was sophomores and juniors, so they'd be experienced seniors and juniors the next year. We had all the pieces in place." Hubbard, as quarterback, took the lead, but everyone on the team knew each position, how a play should develop, what was going to happen before it happened, and if a teammate was struggling or unsure of his assignment, he didn't need to ask for help. All the signs indicated that 1960 would be "our season."

And they were devoted to their leader. "Coach Brown was just like a father," according to Hubbard. "He knew our parents and they knew him. There wasn't much we could get away with, so we had to dedicate ourselves to doing what he required us to do. He was a mentor and just a very good person."

Brown lined the Bulldogs up in the single wing with Hubbard handling the ball in an offense that focused on the running game. Moaning was the blocking fullback. Hubbard rarely threw the ball in 1960, but in the previous season's T formation he had thrown a lot, though admittedly he was much better as a runner. Hubbard acknowledged that he was the reason for the switch: "They changed the offense just for me. The next year we went back to the T. But I was quarterback for one year, and we went all the way."

No brag, just fact. Washington breezed through the season. In several games the Bulldogs seemed unchallenged. Perhaps acknowledging that, Brown sought to test his team against overmatched Hearne Blackshear, slowing the pace in a defensive battle for the first half and then unleashing the Bulldogs after halftime. "Okay, this is your time," he told them as they left the locker room.

Hubbard picked up the pace immediately, returning the kickoff for a touchdown. Conroe put 60 points on the scoreboard for an easy win. For the season, he ran for 2,000 yards and scored 30 touchdowns. Hubbard understood what the coach was up to: "I think he just wanted to see what we could do if we were down. The hardest time we had was in practice. We got hit harder in practice than in the games. We were really hard on each other in practice."

———

Conroe stands forty miles north of Houston where the coastal plain meets the lush, green Piney Woods, which serve as cover for the vast East Texas oil deposits. Oil exploration was done by men like George Strake, a World War I veteran who got his start by working in the oil industry in Mexico. His good fortune in Montgomery County converted a quiet farming and timber community into a bustling hive of delirious citizens, anxious oil speculators, and prosperous new businesses, most of them oil related. Straddling State Highway 75, the town grew up at the junction of the International–Great Northern Railroad and the Gulf, Colorado and Santa Fe Railway. Its residents were descendants of the area's first white settlers, who in the 1830s made their way from states in the Deep South, with slaves in tow, to farm Texas's fertile, cotton-producing soil. As the Civil War approached, they pledged a deep loyalty to the Confederacy and their right to hold on to their slaves. Overwhelmingly, the populace favored secession. Before the war, slaves accounted for almost half the taxable property in Montgomery County, which includes Conroe. Two-thirds of the county's families owned chattel, one of the highest percentages of slaveholding in the state; the 2,106 black people in bondage in 1860 were valued at $1.3 million. When war broke out, Conroe and the rest of the county sent many of its men to join the fight as members of the Fourth Texas Regiment of Colonel John Bell Hood's Texas Brigade, the only Texans who fought in the eastern theater (Virginia). Two-thirds of them ended up dead or maimed. Ironically, the Confederate-leaning town was named after the Union Civil War veteran Captain Isaac Conroe, who came to the area in 1866 and opened a sawmill and a nearby commissary, where he set up shop as the area's first postmaster.

When the war ended, the county, like most of the South, was in economic ruin. The devastation was exacerbated by emancipation, which finally arrived in Texas on June 19, 1865, two and a half years after Lincoln issued the Emancipation Proclamation. Newly freed slaves and their families fled from cotton fields to wherever freedom was and whatever it meant. They scattered and established self-sustaining freedmen's towns such as St. John Colony (in Caldwell County), Shankleville (Newton County), Kendleton (Fort Bend County), and Lincolnville (Coryell County) at Moccasin Bend, but freedmen primarily settled in East Texas. By 1900, blacks owned more than a quarter of Texas farmland. More urban-minded African Americans flocked to Houston, San Antonio, and Dallas to find work and establish freedmen's neighborhoods. Throughout East Texas, blacks found work in the lumber industry, hauling pulpwood and working in sawmills well into the twentieth century.

In 1920, Joe Winters was a mill worker in Conroe. East Texas was not kind to blacks, who suffered intimidation and violence as a consequence of emancipation. Winters became the victim of a grisly public act of vengeance after being falsely accused of rape by the white woman with whom he was having a secret relationship. After a protracted manhunt, reportedly involving thousands of white men scouring the area, Winters was caught and chained to a stake in Conroe's courthouse square, where, in front of hundreds of bloodthirsty, cheering onlookers, including women and children, he was doused with oil and kerosene and burned alive.

In 1886, the Conroe public schools' first classes were held in a one-room structure called the Conroe Mill School, for a five-month term.

Education beyond elementary school was rare for black or white students, so Conroe High didn't have its first graduates—three of them—until 1902. The first school for black children was located in the Central Baptist Church at Madeley Quarters. In 1933, the Mittie J. Campbell School, the first black public school in Conroe, was destroyed by fire. The new school took the name Booker T. Washington. Charles Brown showed up in 1960.

———

A Montgomery County son, Charles Brown grew up in an area called Haynes Chapel, a church community near Lake Conroe that is known primarily for its rare historic public cemetery, Johnson-Haynes Chapel. It includes grave sites of the area's early white settlers as well as of slaves and Hispanics.

"We had our own little community," Brown said. "You listen to what some black folks say, but I didn't know no difference. Shoot, I thought I was living high. We weren't worried about what white folks were doing, and we weren't comparing ourselves. We were competing against each other. They didn't want us around them and we didn't want them around us. Some of them came around on Saturday nights looking for black women and got they butts whupped."

Brown attended Lawson High School in nearby Montgomery. He was an "aggressive and a little mischievous kid" who excelled in math and hard work.

Brown got into football almost by accident: "Mr. Farris taught me, and one day he told me, 'Boy, you going to school!' He meant college. That's just the way they *told* you back then, they didn't *ask* you. So, he called the Texas College president, Robert Glass, who he knew from World War I, and told him, 'I got a big ol' country boy down here, strong as a mule, and I believe he can help your football team.' I had never played a down of football.

"That's how I got to college. I didn't know the game, had never seen it, never heard of it, so help me, God. I'm talking about 1945 in a little ol' place like Montgomery, a country town. I was a lineman and learned to play by observing. I was big and strong and would just come straight ahead and knock the hell out of you. I loved to hit people. I played at around 220, but got up to 233. I was all muscle from hauling pulpwood. But I made All-SWAC my senior year. That's how much I had progressed."

Charles Brown the player had come a long way, but Charles Brown the coach was still a work in progress. When he graduated from Texas College in 1950 with an education degree, he wasn't thinking about a career in coaching. From hauling pine pulpwood with his preacher father and cousins and loading it onto railroad cars, he knew trucking better than Xs and Os. He had been behind the wheel of two-and-a-half-ton and larger trucks since the age of twelve, dreaming of owning a trucking business long before he finished high school. In the evenings, he and a partner would haul a load or two of pulpwood, earning three dollars a load; whoever was driving, usually Brown, pocketed two dollars.

He returned to Montgomery County and worked odd jobs, "trying to get my money right," as he put it. He had in mind to start a trucking business, but an acquaintance who knew of his football success at Texas College drove him thirty-five miles northeast from Conroe to the little town of Shepherd, where Dixon High School needed a football coach. It also needed a football team.

As Brown recalled the interview: "He told the principal, 'This is the man that will make a good coach for you,' and the principal said, 'Okay, you got a job.' That's all the interviewing and everything. That summer, I went to work, and that's how I got into coaching, but I still wasn't convinced that's what I really wanted to do."

Brown started the football program at Dixon in 1950, but his coaching fate was sealed during a stint in the army three years later. With Brown as player-coach, his team won the 1954 Armed Forces Europe championship. He returned to Texas and coached at Livingston Dunbar before landing at Booker T. Washington as an assistant coach for a year. He then spent six years as head coach, compiling a 68–9 record. His thirty-six-year career included later stops at Aldine Carver and Forest Brook, and ended with an overall record of 203–101–1. He and his wife, Carolyn Sadbury, who taught home economics at Washington, were a formidable force. She cooked for the team before every home game, feeding the players at the Brown's home, where she also repaired uniforms, sewing and patching torn game and practice jerseys and pants. The coach refused to accept hand-me-down equipment from Conroe High, so he and Washington boosters purchased what the team needed directly from the local Oshman's Sporting Goods store. Since the school district didn't provide a washing machine, Carolyn stepped in as laundress. The district finally sprang for a washer, but no dryer, so it was not unusual to pass the

Browns' house and see freshly washed football uniforms hanging from the family fence.

That left time for Brown to develop has coaching skills: "I read a lot about football. They didn't allow blacks at the Texas High School Coaches Association meetings 'cause they didn't want to accept us as members, but we could go to clinics, so we went to as many as we could. Carolyn and I just looked at them as vacations. I was a disciplinarian. A kid had to get his lessons, go to class, act right, and I was going to work the hell out of you on the football field. I wasn't worried about you being ready physically, I just wanted to keep you in line. If they got to the field, they didn't believe they could lose."

And they rarely did. Brown installed the single wing offense he had learned from his coach, Alexander Durley, at Texas College, and the Bulldogs' successful execution from that formation brought loyal fans in droves to their games.

"Everybody was getting used to the T formation and got away from the single and double wing. So, they didn't know how to stop it. We went 13-0, and we had more whites at our games, every Thursday night, behind the sidelines, people everywhere. That's how much they cared about our football. There was a bad call one night where the referee called back one of our touchdowns. A white policeman walked up to the ref and told him, 'I don't care what time you leave here tonight, you're going to get a ticket.'"

The Bulldogs "stadium" was a dinky little arena behind the school with bleachers that could hold about six hundred fans, but for the 1960 PVIL 2A state championship game, the school district arranged for Washington to host Midland Carver at Conroe High School's field, where blacks were not normally allowed.

"You could peek through the fence," Brown said, "but you couldn't go in. But the night before the game, they let my daddy in because he was a preacher. He walked around the track, and I found out later that he had been praying for us."

The following evening, Washington was blessed with a divine 16-6 win.

———

Socially, the Bulldogs' first title didn't change a thing. Conroe maintained its segregationist posture, like most of the South, as the civil rights movement picked up steam. So while Washington's white fans supported and in some cases adored the team, their attendance at the games was the extent to which the city promoted race mixing and equality, and whites' tolerant relationship with the team was seasonal.

Hubbard related a particularly galling example: "A white family . . . during football season did everything they could for this one black player, picked him up and took him wherever they went. But, when the season ended, they barely spoke to that child, and it just ate him up. It made you think, is this what it's all about, just athletes with no heart or mind.

"It was what it was back then. It was segregated, but we never let that bother us. In our situation, we won all the time, we had good teams, comradeship. When we'd get in the playoffs the stands would be full of white people who would come out just to watch us practice. They were there all they time, and they followed us on the road. We knew how the times were, but we didn't put a lot of emphasis on that. We were good and they followed us. They wanted to be part of the good things happening in Conroe."

---

Things were pretty good, too, eight miles up the road in Willis, where the A. J. Turner Tigers followed Washington with a state championship of their own in 1967. Coach Julius Shanklin's team, led by quarterback Charles "White Shoes" Young in his signature bright white Converse tennis shoes, knocked off Trinity 30–10 for the PVIL's 1A title, the last state football championship for a Montgomery County school. It was also the only championship team for Turner, which closed at the end of the school year because of integration. Forty years later, the Willis Independent School District presented the Turner champs with rings as a tribute to the program that won its district in six of Shanklin's seven seasons as head coach.

"We were somewhat of a dynasty," Earnest Feggens Jr. said of the team's streak.

In Willis, freedmen farmers built its first church, Thomas Chapel Methodist, in 1867, which was also the first black church in Montgomery County. The first school for blacks in Willis was the Colored School, a log structure that opened in 1889. Before then, in the 1870s, two white men who tried to teach black children came to mysterious ends. According to *A History of Montgomery County*: "In 1870 a Yankee came from Illinois to Montgomery to teach a three month school for the Negroes. In a few weeks he disappeared and was soon replaced by another who taught for a few weeks. One morning the Negro children went to school and their teacher did not arrive. Finally someone reported that the professor had been found drowned in Town Creek. The Negroes were told that the man had slipped from a foot log while crossing the stream and drowned. Other reports were that he was murdered and thrown into the creek by local citizens who resented a Yankee teaching the Negroes."

Turner, named after its principal, opened in 1956, and five years later Shanklin, a Wharton native who was two years out of Prairie View A&M, arrived in a town he had never heard of. He explained how he got the job: "I got a call from Mr. Turner through my aunt because I didn't have a phone. He said they were looking for a coach. This was in December. I said, 'Where are you?' He told me 'Willis,' and I said, 'You mean Wallace.' He told me it was Willis, north of Conroe. Well, I knew where Conroe was because I had been to Boy Scout camp at Camp Strake. Turner showed me the community, and I had never seen a sawmill in my life. He said the kids needed leadership. I had played football in junior college, but we didn't have a football team in high school. I was a student of the game, and Mr. Turner gave me a copy of Dana Bible's book, *Championship Football*, about the total makeup of football, how to organize, and I bought another football book and I read them.

"That first game, I didn't know what I was doing, but one thing I always said was what I didn't know we'd make it up with conditioning. So we ran a lot."

Turner had a measure of success as a strong district contender before Shanklin's arrival, though it had never won a state title. In six of his seven years as the Tigers' head coach he won district championships. Still, Shanklin felt the pressure to keep a winning spirit, and he found motivation at the recently vacated Colored School: "I went down there and saw a plaque where they kept scores of their football games, and it really frightened me. I saw where Willis had been winning games scoring 40 and 50 points. I thought if I come here and we start losing, they're going to run me off right away. But I was fortunate enough that this is really a football town. I found that out when football season started and we won the first game, and people came to me and said this is not supposed to happen, 'cause all the good players had graduated, that these were just the little boys. Somehow we won the district, and the people said,

'You know coach Shanklin, he can walk on water.' But it wasn't something that I did. The seed was already here, and I just happened to walk into it, 'cause they love football here."

A love of football has never been a problem in Montgomery County or anywhere else in the Lone Star State, but crossing the color line to openly express admiration for black achievements always saw white supremacy put up an impenetrable goal-line defense.

"When you have a winning tradition in a small town like this, everybody knows everybody and you're going to have a lot of followers," Jerry Blair, a Turner fan, recalled. "The sidelines were full, white and black fans, but when we won state, it was no big deal, no celebration."

The Tigers had no reason to expect one, and neither did their PVIL peers in Conroe. Memories of both championships quickly faded into a hidden, unspoken history. The anomalous congratulatory gestures offered by the Conroe and Willis school districts came much, much later. They symbolized what should have been. But at the time, the champs were left to revel in victory among themselves. For those who continued their athletic careers, other championship platforms would lift them up and acknowledge their hard work, skills, and accomplishments.

Frank Moaning was a good example. After he graduated from Conroe Washington, Coach Billy Nicks got him to Prairie View, where Moaning played on the Panthers' 1963 NAIA Championship team, which included Otis Taylor, Ken Houston, Jimmy Kearney, Alvin Reed, and Horace Chandler, all PVIL school grads. In 2007, Moaning was inducted into the Prairie View Athletic Hall of Fame, and in 2011 into the PVIL Coaches Association Hall of Honor.

Moaning recalled his earliest football experiences: "I didn't know what a football was until I went to Conroe. All we ever played in Tamina was baseball, but when I got to Conroe in fifth grade, we'd be playing football at recess and lunch time, and I just liked the game and I was good at it. I liked the game, it was rough and tough. I was just a ol' country boy. I cut pulpwood, that's what my daddy did, pulpwood contractor, and he was a hell of a baseball player, came along during Jackie Robinson time. He'd bust a mitt he could throw so hard. We played a little basketball, but I wasn't too good at that."

Tamina is a straight shot ten miles south of Conroe. The mostly black community was named for the late eighteenth-century New York City political organization Tammany Hall, which was founded to help the

Irish. When the town applied with the postal department for service, its name was misspelled on the application. The pronunciation stuck, and so did the errant spelling. The one-room black school in Tamina was named for Phillis Wheatley; a single teacher instructed grades one to six until 1949. When the school closed, its students were bused to Conroe. The lack of teachers in Tamina put them at a disadvantage, Moaning recalled: "The smartest kids in sixth grade helped by teaching first and second grades, so a lot of us were behind."

Once Moaning got to Washington, he was on a fast track to success, playing three seasons on teams that lost only two games. "James Barnhill was head coach when I first started playing. The white school gave us secondhand stuff, all the football gear. Barnhill got mad one day, took all that stuff back to the district and threw it over the fence. They got rid of him."

Accolades were nothing new to Moaning, but the rings and city proclamation were "one of the greatest things that ever happened to us, because we were Conroe's team, the only team in Conroe to ever win a state championship, and we won two. Another thing I liked about it was that it gave coach Brown a good recommendation, 'cause he was a hell of a coach."

It wasn't so much that the honors came, or when they came, but from whom they came: the Conroe Independent School District, local businesses, and white citizens. The night of the ceremony in 2014, "Conroe's Team" was officially presented to its fans, and finally the city could exhale, exorcise a few racial demons, and publicly express a long overdue show of pride.

"I will never forget that particular night," Ellis Hubbard said. "It's hard to imagine. We had mayors and councilmen there, and one guy walked up to me and said, 'The guy that was number 12, I want to meet him.' So he came up to me, 'You're Ellis Hubbard, I have been wondering what happened to you. I was a kid when you won the state championship, and I tried to get out there on the field so I could shake your hand, just touch you, but my dad told me we weren't allowed on the field. I waited all these years, and now I'm going to shake your hand.'

"My wife was there, and he went over to her, took his hat off, bowed to her and said, 'I got a chance to bow to the woman who married number 12.' He was a councilman, and all of his life he'd wanted to know what happened to us. That made me feel good, made me wish that more of our people could have been at the game. We just took it all in. There were a lot of white people back in those days who didn't want to be in the situation they were in. They were wishing we all played together so they'd be in a winning tradition. I believe our attitude and their attitude towards us back then in that small town may have sparked a consciousness in a lot of people to come together.

"That night you wouldn't know there had been segregation. Everyone was sitting together. Afterwards you went back to your own traditions, and that was the sad part. But that night everybody came together."

## Educating Negroes . . . Or Not

*Education came to be one of the great preoccupations;*
*enlightenment was viewed as the greatest single opportunity*
*to escape the indignities that whites were heaping upon blacks.*
*Children were sent to school even when it was a great inconvenience*
*to their parents. Parents made untold sacrifices to secure the*
*learning for their children that they had been denied.*
JOHN HOPE FRANKLIN, *From Slavery to Freedom*

Racism and segregation were the only forces able to hold back the Bulldogs, the Tigers, and other teams in the PVIL from receiving their just due in an era when even recognition for excelling in Texas's beloved state pastime, high school football, was kept in check. A quick glance at PVIL history reveals that the league featured a stunning number of players, coaches, and teams worthy of rings and city proclamations—Austin Anderson's back-to-back 3A titles in 1956 and 1957, and Livingston Dunbar's 1953 and 1954 1A champs immediately come to mind. Yet accomplishments such as those remained invisible, hidden behind the veil of discrimination, considered inconsequential and disposable. When integration forced the closure of most PVIL schools, remnants of their glory days—trophies, yearbooks, photos, banners—their histories, were tossed in garbage bins as the buildings were demolished. Perhaps their perceived lack of worth was so ingrained that in some instances officials, former coaches, and players, did not think to preserve the representations of their history. The PVIL was a throwaway league of unvalued schools, but the people who taught, mentored, coached, and competed therein nonetheless thrived in the vacuum of a parallel society, just as black people had always done. The black academicians who met in 1920 to form the Texas Interscholastic League of Colored Schools, which would provide organized éxtracurricular events for high school students, were undoubtedly excited about the prospect of shaping the athletic destinies of generations of black kids.

At a November 1920 meeting in Houston, men from the Colored Teachers State Association of Texas sought to provide leadership for black high school student competitions in the same manner that the University Interscholastic League, based at the University of Texas, had done for white students since 1910. The UIL initially oversaw debating competitions and added athletics, music, and other academic contests later. Prairie View's president served as the chief officer, with the title of executive secretary. Also like the UIL, the TILCS had District and State Executive Committees to oversee the league's constitution and rules, and a Legislative Advisory Council to study and maintain compliance. The TILCS began to solidify at a state track meet in 1921 at Prairie View State Normal and Industrial College, though both the TILCS and the UIL would rest their ten-gallon hats on football. The course of the TILCS paralleled black history in Texas, and its schools resulted from the struggles to educate African Americans after emancipation. Much of the driving force for those struggles originated from the all-black former plantation community of Prairie View.

————

After purchasing a first-class ticket on June 7, 1892, and boarding the East Louisiana Railway train in New Orleans, a light-skinned Creole of color attempted to seat himself in the "whites only" coach. Immediately ordered to leave the coach, Homer Plessy refused. He was arrested and charged with "violating the Louisiana segregation statute of 1890." Plessy's arrest was a coordinated effort by the Citizens' Committee of New Orleans (Comité des Citoyens), which wanted to test and overturn Louisiana's Separate Car Act, which required "equal, but separate" train car accommodations for blacks and whites. The committee filed a writ arguing the law violated the Thirteenth and Fourteenth Amendments to the US Constitution, specifically the Equal Protection Clause of the Fourteenth Amendment. The case, styled *Plessy v. Ferguson*, was appealed to the Louisiana Supreme Court, which held that the law was constitutional.

(Ferguson was the judge who presided over Plessy's criminal trial in New Orleans.) The committee then appealed the case to the US Supreme Court. A decision in Ferguson's (Louisiana's) favor was handed down on May 18, 1896. The ruling upheld the "separate but equal" doctrine and legalized racial segregation in public accommodations. For education, that meant separate schools for black and white students, a principle that held until 1954, when it was overturned by the Supreme Court case *Brown v. Board of Education*. Writing for the majority in Plessy's case, Justice Henry Billings Brown wrote: "The object of the Fourteenth Amendment was undoubtedly to enforce the absolute equality of the two races before the law, but in the nature of things it could not have been intended to abolish distinctions based on color, or to enforce social, as distinguished from political, equality, or a commingling of the two races upon terms unsatisfactory to either."

Thirty years before *Plessy*, postbellum Texans had not been too keen on "commingling" with newly freed slaves or providing them with education. The Supreme Court's 1896 decision only strengthened whites' resolve for racial separatism and supremacy, especially in the Deep South. Black codes in place throughout the region during the first years of Reconstruction prohibited academic instruction for blacks. But Texans weren't champing at the bit to educate most of their kids, black or white.

In 1821, Stephen F. Austin inherited his father's grant from the Mexican government for land in what is now Fort Bend County in Southeast Texas, where he was to settle 300 families—the "Old 300," as they came to be called. The colony established the first school in Texas in 1823. Rural families nonetheless preferred homeschooling, private schools, tutors, or itinerant teachers. Public school systems didn't begin to develop until 1871, and it was another sixty years before the schools extended studies to twelve grades. By 1930, black children made up two-thirds of the school-age population in East Texas, where the great majority of freed slaves had settled, though 97 percent of the area's segregated schools excluded blacks. Racially, as with all other aspects of education during that period, salaries for teachers were lopsided. Pay increases averaged $8.98 for rural white teachers per student, but only $0.16 for rural black teachers.

That any high schools for black children were established was a major accomplishment, and the communities had learned black men and women and Northern Christians to thank. In 1860, there were over four million blacks in the United States, 14 percent of the country's population; 90 percent of them lived in the South as slaves, including 169,000 in Texas, 30 percent of the state's population. Nearly all were illiterate farmhands in East Texas.

Before the Civil War, only twenty-eight blacks in the United States were known to have received baccalaureate degrees. When the war began, every Southern state except Tennessee prohibited the formal instruction of slaves or free blacks. There were only two black colleges in existence before the Civil War—Wilberforce, opened in 1856 by Methodist Episcopalians in Ohio, and the Ashmun Institute, started in 1854 by Presbyterians in Pennsylvania. After the war, Ashmun changed its name to Lincoln University, in honor of the late president; it became the alma mater of such luminaries as Thurgood Marshall, Langston Hughes, Cab Calloway, and one of the greatest running backs in black college football history, Franz "Jazz" Byrd.

The Episcopalians' and Presbyterians' involvement in starting those schools was trendsetting. Church groups (both black and white) became central to the establishment of black colleges, particularly throughout the South. A traveling group of African Methodist Episcopal pastors founded the first black college in Texas, Paul Quinn College in Austin in 1872. One year later, Methodist Episcopalians opened Wiley College in Marshall. The churches were eager to help freedmen adjust to life after bondage while simultaneously fueling their religious faith and creating ready-made congregations. Elder freed slaves were happy to see religious instructors because they wanted nothing more than to learn to read and study the only book often found in black homes—the Bible. Coming out of mass repression, former slaves had an unrivaled thirst for education, and it was a bonus that many of its facilitators carried spiritual messages. The fervor for knowledge was described by one historian: "Their interest in education was as though an entire race was trying to go to school."

Not long after the Civil War, black colleges began sprouting throughout the Deep South. From 1865 to 1890, more than two hundred private black institutions were founded there, some meeting first in abandoned barns or other rural buildings with only a handful of eager students. Atlanta University, for example, opened in 1865, holding its first classes in a railroad boxcar. The prestigious Fisk School, in Nashville, opened six months after the close of the war in an army barracks that had housed black cholera victims. Its first students ranged in age from seven to seventy, and classes could include parents and their children, all learning basic skills. That was also a common trait among the schools founded in East Texas.

Yet southern and Texas attitudes toward it all could not have been more hostile, to put it mildly. When the Union general Gordon Granger arrived in Galveston on June 19, 1865, to deliver the news of emancipation to Texas slaves, a panic quickly spread among whites, who feared that the reality of free black people would be nothing short of an apocalypse. Mass illiteracy among blacks was of great comfort to the psyches of white citizens, who carried a deep-seated fear of educated blacks—somewhat paradoxically, since white supremacist thought was that Africans did not have the capacity to learn. In addition, suppressing black education was another means of maintaining an industrial status quo: keeping black laborers in check while also perpetuating stereotypical myths of racial superiority. An illiterate Negro was a Negro who, socially, knew and stayed in his place and would remain a productive and compliant laborer. Formal education for the Negro was a threat—an affront—to the very being of white civility, such as it was where Negroes were concerned. But education would be an unstoppable force and an invaluable means of escape from bondage—both mental and physical.

In a typical southern newspaper editorial, a *Norfolk Virginian* piece in 1866 railed against Northern intrusion in the affairs of the South: "Of all the insults to which the Southern people have been subjected, this was the heaviest to bear . . . to have sent among us a lot of ignorant, narrow-minded, bigoted fanatics, ostensibly for the purpose of propagating the gospel among the heathen, and teaching our little negroes and big negroes, and all kinds of negroes, to read the Bible and show them the road to salvation." Texans concurred.

Texas's Constitution of 1866 provided that "the income derived from the public school fund be employed exclusively for the education of white scholastic inhabitants," but favorable legislation meant nothing to some Texans, who boldly made their feelings crystal clear: "I'd rather put a bullet in a Negro than see him educated." With slave-era sympathies still running high, that kind of mentality materialized as schools for blacks were burned, teachers and students were threatened and attacked, and newspaper editorials stirred up readers against "zestful idealists" from the North. From June 1865 to December 1866 in the Houston area, there were over twelve homicides and thirty-nine physical assaults related to attempts to educate Negroes. In an 1869 editorial, a Waco newspaper decried educating Negroes, because "we do not approve their sending their children to school for a mere hifalutin' idea of making them smart and like white folks." German communities welcomed northern teachers, who otherwise took their chances by staying in hotels and boarding-houses, where they risked being insulted, or worse if their missions were discovered. In Hempstead, a female teacher from Wisconsin was chased from her room at a boardinghouse in the middle of the night by the owner's son, who was returning from service in the Confederate army.

Enter the US Bureau of Refugees, Freedmen, and Abandoned Lands, established in 1865 to help slaves from Texas to the District of Columbia make the transition to freedom. The Freedmen's Bureau championed black education, and by 1867 had taught ten thousand adults and chil-dren in Texas to read and write. There were only 16 schools for blacks in 1866, but that figure had increased to 150 when the Freedmen's Bureau closed after a five-year run. The schools offered instruction in arithmetic, reading, writing, history, and geography from the elementary to the col-lege level. Julius Rosenwald, president of Sears, Roebuck, established the Julius Rosenwald Fund in 1917 because of his interest in educating blacks. He believed that America could not prosper "if any large segment of its people were left behind." His fund paid for the construction of more than 5,000 "Rosenwald schools" in fifteen southern states, including 464 in Texas, which affected 57,330 black students.

J. T. Kirkman, state superintendent of education in June 1867, painted this picture in describing the Freedmen's Bureau's success: "A very great number of the planters, seeing the eagerness of the Freedmen for edu-cation, have offered to furnish school buildings and have applied for teachers. At Gonzales, Seguin, Liberty, Marlin, and other places dona-tions of land on which to erect school houses have been made by white citizens."

———

As school systems evolved in the 1920s and 1930s, the state spent an average of $3.39 per student to educate black children, about a third less than for white students. Black teachers were paid significantly less than white teachers ($91.60 a month, compared with $121.03).

By 1870, black communities had spent more than a million dollars on private school education, raising money through churches as well as donations from craftsmen and other paid laborers. They purchased land, built schools, and paid teachers, accommodating trade, elementary, and secondary-level classes. Texas's Constitution of 1876 called for an "Agricultural and Mechanical College" while pledging that "separate schools shall be provided for the white and colored children, and impartial provisions shall be made for both." That marked the founding of the Alta Vista Agricultural and Mechanical College of Texas for Colored Youth, which was established on land where the Alta Vista plantation had been located in Waller County. In 1879, the school took the name Prairie View Normal and Industrial Training School.

It would become the academic and athletic mecca for black Texans.

## Welcome to the Hill

Geographically, it has always been easy to miss the tiny rural black cultural oasis wedged between Waller and Hempstead. Prairie View lies forty miles or so northwest of Houston and is almost as remote as the northern Louisiana black college Grambling, of which it is said that in order to get to campus, "you have to be going somewhere else."

Black Texans had no problems finding their way to Prairie View. The school was a beacon for education that was first lighted in 1876, a decade after Texas slaves were finally notified of their freedom. Emancipation coincided with a push for higher education in Texas, an issue firmly addressed by the Constitution of 1876. Article 7, section 14, decrees: "The Legislature shall also when deemed practicable, establish and provide for the maintenance of a College or Branch University for the instruction of the colored youths of the State, to be located by a vote of the people; *provided*, that no tax shall be levied, and no money appropriated out of the general revenue, either for this purpose or for the establishment and erection of the buildings of the University of Texas."

A three-member board at the newly established Agricultural and Mechanical College at Bryan (Texas A&M) was charged with finding a location for the "branch" school and appointing an administrator for one hundred students. The land that they chose, the Alta Vista plantation, was ripe for producing cotton, rice, and timber, but also had a large African American population as a result of the many plantations in the Hempstead area before the Civil War.

After the death of Jared Kirby, Alta Vista's owner, his widow, Helen Marr Kirby, transformed the plantation into a school for young ladies. It failed, which made it easy for the committee to purchase its 1,388 acres. Mrs. Kirby later became the first dean of women at the new University of Texas. On November 17, 1877, the board organized the college for colored youths, and the following January selected as the school's one professor L. W. Minor. Thomas Gathright, the president of Texas A&M, described him as "a colored man, whom I know well." Minor, who was said to be "a man of fine education and excellent character," had known Gathright in Mississippi. Little else is known about him.

To attract the first students, ads were placed in the Hempstead newspaper, and circulars were posted in the area. Minor sent notices to other press outlets and personally wrote to black community leaders. On March 11, 1878, eight students enrolled, playing $130 in tuition for nine months of instruction, board, and "one suit of uniform." The first class was successful, but the fall class was smaller, and all the students left school to make money picking cotton. This development greatly disappointed Gathright and the board of directors, which was already unhappy with the low enrollment, leading it to assume "there is no demand for higher education among the blacks." There were discussions of converting the school into a manual labor institution or a normal school, that is, one for training teachers, or even relocating the school to Austin or another large city, where students could earn their board and the institution perhaps become coeducational. Ironically, the Alta Vista school's first enrollment was two students more than Gathright had attracted for the first classes at his campus in College Station two years earlier.

George Ruble Woolfolk, in his book *Prairie View: A Study in Public Conscience, 1878–1946*, wrote, "If the Negro boys were not ready for college work, the same could be said for the whites attending the main college. . . . The Agricultural and Mechanical College for the benefit of colored youths at Alta Vista was not given a fair chance to demonstrate its feasibility as an educational experiment."

Minor's tenure lasted one year. Gathright and the A&M board, convinced that the experiment in higher education for Negroes had failed, suggested renting out the property until the school could be reorganized. One board member reasoned, "I assume and sincerely trust that this institute will receive a generous support from the state, having always felt that it was our duty, claiming to be the superior race, and having control of the government, to do all in our power that promised beneficial and practical results to educate and elevate our colored citizens."

The board met in Hempstead on August 28, 1879, and reorganized the school as Prairie View State Normal School. "Normal," a designation for teacher-training schools, referred to the norms or models of instruction that all students were expected to emulate. The first normal school (*école normale*) was established in France in the late seventeenth century. Most historically black colleges were founded as normal schools. The new Prairie View was led by the Memphis native and Fisk graduate E. H. Anderson as principal. Sixty students were taught in thirteen subjects on the elementary and secondary levels. Forty years later, in 1919, Prairie View began its four-year senior college program. After several additional name changes, it formally became Prairie View A&M University in 1973.

Historically black colleges fulfilled the need for black teachers in every corner of the state, and for several decades, the bulk of them had degrees from Prairie View. Once the school began its football program, in 1906, many of those teachers doubled as coaches for all sports. First and foremost, Prairie View and other black colleges gave black kids a chance to learn, prosper, and advance their people in the face of racism.

A former Prairie View mayor, Frank Jackson, was one of those kids: "The folks that have worked at Prairie View have given their time and their lives, not for the money but for a mission. They help kids like Frank Jackson who came out of Luling, Texas, out of the watermelon and cotton fields. Couldn't go to UT, didn't have the grades to go there, but Prairie View said, 'Bring that boy on down here. Do you want to be an engineer?' I didn't know what an engineer was. The only engineer I knew was the one that drives a train. They gave me an opportunity to make something of myself and change my life. All of us come here, we've got stories to tell. The beauty of working here is that when these kids come here they're just like diamonds in the rough. They graduate and ten years later they come back and say, 'Do you remember me? This is my wife, this is my son, and I'm an engineer. I'm doing good.'"

## "Any Public White School"

On November 6, 1869, in New Brunswick, New Jersey, the boys from Rutgers University brawled with the guys from Princeton, twenty-five to a side, wearing street clothes, kicking, heading, batting with their open hands, and punching with closed fists a round leather ball. Running or throwing the ball was not allowed. They called the game football, an extremely violent pursuit that quickly gained popularity—and a propensity for mortality. By 1900 there was a drastic rise in football-related deaths. At least forty-five men died from playing the game from 1900 to 1905 as a result of internal injuries, broken necks, concussions, or broken backs. President Theodore Roosevelt was an avid fan, but even he wanted to temper the game's violent nature. He called two White House conferences in October 1905, at which university coaches, including Yale's Walter Camp, and athletic "advisers" discussed reforming game play for the sake of safety. The conferences led to rule changes and other meetings involving larger groups. A December 1905 meeting in New York City of representatives from sixty-two schools led to the formation of what became the National Collegiate Athletic Association.

Football made its way to Texas high school campuses in 1892 when Galveston Ball fielded the state's first organized team. In the same year, in Salisbury, North Carolina, the first intercollegiate football game between historically black college teams was played by Biddle College (now Johnson C. Smith) and the host team, Livingstone, which lost 5–0. The first public school system in Texas was organized in 1875 in Brenham, and it included Brenham High School for the Colored (later named for its principal A. R. Pickard), the first high school for African Americans in Texas. It isn't clear which black school first adopted the football trend. One of the earliest games pitted Dallas Colored High School (which became Booker T. Washington) against a team from Wiley College in 1908. The UIL crowned its first football state champion in 1920—actually, cochampions, since Houston Heights and Cleburne played to a 0–0 outcome. That was two decades before the PVIL produced its first official state champion, Fort Worth Terrell, coached by Marion "Bull" Bates, which defeated William Pigford's Austin Anderson team 26–0.

The TILCS was formed in 1920 because UIL membership was open only to "any public white school," a stipulation added in 1913 to its original 1910 charter, which had no restrictions on race for membership. Even so, the UIL offered backdoor guidance to the TILCS, in an undefined and probably uncomfortable relationship for both sides. The UIL ended up turning over responsibility for the TILCS to the Negro School Division of the State Department of Education. The UIL considered insurmountable the difficulties of supervising and administrating events for black schools and doubted whether future progress would be made, because of a lack of interest from the schools. However, the UIL continued to offer assistance to develop the TILCS, which did not officially take the name Prairie View Interscholastic League until 1963, seven years before it went out of business. Yet the league was referred to by many throughout its existence as the Prairie View League, the Scholastic League of Colored Schools, the Negro Interscholastic League, or the Negro League.

With Prairie View professor L. W. Rogers leading the way at the November 1920 meeting in Houston, a committee was formed to set the structure of the TILCS. In March 1921, plans were finalized in Austin to hold the league's first state academic and track meets at Prairie View the following month. The meets drew black students from more than fifteen counties to compete in declamation, spelling, and track and field events. League officials were so pleased at the meets' outcomes that they immediately began planning the next year's state-level event, which would be preceded by county and district competitions. Football and basketball received no such structure at that time.

Rogers stepped down two years later, turning over league control to Prairie View principal J. G. Osborne and members of the school's faculty.

## Structure for the PVIL

*For some years Negro High Schools in Texas have been carrying on football and basketball programs with no form of organization or association, with no official method of deciding championships . . . and disputes. The conditions have grown, as you may well imagine, quite out of hand. . . . My local supervisor . . . suggests that I ask you to grant us a few minutes of your time in Austin . . . so that we may become better acquainted with your University League . . . [which] under your direction is quite the largest and best organization of its kind in the country.*

PALMER D. WHITTED, TILCS Rules Committee member, to Roy Bedichek, head of the Bureau of Public School Extracurricular Activities at the University of Texas, April 14, 1938

The UIL's membership restriction based on race stood for almost sixty years. Nonetheless, the league helped the TILCS solidify its structure for deciding champions in football and basketball, a process whose form had been chaotic at best and resembled, as one coach put it, "outlaw stuff." Any team that had a good season could self-proclaim its statewide supremacy, even if it had played only a local schedule with rosters that could include players well over twenty years of age, some in their thirties, and athletes who attended school only during football or basketball seasons. Some players set foot on campus only for afternoon practices and on game days.

On March 19, 1938, Houston Yates's coach Pat Patterson and several other coaches, including Galveston Central's Ray Sheppard, John Codwell of Houston Wheatley, and Herman Holland of Dallas Washington, met at Bishop College, in Marshall, in conjunction with the state basketball tournament and emerged with a plan for organizing athletic programs for black high schools. The proposed name for the new league was to be the High School Athletic League, but later in the meeting, the group adopted the name Lone Star Interscholastic Athletic Association. The next month, Holland submitted his suggestions for district alignments, similar to a plan that Patterson had submitted, though it is unclear from available records which plan came first or what happened to the proposed new names. It is also possible that Patterson, through his principal, W. H. Holland, presented his suggestions at a Rules Committee meeting in 1938 at Sam Huston College (later Huston-Tillotson), in Austin.

The following setup, credited to Patterson, was approved by the committee in either 1938 or 1939, to take effect in the 1940 season, erroneously considered by many the creation date of the PVIL:

| DISTRICT 1 | DISTRICT 2 |
|---|---|
| Kilgore Dansby | Dallas Lincoln |
| Longview Womack | Dallas Booker T. Washington |
| Marshall Pemberton | Forth Worth Terrell |
| Paris Gibbons | Wichita Falls Washington |
| Texarkana Dunbar | |
| Tyler Emmett Scott | |

DISTRICT 3

Beaumont Charlton-Pollard
Galveston Central
Houston Washington
Houston Wheatley
Houston Yates
Port Arthur Lincoln

DISTRICT 4

Austin Anderson
Corpus Christi Solomon Coles
San Antonio Wheatley
Victoria Gross
Waco Moore

The PVIL finally had a formal structure. At UIL schools, football myths and legends were born, and touchdown-scoring heroes were deified statewide on Friday nights in big city stadiums and in small farming communities whose identities were shaped by what happened on patches of grassy turf flanked by creaky wooden bleachers. There was no shortage of related newspaper and magazine articles, books, and movies about high school football in Texas as fans of UIL schools and a fawning statewide mainstream media delighted in telling tales of "Slinging" Sammy Baugh, Doak Walker, Bobby Layne, "Super Bill" Bradley, and Ken Hall—the "Sugarland Express"—and others, and the programs that produced players like them in Odessa, Brownwood, Daingerfield, and Cleburne. It didn't hurt that most of the UIL's blue-chip players continued their brilliance in major college programs of the Southwest Conference, an alliance of seven Texas schools and a northeastern border neighbor, the University of Arkansas, which began in 1914 and existed for eighty-two years. The white boys who were Friday night's heroes could easily stay in state and make seamless transitions to Saturday-afternoon performances that would bring acclaim to their high school teams and coaches, too.

For the PVIL, weekly black newspapers such as the *Houston Informer*, with Lloyd "the Judge" Wells's "Dateline Sports" column; the *Houston Forward Times*, home of Bud Johnson's "Bud's Eye View" column; the *San Antonio Register*; and other black media outlets were dedicated to trumpeting black schools. They reached far fewer people than the state and national wire services and large dailies such as the *Houston Post* and the *Dallas Morning News*, whose coverage of PVIL games was limited to a few paragraphs from "special correspondents" who phoned in scores or submitted game details to someone at the sports rewrite desk. Playoff and championship games got more attention than regular-season matchups, but not by much. Small-town papers were often more generous in devoting space in their publications to the PVIL games. At times, the big papers relegated black high school results to the "scoreboard" pages and their made-for-reading-glasses agate type.

The PVIL languished in the shadow of the UIL, which went about building and maintaining its "Friday night lights" image of high school football. It would proclaim Texas to be the prep football capital of the nation. Folks in California, Ohio, Florida, and Pennsylvania still think otherwise. Yet, arguably, the UIL wasn't even the most talented football league in its own state. It was the most organized, most publicized, most funded, without question. But the PVIL could stake a legitimate claim to its own prowess, with programs that featured speed, athleticism, and a taste of showmanship—to the acknowledgment of no one.

Except black colleges.

Segregation meant success for black college programs, in athletics and academia, since they automatically got the best and brightest students from black communities and built golden recruiting pipelines connected with black high schools and their blue-chip talent from Texas to Florida to Maryland. In Texas, that meant schools like Prairie View, Wiley, Texas Southern, and Texas College, all of which at one time or another belonged to the Southwestern Athletic Conference (the SWAC) and won black college national championships—five for Prairie View before integration. The schools existed in a recruiting paradise where access to quick, speedy running backs, strong-armed quarterbacks, sure-handed receivers, and bone-jarring tacklers often came through casual conversations or "advice" from relatives or teachers all eager to nudge a good player toward their alma mater. Any young black kid who showed promise of any kind was encouraged and helped along by a nurturing community that did all it could to help its youngsters beat the odds, beat racism, and succeed in a climate that overwhelmingly said he could not. Black college athletic programs thrived in that system. Their no-budget budgets didn't allow for extensive recruiting trips, but the coaches could be just as effective at bringing in talent for the cost of lobbing a long-distance phone call.

If he wanted a player for Prairie View, Coach Billy Nicks would pick up the phone and wind up: "This is Nicks talking." Then he would pitch: "Listen, you've got a good boy there, and I'd like to have him. You coaching? How'd you get that job?" His former pupil would meekly answer, "Well, you recommended me, coach." Then the delivery: "Well, you bring that boy out here Saturday!" Nicks summarized the result: "I'm through with that conversation. And he'd have that boy there and glad to talk to me."

The SWAC, which spread from Texas into Mississippi and eventually Alabama, was the biggest benefactor of PVIL talent. But before integration, PVIL players would also migrate to more accepting programs in the Midwest, the mountain states, the Far West, and the Pacific Northwest, places where the sight of black players was not uncommon. The Nebraska Cornhuskers suited up George Flippin, the son of a freed slave, in 1891; George Jewett started at fullback for the University of Michigan in 1890; and Walter Gordon was an all-American lineman for the University of California, Berkeley, in 1918. Ben Kelly, in 1953, became likely the first black player for a predominantly white school in Texas, and maybe the Deep South, when he suited up for San Angelo College after graduating from Blackshear, the PVIL school in San Angelo.

> *I was in tenth grade playing nose tackle, but I wasn't straight over Bubba [Smith]. He was playing center. James Sykes was one of our linebackers, and he noticed Bubba was kind of limping. He said, "Coger, hit him on that leg!" Bubba heard him and looked at me like, "You try it." When the ball was snapped, I dived on the ground. Bubba was nine feet tall. I'm not hitting Bubba, I said to myself, but I'm gon' make it look like I'm trying.*
>
> COGER COVERSON, Jack Yates High School

The stream of PVIL talent leaving the state picked up in the 1960s. Mel Farr of Beaumont Hebert went to UCLA, where he was a consensus all-American running back in 1966. Future Pro Football Hall of Fame wide receiver Charley Taylor, from Dalworth High School in North Texas, headed to Arizona State as a running back in the early 1960s. There might not have been an overt acknowledgment around Texas of that kind of talent, but coaches and recruiters from the Big Ten, the Big Eight, and the Pacific Eight were very well acquainted with what PVIL programs had to offer.

"Duffy Daugherty lived in Beaumont," Jerry LeVias said jokingly about the great Michigan State coach who, through his many trips to conduct coaching clinics in the area, landed several Golden Triangle players for the Spartans, including Bubba Smith and running back Jess

Phillips (both from Beaumont Charlton-Pollard) and Gene Washington (Baytown Carver) in 1963. (The Golden Triangle is the area of south-eastern Texas bordered roughly by Beaumont, Port Arthur, and Orange.) LeVias was as elusive in the recruiting battles for his services as he was when running on the field for Beaumont Hebert. He got away from Daugherty and dozens of other out-of-state coaches when he chose to play for Hayden Fry at Southern Methodist University in 1965, the first black scholarship athlete in the Southwest Conference.

LeVias was deemed too small by the SWAC schools and University of Texas coach Darrell Royal. But at that point, all roads from the PVIL generally led directly to black colleges: Angleton Marshall quarterback Emmitt Thomas (Pro Football Hall of Famer as a defensive back) went to Bishop College (by then in Dallas); lineman Alphonse Dotson, from Houston Yates, went to Grambling; defensive back Ken Houston (Pro Football Hall of Fame), from Lufkin Dunbar, went to Prairie View; quarterback Eldridge "the Lord's Prayer" Dickey, from Houston Washington, went to Tennessee State; and San Antonio Wheatley running back Odie Posey went to Southern University in Baton Rouge, just to name a few. Coach Nicks's five black college national championships at Prairie View came between 1953 and 1964 with rosters well stocked with former PVIL players, including Jimmy Kearney (Wharton), John Payton (Livingston Dunbar), Charles Garcia (A. W. Jackson, Rosenberg), and John "Bo" Farrington (Houston Yates). Farrington died in an auto accident in 1964, along with famed running back Willie Galimore, as the players were returning to the Chicago Bears training camp in Rensselaer, Indiana.

If you were looking for a football player during the offseason, you only had to attend a PVIL track meet, where players like Cliff Branch dominated the sprint events. Branch had an unprecedented 9.3 clocking in the 4A 100-yard dash at the 1966 PVIL state meet, making him the first Texas schoolboy to record such a time. But in the very next heat, for 3A sprinters, Wichita Falls Washington star Reggie Robinson bested Branch's time with a blistering 9.1. Branch found his true calling on the football field, earning three Super Bowl rings as an All-Pro receiver with the Oakland Raiders. Collegiately, after a brief stop at Wharton Junior College, Branch chose the University of Colorado Buffaloes.

"We didn't recognize that we had a special league but we did," he said. "We had a league of our own, on Wednesday and Thursday nights at Jeppesen Stadium. We didn't feel slighted, because the competition was so strong—Yates, Wheatley, Kashmere, the Beaumont schools. It was special football, and a lot of the athletes that came out of the PVIL went on to great careers in colleges and Pro Bowl–type careers in the pros. There were a lot of great athletes that came out of this league."

While it was not unusual for some of the woefully underfunded black schools to outfit their teams with hand-me-down equipment (including jockstraps) from white schools, the quality of play at black schools proved to be anything but second rate. For fifty years, the PVIL produced a wealth of outstanding players and coaches that few in the Lone Star State, outside local black communities, cared to acknowledge.

"There was the black side of town and the white side, and you just dealt with what was laid out there for you," Bubba Smith told the *Houston Chronicle* in a 1992 interview. "You didn't have time to think, 'Why can't I do that, or why is it like that?' Sometimes I think a large part of my life was lost by that. But you could always show what you had on the football field.

"[And in the PVIL] you're talking about people who could righteously play the game. None of the teams were diluted back then. Everyone on the field could play. If you blink, they were gone. It was more physical and tougher. And it always meant something if you could outrun somebody, because everybody could run."

With integration encroaching, the league ran out of time in 1967, and the UIL received a sudden infusion of, as the great Florida A&M coach Jake Gaither described his ideal player, "mo-bile, a-gile, and hos-tile," blue-chip black players who would legitimize the league's claim of having the best high school football talent in the land. Integration brought a symbolic end to a contentious social era, though the struggles and debates continue, and grandsons descended from PVIL athletes are now celebrated for their play at UIL schools.

The PVIL went out in style, and true to form, no one noticed.

# CHAPTER 2

# Night Train, Choo-Choo, and Ridin' the Yella Dawg!

*If it hadn't been for the race problems, I would have been the third-best, and the twins would have been the fourth- and fifth-best athletes in the family. Two of them were better than I, but they got caught up in the race thing and never got the chance. My two older brothers didn't get the same opportunity I got, or they probably would've gone farther than I went as far as pro ball.*

EARL CAMPBELL, talking about his older brothers, Willie and Herbert

That an organization called the Prairie View Interscholastic League acted as the governing body for competitions among black high schools in Texas seemed a well-kept secret to the general public. It nonetheless showcased some of the best prep-school football talent in the country. From the Kelley brothers at Abilene Woodson on the South Plains of West Texas to the petroleum-rich Gulf Coast and Golden Triangle with its wealth of insanely gifted players—Bubba Smith, Jerry LeVias, Joe Washington Jr., Ernie "Big Cat" Ladd, Ray Dohn Dillon—to the Hill Country and Dick "Night Train" Lane's clothesline tackles at Austin L. C. Anderson to Jeppesen Stadium's weeknight Houston inner-city electricity juiced by players such as Otis Taylor, Eldridge Dickey, Otis Pointer, Allen Merchant, Ural "Sloppy Joe" Johnson, and Leo Taylor.

The PVIL football honor roll reads like a who's who of national prep, college, and professional gridiron greats. Six of its alumni are in the Pro Football Hall of Fame, including "Mean" Joe Greene (Temple Dunbar) and Ken Houston (Lufkin Dunbar). The great Ollie Matson played a year at Houston Yates before moving to San Francisco and becoming a star, leading the 1951 University of San Francisco Dons to an undefeated season as the nation's top rusher and finishing ninth in the Heisman Trophy voting. Homer Jones played at Douglass High School in Pittsburg, Texas, and his world-class 9.3 100-yard dash speed brought revolutionary changes to NFL defensive coverages when he joined the New York Giants as a wide receiver in 1964. He also became known as the player who started the end-zone touchdown celebration of spiking the ball. Alphonse Dotson, a lineman from Yates, was the first small-college player named to a major all-American team—the one chosen by the Newspaper Enterprise Association—as a Grambling senior in 1964. Houston Washington's Eldridge Dickey was the first black quarterback drafted in the NFL's first round, taken by the Raiders ahead of Alabama's Kenny "the Snake" Stabler.

There has never been a shortage of newspaper and magazine articles, books, and movies about high school football in Texas. Most famously, Buzz Bissinger's book *Friday Night Lights* spawned a film of the same name about football at Odessa Permian High School, and a television series set in fictional Dillon, Texas. The media focused overwhelmingly on white players and coaches while unashamedly ignoring the PVIL for fifty years. It wasn't for lack of material. There was plenty to write about, whether or not the white public and the mainstream media were interested (generally, they were not). "If you found anything about us in the papers, it was just the championship game or the major scores," Luther Booker, the late Yates head coach, said. "Mostly we were totally ignored, and I think that was terrible."

Black high school football flourished in a time when it seemed no one outside the black media and its audiences cared about or was in any way willing to acknowledge the abundance of talent bursting from the under-funded schools that competed under the PVIL banner, or as most whites called it, in polite company, the "Negro League" or the "Colored League."

The PVIL created pride and ambition, and its games revived spirits battered by the day-to-day burdens of racism. African American fans enjoyed football just as much as whites, but for black players, the game was a vehicle to propel them from poor hardworking disenfranchised communities into better lives that could include a college education. Many of the players became the first in their families to set foot on a college campus as a student or to secure a high school diploma. Their degrees came from historically black colleges—Prairie View, Texas Southern,

Wiley, Texas College, Bishop, and Jarvis Christian. For the most part, they were East Texas institutions serving local African American communities populated by direct descendants of slavery. The shortage of college options for black Texans made for a true sense of family among PVIL coaches and educators, most of whom had been classmates, teammates, and competitors at black colleges. Their families knew one another, they married their college sweethearts (in many cases, whom they met through a teammate's sweetheart or relative), and they had knocked heads and broken bread long before they stood across the sidelines from one another and matched football wits.

And they got college degrees.

The National Football League, from the late 1920s to the mid-1940s—roughly from Fritz Pollard (one of the first black players in the NFL and the league's first black head coach) in 1928 to Kenny Washington, who signed with the Los Angeles Rams in 1946—had no black players, so there was no pro football dream for blacks to chase after college. Instead, black players enjoyed whatever glory they earned on the gridiron in college and then walked away with degrees from black colleges and went home or elsewhere in the state to teach and coach at PVIL schools. In return, they would send their best players to their alma maters.

Prairie View had a run of eighty consecutive losses from 1989 to 1998, the worst losing streak in college football history. But during the 1950s and 1960s, Billy Nicks used homegrown talent to establish a Panthers' reign that was the most feared program west of Eddie Robinson and Grambling, whom Nicks beat in eight of their fourteen meetings, outscoring the Tigers 370–99. Nicks won five black college national championships at Prairie View with guys such as Kenny Houston (Lufkin Dunbar), Jim Kearney (Wharton), Alvin Reed (Kilgore), Charlie "Choo-Choo" Brackins (Dallas Lincoln), Clem Daniels (McKinney), and Bo Farrington (Yates).

White boys wanted to play for Texas A&M's Bear Bryant or Darrell Royal at Texas, but Wiley's Pop Long, Texas Southern's Alex Durley, and Nicks were the coaches black boys admired.

## From the PVIL to the NFL

The 1967 professional football draft was a historic event. It brought together for the first time the National Football League and the upstart

American Football League for the annual meeting where teams staked their claims to the best senior collegiate players. The two-day affair, March 14–15, in midtown Manhattan in the Gotham Hotel ballroom had none of the overproduced glitz and glamour of the contemporary made-for-television version. There was no throng of analysts, and certainly no green room for the supposed best-of-the-best prospective picks to park themselves and their entourages while nervously waiting for their names to be called—sooner rather than later. In fact, there were no players anywhere near the premises in 1967, and to announce the picks, NFL commissioner Pete Rozelle scribbled the name of each team's selection furiously in chalk on a portable blackboard positioned on an easel.

The leagues' merger would not be finalized for another three years, but their first common draft was a truce that put an end to the big-money bidding wars to sign the most prized players and brought to a screeching halt the associated recruiting high jinks. Future Oakland Raiders owner Al Davis was a young San Diego Chargers assistant when he secured the signature of Arkansas halfback Lance Alworth on a contract in an end zone of New Orleans' Sugar Bowl Stadium in 1962 immediately after the Razorbacks' season-ending loss handed Alabama's Bear Bryant his first national championship. Alworth had been drafted by the San Francisco 49ers a month earlier, and sitting in the stands was an aghast Red Hickey, the Niners' head coach, whom Davis had just beaten to the punch. And imagine the Dallas Cowboys' surprise before the 1965 draft when Kansas City Chiefs scout Lloyd "the Judge" Wells, a PVIL alum from Houston Wheatley, managed to grab his protégé wide receiver Otis Taylor out from under the noses of his Cowboy sitters, who had stashed the Prairie View great in a Dallas-area hotel until they could officially draft and sign him. Around 3:30 in the morning, Wells talked his way past the Cowboy gatekeepers and into Taylor's room, and then helped him escape through the room's rear window and off to Kansas City to sign with the Chiefs.

The 1967 draft, with its newfound measure of civility between the two leagues, was witnessed by a crowd of none. No fans or clamoring media assessed and celebrated each pick, and certainly there was no Internet immediacy. So low key was the event, most of the players selected weren't aware it was happening. Michigan State receiver Gene Washington, from Baytown Carver, just happened to be in the school's athletic department when he got a call that day. Some players didn't hear about their good fortune for several days after the draft, and while most fans, players, and an otherwise unaware US populace went about their business that day, waiting for news of the daily body count in Vietnam, there was much to get excited about in Texas, whenever the news arrived. Rozelle, in an unprecedented action, chalked the names of three first-round players who began their careers in the PVIL.

Knowledge of that link would have been a huge revelation to Rozelle, everybody else at NFL draft central, and more than a few handfuls of folks in Texas, black and white—though six PVIL alums had played for the Kansas City Chiefs in Super Bowl I earlier that year:

- Aaron Brown, defensive end (Port Arthur Lincoln)
- Willie Mitchell, defensive back (San Antonio Wheatley)
- Andy Rice, defensive lineman (Halletsville Stephens-Mayo)
- Fletcher Smith, defensive back (Hearne Blackshear)
- Otis Taylor, wide receiver (Houston Worthing)
- Emmitt Thomas, kick returner / defensive back (Angleton Marshall)
- Jimmy Hill, defensive back (Dallas Washington)

The PVIL had built a star-studded lineage by 1967, and its most notable alumnus was Detroit Lions defensive back Dick "Night Train" Lane, the most feared defensive back in NFL history. Vince Lombardi called him "the best cornerback I've ever seen." At six-two, two hundred pounds, Lane was big for a cornerback but could run and brutally punish receivers and ball carriers with a decleating shoulder to the chest or his signature "Night Train Necktie," a vicious clothesline hit—his forearm applied with great force to an opponent's head—traumatically impeding the player's progress. At the time, the NFL game was a rough, no-holds-barred affair, but Lane's move was deemed so dangerous that the league later banned the tackling method. Lane could hit, but he was also an extraordinary ball hawk who, as a rookie in 1952 with the Los Angeles Rams, intercepted 14 passes in only twelve games, a single-season league record that still stands. Of the top five leaders in that category, three are from PVIL schools:

1. Lane, 14 interceptions, 1952 (Austin Anderson)
2. Lester Hayes, 13 interceptions, 1980 (Houston Wheatley)
5. Emmitt Thomas, 12 interceptions, 1974 (Angleton Marshall)

Another Pro Football Hall of Fame defensive back, Lem Barney, played for the Lions after Lane. He recalled, "Train will always be the Godfather of cornerbacks. He was as large as some linemen of his era. He also was agile and very fast. His tackling was awesome. He did the clothesline and other tackles that just devastated the ball carrier."

Lane's life began in an East Austin garbage bin, where he had been left as a baby by his prostitute mother. At first, a widow named Emma Lane mistook the baby's cries for a cat's howling, but retrieved the child and raised him as her own. Lane reunited with his mother in Scottsbluff, Nebraska, after playing football for W. E. Pigford and graduating from L. C. Anderson High School in 1946. He played football for a year at Scottsbluff Junior College before serving four years in the army. Lane settled in Los Angeles, working in an airplane factory before wandering over to the Rams' training camp. He became one of the league's most heralded free-agent signings, impressing offensive coaches as a wide receiver and defensive coaches with his play in the secondary. He played in seven Pro Bowls and finished his career with 68 interceptions, and was named first- or second-team All-NFL every year from 1954 through 1963. Lane was the first PVIL superstar.

———

Before 1967, only two PVIL alums had been first-round picks. In 1964, Charley Taylor from Grand Prairie Dalworth, in North Texas, went to the Washington Redskins, and two years later Aaron Brown, from Port Arthur Lincoln, was taken first by the Chiefs. There was nothing odd about either transaction. In 1946, the Rams had signed free agents Kenny Washington and Woody Strode out of UCLA as the league's first black players in the post–World War II era. Three years later, Indiana University halfback George Taliaferro became the first black player drafted by an NFL team when the Chicago Bears took him in the thirteenth round, though he chose to play in the rival All-America Football Conference. Six rounds later, in the same draft, Penn State's Wally Triplett, also a halfback, was chosen by the Detroit Lions; he became the first drafted African American player to play in the league. The NFL didn't begin warming to black talent until the 1960s, and then did so in large part because of the success of the AFL, which made liberal use of black college players. On October 23, 1955, the Green Bay Packers made Charlie "Choo-Choo" Brackins the league's fourth black quarterback when he played the final minutes of a game against the Cleveland Browns. Brackins, a sixteenth-round pick that season, starred at Prairie View after attending PVIL-member Lincoln High School in Dallas. Brackins was also the first black college quarterback to play in the NFL.

The league's checkered racial history and the PVIL's struggle to be recognized quietly collided in the 1967 draft. And the PVIL's bonanza began immediately.

With the first pick, the Baltimore Colts selected the most feared defensive lineman in college football, Michigan State's Charles "Bubba" Smith, out of Beaumont's Charlton-Pollard High School. He came from a football family led by Smith's father and coach Willie Ray Smith Sr. Four years later, Bubba's younger brother Tody (Charlton-Pollard and Southern Cal), a defensive end, would be a first-round pick of the Dallas Cowboys.

With the seventh pick in the 1967 NFL draft, the Detroit Lions took another Beaumont native, UCLA running back Mel Farr, of Hebert High School, the younger brother of Miller Farr, who was a 1965 free-agent cornerback for the Denver Broncos but became a three-time AFL All-Star.

With the eighth pick, the Minnesota Vikings took wide receiver Gene Washington, from Baytown Carver and Michigan State.

The Los Angeles Rams did not have a pick in the first round, but their initial pick in the second round was Texas Southern University running back Willie Ellison, from Lockhart Carver, another PVIL school.

By draft's end, at least a dozen former PVIL guys had been selected, including David Lattin. The Chiefs took "Big Daddy D," who had been a basketball teammate of Otis Taylor's at Worthing, as a wide receiver with the 443rd of the draft's 445 picks. Lattin waited another couple of months for the NBA to call, and when it did, the Golden State Warriors were on the other end informing Lattin he was their first-round pick, the tenth overall selection.

## "The Judge"

It was no coincidence that the Chiefs took a flyer on Lattin and expressed intense interest in drafting Taylor. Both players were products of Lloyd Wells's stable of PVIL and black-college athletes collectively known as the "League." As the group's commissioner, the flamboyant Wells was mentor, agent, publicist, confidant, sartorial guide, and social director. In his biography, *Slam Dunk to Glory*, Lattin said of Wells, "Lloyd was the hardest-working man I ever knew. He was a cheerleader and a one-man public relations operation for the black community. Lloyd saw to it that we young black athletes received state and national attention. He took us under his wing, nurtured us, showed us the value of hard work, and turned us into men. The only vacations Lloyd took were with us, his 'league,' his 'sons' as he called us. On weekends, he drove us in perennially new cars, usually a Cadillac, to Galveston, where he laid out a huge lunch and we spent the day hanging out at the beach."

Wells was a lot of things to a lot of people, and some of the descriptions are not flattering, but he was praised as the man who directed PVIL players to black colleges and black college players throughout the South to the American Football League, specifically the Chiefs. The team hired him as its first black scout, and he delivered eight All-Pro players and three Pro Football Hall of Famers: Buck Buchanan, Willie Lanier, and Emmitt Thomas. Head coach Hank Stram took to calling him "Outta sight!"—a reference to Wells's assessment of every player he presented to the coach—but the nickname that stuck was the "Judge."

Lloyd Clarence Alex Wells was himself a PVIL and black-college alum. He graduated from Houston Wheatley in the 1940s and played football at Southern University. As a freshman at Southern, Wells roomed with Collie J. Nicolson, the man who became the publicist for Eddie Robinson's Grambling football teams and was largely responsible for the team's and the university's national image. Both men had been marine sergeants in World War II, and both had mastered working with the black media. Besides being a columnist for the *Houston Informer* and then the *Houston Forward Times*, Wells was instrumental in starting the PVIL all-star football and basketball games. Wells the civil rights activist used his column to advocate for open seating at Jeppesen Stadium, where black fans were relegated to bleacher seats in the end zone, and at Colt Stadium, where black fans were confined to outfield seats. Wells also desegregated the Astrodome press box.

In the midst of the Chiefs' locker room celebrations after their Super Bowl IV conquest over the Minnesota Vikings, TV crews interviewed Stram, owner Lamar Hunt, players, and even the scout who helped assemble the Chiefs' championship roster, the Judge. Everybody recognized Wells's importance to the Chiefs, but his persuading black college stars to choose the AFL over the NFL, well before the common draft, gave the young league an edge over its older rival, which only marginally used black players. Michael MacCambridge, author of *Lamar Hunt: A Life in Sports, and America's Game*, explained: "It was also no accident that the teams that were most successful were the teams that had the largest contingent of black players, because they were truly looking for the best players. That 1969 Super Bowl team was the first team in Pro Football history to win a championship with the majority of the starters being African-American."

———

There are no clippings to indicate otherwise, but it is likely that even the PVIL had no immediate sense of what had been its best showing in the pro football draft. Its accomplishment in 1967 was quickly overshadowed by black student unrest in Houston and turmoil in northern cities. In April in Seattle, Stokely Carmichael first uttered the phrase "black power," one month before 488 Texas Southern University students were arrested after clashing on campus with Houston police, killing Louis Kuba, a twenty-four-year-old rookie officer. In July, back-to-back race riots saw Newark and Detroit "burn, baby, burn." On the positive side, the first black US Supreme Court justice, Thurgood Marshall, was seated in October, appointed by Lyndon Johnson.

Amid the black community's aggressive push for social change, the PVIL began preparations for its demise, looking ahead to the fall 1967 football season, when the bulk of its member schools would switch to the UIL. Black players had been trickling into previously all-white schools for several years after the *Brown v. Board* decision in 1954. Increasingly, black teams would compete against white teams, some integrated, as the PVIL entered a three-year fade to black.

A new era for pro football was underway, too. The two pro leagues integrated, taking a big step toward making football the country's new national pastime and a multibillion-dollar sports and marketing behemoth. The specter of school integration in Texas, however, cast a pall over the proud, exhilarating two days of the NFL draft for the PVIL, bound for a merger with the UIL. The two organizations had spent several decades going about their separate but equal businesses of staging high school sports events and promoting Texas football. But as the 1966–1967 school year came to a close, the PVIL and its members crept closer to a day they had all seen coming. Their sense of sadness came cloaked in a shroud of fear for the future of education—academic and cultural—for their students as well as employment for the teachers and coaches at all-black schools facing closure. A system powered by segregation had necessitated the PVIL's creation in 1920, and half a century later integration was ordering the organization's demise.

The historic fall season was the first time in Texas history that black schools competed against white schools. White programs had integrated rosters, along with coaching staffs that included PVIL all-stars and exceptional coaches.

But as a result, the black community experienced a sense of loss that went well beyond athletics. "When integration came, I felt that they threw us a curve," said Coach Joe Washington Sr., who watched the transition in Port Arthur, where he led the Lincoln Bumblebees. "The way I took integration, they said, 'We're going to fix you, we're going to do away with your schools and bring your kids over to us.' They put those kids in situations that were new to them, and some of them were not able to handle it. Yes, we were probably better off educationally, but not as a race. We lost too many people in the shuffle. Coaches and teachers lost jobs, kids dropped out of school."

Visibility for both the PVIL and UIL was based on athletics, especially football, but PVIL coaches and teachers and their descendants had always had a much larger mission—educating and preparing young black minds for citizenship in a social environment that neither welcomed nor encouraged them. Where academics were concerned, that preparation had been done successfully for almost a century. Football came along for the ride, emerging as the lead vehicle for transporting thousands of young black boys into manhood.

Black men were the driving force, the gridiron their highway to success.

## The "Race Thing" and All-Stars

That one of the most celebrated running backs in football history, at any level, could confess that he wasn't the best player in his own household speaks to the crux of the PVIL legacy—too many talented players whose careers and recognition were handcuffed by segregation. In the Campbell household, a "Tyler Rose" by any other name would have been Willie or Herbert. Earl came along in time to play at the newly integrated John Tyler High School, which he led to a UIL 4A state championship as a senior in 1973. His older brothers were both linemen who played at the PVIL's Emmett Scott High School. Willie, a team captain and all-district defensive performer, graduated in 1965; fifty years later, he was inducted into the Tyler ISD Hall of Fame. The citation called him the best athlete in the Campbell family, which included twin brothers Steve and Tim, who followed Earl to the Longhorns' program.

The PVIL, not just the Campbell brothers, was obscured by the "race thing," from its inception in 1920. It created local heroes for proud, struggling black communities and the few white fans who appreciated the wide-open style of play and athleticism of PVIL teams. The latter group liked winners, no matter their color, and particularly in small towns with one black school and one white school, it was acceptable for whites to cross the tracks and for a few moments suspend racial judgment and appreciate black culture. What better venue was there than a black high school football game, with its display of athletic flash and style in a party atmosphere complete with the pulsating, soulful beats of marching bands? For white fans, the exchange was an opportunity to back a winner.

But news of what they saw there didn't spread. There was no buzz about black high school players or coaches. But there should have been. In swarms.

As an example, here are possible dream-team depth charts for an all-time preintegration PVIL all-star game, North versus South. Most of the familiar names are famous for their accomplishments after their PVIL days. The names likely to be unfamiliar are a testament to the lack of recognition for outstanding players who got no exposure at the pro or major-college level, and no ink from local media, but who were among the best—in some cases, the best produced by their schools.

NORTH TEAM

*Offense*

Wide receiver: Reggie Robinson, Wichita Falls Washington
Wide receiver: Homer Jones, Pittsburg Douglass
Tight end: Alvin Reed, Kilgore Dansby
Running back: John Payton, Livingston Dunbar

Running back: Clem Daniels, McKinney Doty
Running back: Abner Haynes, Dallas Lincoln
Kick returner: Ron Shanklin, Amarillo Carver
Kick returner: Carl Garrett, Denton Moore
Kick returner: Charley Taylor, Grand Prairie Dalworth
Lineman: Ed Holland, Sherman Douglas
Lineman: Herbert Campbell, Tyler Emmett Scott
Lineman: Harry Wright, San Angelo Blackshear
Lineman: Winston Hill, Gladewater Weldon
Quarterback: Audrey Ford, Tyler Emmett Scott
Quarterback: Charlie "Choo-Choo" Brackins, Dallas Lincoln
Quarterback: Charles Green, Marshall Pemberton

*Defense*
Lineman: Willie Campbell, Tyler Emmett Scott
Lineman: Andy Rice, Hallettsville Stevens-Mayo
Lineman: Joe Greene, Temple Dunbar
Lineman: Elijah "Big Chill" Childers, Abilene Woodson
Linebacker: Arthur Ray Henderson, Livingston Dunbar
Linebacker: Johnny Harper, Linden Fairview
Linebacker: Pete Barnes, Longview Womack
Back: Rich Sowells, Huntsville Sam Houston
Back: Carl "Spider" Lockhart, Richardson Hamilton Park
Back: Ken Houston, Lufkin Dunbar
Back: W. K. Hicks, Texarkana Dunbar
Coach: Lewis "Les" Ritcherson, Waco Moore
Coach: Damon Hill, Lubbock Dunbar
Coach: Marion "Bull" Bates, Fort Worth Terrell

SOUTH TEAM
*Offense*
Wide receiver: Otis Taylor, Houston Worthing
Wide receiver: Warren Wells, Beaumont Hebert
Wide receiver: Cliff Branch, Houston Worthing
Running back: Ray Dohn Dillon, Galveston Central
Running back: Willie Ray Smith Jr., Beaumont Charlton-Pollard
Running back: Mel Farr, Beaumont Hebert
Kick returner: Jerry LeVias, Beaumont Hebert

Kick returner: Leo Taylor, Houston Yates
Kick returner: Paul Gibson, Conroe Washington
Lineman: Gene Upshaw, Robstown
Lineman: Coger Coverson, Houston Yates
Lineman: Clifton Ozen, Beaumont Hebert
Lineman: Sam Adams, Jasper Rowe
Quarterback: Eldridge Dickey, Houston Washington
Quarterback: Jimmy Kearney, Wharton Training School
Quarterback: Karl Douglas, Houston Worthing

*Defense*
Lineman: Alphonse Dotson, Houston Yates
Lineman: Bubba Smith, Beaumont Charlton-Pollard
Lineman: Aaron Brown, Port Arthur Lincoln
Lineman: Ernie Ladd, Orange Wallace
Linebacker: Godwin Turk, Houston Wheatley
Linebacker: Anthony Guillory, Beaumont Hebert
Linebacker: Garland Boyette, Orange Wallace
Back: Dick "Night Train" Lane, Austin Anderson
Back: Miller Farr, Beaumont Hebert
Back: Bivian Lee, Bastrop Emile
Back: Leroy Mitchell, Wharton Training School
Coach: Andrew "Pat" Patterson, Houston Yates
Coach: Ray Timmons, Austin Anderson
Coach: Willie Ray Smith Sr., Beaumont Charlton-Pollard

In reality, the PVIL sanctioned five all-star games, 1961–1966 (there is no record of a game in 1964). The first was played at Beaumont South Park's Greenie Stadium, the second in Galveston, and the final three at Houston's Jeppesen Stadium. Held in conjunction with meetings and coaching clinics at Prairie View for the Lone Star Coaches Association— the organization for black high school coaches, who were prohibited from joining the Texas High School Coaches Association—the games pitted Houston-area standouts against those from the Golden Triangle. College recruiters from outside Texas and black-college coaches were present in abundance, and their numbers increased as the Southwest Conference began cautiously embracing integration. The final PVIL all-star game, in 1966, was played one year after LeVias was offered his groundbreaking scholarship to SMU and one year before the PVIL-UIL merger. The last game featured Dallas Lincoln running back Duane Thomas, the future Dallas Cowboys star, who was headed to West Texas State University.

The 1966 midsummer showcase gave fans one last look at some players and coaches whose careers were coming to an end, and at a league on the wane. But the players, coaches, and teams from historically black schools around the state had shaped the PVIL's image and left indelible athletic and social imprints with their speed, athleticism, strong arms, and style.

## Dickey

No one knows, or is willing to admit, what really happened to the best quarterback in PVIL history, Booker T. Washington's Eldridge Dickey, and why the Fourth Ward's "can't miss" kid with the divine nickname and electric arm never played a regular-season down at quarterback in the National Football League. It isn't unusual for hotshot college quarterbacks, first-round draft picks, to crash and burn at the pro level. Some leave before the end of their first and only contract, and others become journeymen, shuttling from training camp to training camp, their extended backup duties including manning clipboards. They never see the end coming that quickly, and have no reason to, given their impeccable résumés. Dickey's was as brilliant as any, and more so than most. The six-two, two hundred pound quarterback racked up 6,523 yards passing and 67 touchdowns at Tennessee State. A three-time black-college all-American, he led his team to an undefeated black-college national championship season. He had a reported IQ of 130.

One scout observed before the 1968 draft: "If Eldridge Dickey was a white boy, 26 pro teams would be chasing him. But there aren't many clubs willing to risk signing a Negro quarterback—especially if he's better than anything they've got."

At the time, Raiders' owner Al Davis had all-AFL quarterback Daryle Lamonica, the "Mad Bomber," coming off a Super Bowl season. Lamonica, still in his prime, was backed up by the aged veterans George Blanda (age forty-one) and Cotton Davidson (thirty-seven). Davis nonetheless chose two quarterbacks in the first two rounds of the draft: Dickey, number one, and Alabama's Ken Stabler, number two. Taking Dickey was a bold statement by an owner with maverick tendencies. No black quarterback had ever been drafted in the number one slot, and certainly not one from a historically black college ahead of a white peer from a major program like Bear Bryant's Crimson Tide. Then the story took an odd turn. Whatever Davis saw in Dickey at TSU, he saw differently in the Raiders' training camp. Or maybe shifting Dickey to wide receiver was Davis's design all along, because of his extraordinary athleticism. Dickey was still allowed to work with the quarterback group. Stabler left the Raiders during training camp, possibly because he was being outplayed by Dickey, and spent the first two seasons of his career in Spokane, Washington, in the Continental Football League. After the preseason, Dickey never played quarterback again, spending the remainder of his star-crossed career as a wide receiver and kick returner.

If the team planned to keep three quarterbacks on the roster, a young, exciting Dickey with the skills to operate an offense that featured the long ball—Lamonica to PVIL alum Warren Wells—wasn't good enough to warrant grooming ahead of at least one of two geezers? In his biography, *Just Win, Baby*, Davis explained, "We were good at every position and Eldridge never found a niche in the four years we carried him . . . Eventually I traded him to Kansas City. He never really made it in the league."

Davis had beat Chiefs head coach Hank Stram to Dickey in the 1968 draft, and maybe that went to Davis's motive: keeping the talented Dickey away from the Raiders' most hated rival. Davis knew Stram had been interested in drafting Dickey. Stram was deeply troubled about Dickey's plight, and he wasn't shy about expressing how he felt: "What happened to Eldridge Dickey has to go down in history as one of the greatest sports crimes ever committed. The entire sports world and Eldridge Dickey was robbed by the Oakland Raiders in 1968. During the preseason, he out-performed nearly every quarterback in the AFC and NFC. I was not surprised when Kenny Stabler quit. Dickey was special and just too talented. He was fast, had a powerful arm and could throw a football with both hands. He was truly one of the most accurate passers I've ever seen. I wanted him badly but Oakland selected him first. By the time I did get him four years later Dickey really wanted out of the NFL. Deep down he never forgave the Oakland Raiders."

Stabler came back to the Raiders and had a career that would land him, posthumously, in the Pro Football Hall of Fame.

Dickey died in 2000 at age fifty-four from a stroke, exacerbated by a broken heart from a pro career that never was. It wasn't supposed to end that way. Dickey's fate was not an anomaly among black quarterbacks of his era and before, outstanding players in high school who found themselves at other positions, first in college then in the pros. Hebert's Miller Farr went from quarterback to defensive back at Wichita State, and Yates's Leo Taylor from quarterback to wide receiver at North Texas State. Wharton's Jimmy Kearney was also a brilliant quarterback at Prairie View, but had an NFL career as a defensive back, the same as Emmitt Thomas, who quarterbacked at Angleton Marshall and Bishop College, but is in the Pro Football Hall of Fame as a defensive back. Grambling's James "Shack" Harris didn't have his professional breakthrough—the first black quarterback to start a season—until 1969 with the Buffalo Bills.

It was an accepted fact among black quarterbacks that playing the position was a dead-end gig with no future beyond high school or college. The reason was overtly simple. Racist thought was that black quarterbacks didn't have the smarts to play the position in professional football; in fact, pro teams did not want a black player as a team leader and the face of a franchise.

It didn't matter that Dickey was bright, a pure pocket passer with mobility, and a proven leader.

He first started throwing "footballs" on Cleveland Street in Fourth Ward by using milk cartons stuffed with newspapers. He became a must-see at Lockett Junior High School and then at Washington, using his goal-line-to-goal-line arm strength to throw spirals so tight you couldn't see the spin. He entertained as much as he controlled an offense. Before every game, he led the team in the Lord's Prayer, and a nickname was born. Tennessee State's stogie-chomping head coach, John Merritt, thought that Dickey was the answer to his struggling program's prayers.

Bo Humphrey, an assistant coach at Washington, grew up in Fourth Ward. He knew Dickey's family and had watched the kid everybody began calling "Man" from his childhood. He recalled some early impressions: "There were telephone wires crossing the streets, and he was throwing over the wires for a whole block. He used to ride to school with me. I had a station wagon and carried a load of kids. He was a smart young man. One game when he got his ankle hurt, he asked for tape over his shoe for more support. We did that, but he wanted tape over the other one too so they wouldn't know which one was hurt. It looked like he had spats on, so everybody started looking at that, and the next thing you know it was white shoes . . . everybody wanted white shoes.

"He was ahead of his time."

Karl Douglas, a quarterback at Worthing, remembered Dickey with great admiration: "He was my idol. Coach [Oliver] Brown told us, 'I want you to see Dickey,' so he took a couple of us to see him play when he was at Booker T. Washington. They came out to warm up, and Dickey was the last one, not wearing a helmet. He was sitting alone in the middle of the field. He ran to the center of the team's circle, put on his helmet, and started leading calisthenics. I was in awe. On the first play of the game, they broke the huddle, and he stopped about two feet from the center and said, "Good evening line"—you could hear him. He gave a quick count, sprinted left, waved his receiver to go deep on the right, and hit "Sloppy Joe" Johnson on the run down the sidelines for a touchdown. And the two-point conversion was beautiful. He took the snap, jumped up like he was going to hit the tight end, but came down and lobbed the ball toward the corner of the end zone, turned around, looked at the sideline, and started clapping while the ball was still in the air. He never turned around to watch the pass be completed, and ran to the sideline. I wasn't trying to emulate Dickey, but I wanted just a little bit of that swagger."

## The Yellow Jackets Sting

*Look at Charlie Bonner, run that ball,*
*He run so fast, look like escaping gas*
*His number shines so bright, just like a guiding light*
*If you don't get him now, you ain't got a chance, no how!*
"SEVEN YEARS OF YELLOW JACKET GREATNESS"

L. C. Anderson was the designated high school for Austin's black students, many of whom lived in the capital city's Negro District, a zone set off in 1928 by an urban planner to segregate residential neighborhoods. Several postemancipation neighborhoods had been founded in the city by freedmen, most prominently Wheatsville and Clarksville, both west of the University of Texas. Whites lived in some of the freedmen neighborhoods, which were scattered around town, but the existence of integrated neighborhoods did not negate the effects of Jim Crow throughout the city. The plan set up zones separated by East Avenue, which in 1962 became Interstate Highway 35, an unofficial racial demarcation line between blacks and Mexican Americans to the east, and whites to the west. The resulting mindset was West Austin, good, and East Austin, bad. As vacant properties west of East Avenue were redeveloped, rents were increased, and restrictive covenants blocked black families from becoming residents. Black businesses were intimidated by the threat of city services such as public utilities being withheld if they did not "voluntarily" relocate.

The migration saw East Austin's population grow quickly as families, churches, schools, and prospering black-owned businesses moved in. Within two decades, well over a hundred businesses were operating in the area, many of them lining the busy 11th Street corridor. There were restaurants, bakeries, a beauty school, newspapers, grocery stores, and professional offices (doctors, dentists, attorneys, and others). Ambitious black entrepreneurs helped build East Austin into a vibrant, self-sustaining neighborhood in segregated Austin. The iconic Victory Grill opened in 1945 on V-J Day. A band manager named Johnny Holmes converted an icehouse to a club venue for African American servicemen on R&R and those returning from World War II. Blacks and more than a few whites frequented what became the most popular entertainment stop in East Austin. A renowned blues and jazz venue, the Victory Grill, at its peak in the 1950s, presented some of most of the popular national R&B and jazz artists as part of the so-called Chitlin' Circuit. Ike and Tina Turner, James Brown, Etta James, Billie Holiday, and Chuck Berry were among the many performers who played shows there.

The true rallying point for East Austin was Anderson High School athletic and band events. Anderson's marching band, directed by Ben Joyce, included such future music luminaries as the trumpeter Kenny Dorham and the Motown arranger Gil Askey. And it won seven PVIL state competitions. For several years, Joyce organized popular summer band concerts at East Austin's Rosewood Park. In the fall, of course, the band performed at the halftime of Anderson football games for sold-out Friday-night affairs at Yellow Jacket Stadium, where occasionally Longhorns' football coach Darrell Royal could be spotted watching the game from a nearby hillside.

The first two schools for African Americans in Austin both opened in 1881 in West Austin. Black children on the east side attended Robertson Hill School, which opened in 1884. A high school was added to Robertson Hill in 1889. That high school opened in a new building in 1907, and was named after E. H. Anderson, educator and brother of L. C. Anderson, both natives of Memphis, Tennessee. They were the second and third principals of Prairie View College. L. C. Anderson left Prairie View to become principal at Anderson, where he stayed for thirty-three years, stepping down in 1929. The school took his name in 1938. L. C. Anderson was also the first president of the Colored Teachers State Association, the group that formed the Texas Interscholastic League of Colored Schools, forerunner of the PVIL.

Anderson had had football teams since the 1920s, but the arrival of William Pigford as head coach in 1940 signaled the beginning of the program's rise to PVIL dominance. Supposedly, his 1944 squad, which featured Dick "Night Train" Lane, scrimmaged the Longhorns on the University of Texas campus and scored the only touchdown. In the first six seasons of the league's structured playoffs, beginning in 1940, Pigford led Anderson to the 2A state finals three times, winning in 1942 with an 11–0 squad that trounced Paris Gibbons 40–0. Willie "Zipper" Wells Jr. (son of the Negro League baseball star) caught five touchdown passes and kicked four extra points.

Lonnie Jackson, an end on the 1942 team, recalled some of his coach's training techniques: "Coach Pigford was real good at making things, and he built a seven-man blocking sled that must have weighed 1,000 pounds or more. And he had a tackling dummy that had pulleys attached to a bell. If you couldn't tackle with the technique and force to ring that bell, you didn't play for him. All the years he coached, you could see the fundamentals come into play. When opposing players were blocked and tackled, they stayed blocked and tackled."

When Pigford became principal in 1955, his assistant, Raymond Timmons, took over and won back-to-back state championships in 1956 and 1957 and another in 1961. Across town, Austin High was the 2A state champion in 1942 in the UIL, which led *Austin American-Statesman* sportswriter Wilbur Martin to ask, "Now why ain't there a high school bowl game?"

For these two teams, the answer was obvious, but the kids from the Negro District didn't need that kind of validation of their powerful program. From 1940 until integration in the 1960s, Anderson was clearly the best program in the city. No other Austin high school team came close to matching its consistent winning. From 1956 to 1961, Anderson won sixty-five of seventy-seven games, including a PVIL-record twenty-four straight in 1956–1957. The Yellow Jackets won their district five times, held thirty opponents scoreless, won seven games by sixty-one or more points, and won the three state titles under Timmons.

Leroy Bookman, who followed in his father's footsteps to play for the Yellow Jackets, recalled the feeling: "It was a privilege to play for Anderson. Winning was a tradition. The games had a family atmosphere because everyone wanted to be a Yellow Jacket."

Anderson running back John Harvey, considered the greatest Austin athlete in the mid-1960s, was the first African American football player offered a scholarship to the University of Texas. He didn't qualify academically, so he headed to Tyler Junior College and then played in the Canadian Football League. The 1968–1969 Anderson roster included underclassman Thomas "Hollywood" Henderson, a future Dallas Cowboy, who left Austin after his sophomore year for Oklahoma City's Douglass High School.

The Yellow Jackets' fantastic run in the late 1950s featured three incredible players who successively wore number 44. Each played on offense (running back), defense (safety), and special teams: Charlie Bonner, 1955–1957; Andrew Brown, 1958–1959; and Roy Horton, 1960–1961. Kids literally sang Bonner's praises, as described in a Yellow Jacket memoir that notes his "pause, stop, dance, reverse field" moves: "[The] lyrical rap-like lines were being sung by kids [in black neighborhoods] all over town—East Austin, St. Johns community, Pilot Knob, Clarksville, Black Land and others—while emulating the moves, mannerisms and cool of one of Anderson High School's greatest football players, Charlie Bonner. The verses of the song lyrically varied from neighborhood to neighborhood, pick-up game to pick-up game, even player to player, but the message, [was] always the same, Bonner, the greatest. The kids carried the word. If you missed his play, you have a definite void in your repertoire of athletic memories. For those that saw him play, cherish a memory for life. Talk'n 'bout Charlie Bonner y'all!"

The flashy Bonner set the school record in 1955 when he scored 146 points, but Brown was considered an even better runner, and Horton was the best all-around player. Besides running, passing, and kicking, he led a 1961 defense—along with Orsby Crenshaw—that shut out eight opponents. In that final state-championship season, Crenshaw scored 120 points and a school-record 20 touchdowns. In the 20–13 win over Yates, Crenshaw scored a touchdown and had two of Anderson's six picks that night.

## Huddling Up in Abilene

*Any time you got hurt, Coach [James] Valentine would come over, look at you, and say, 'Run it out, boy!' We had a hurdler, he was jumping those wooden hurdles, and some kinda way he misstepped and hit his leg on a hurdle and fell real hard. They were practicing in the gym 'cause it was raining. When he fell, his hip hit real hard, so he was laying down. Coach Valentine came over, looked at him, and told him, 'Run it out, boy!' The boy had broke his hip! We thought we'd never get through laughing.*

JAMES THOMAS

On a cold December West Texas night, several black men made their way into the modest dining hall of Pastor Andrew Penns's Valley View Baptist Church in Abilene. They were there for some football-based fellowship. Their time suiting up for the Abilene Carter G. Woodson Rams was half a century in the past, but this was not a reunion. They all still lived in Abilene and saw one another often. They were former teammates and lifelong friends. The evening was another opportunity to swap some tales from back in the day when they were close-knit, carefree young boys enjoying the glory of playing a game in a town that offered them little else.

Their playing days were a long time ago, but they were so comfortable with one other at Valley View Baptist that it could have been just yesterday that they were riding the "yella dawg" school bus to represent the green and white in Midland, Odessa, Fort Worth, Grand Prairie, Wichita Falls, or Langston, Oklahoma. They would make up songs to entertain themselves on the long rides that ended back at Woodson in the early morning hours, sometimes just before dawn at the beginning of another school day.

On that night, Pastor Penns's dining hall was the Rams' locker room. All that was missing was steam from the showers and the aroma of analgesic ointments. The stories came rapid-fire from Billy Thomas, Robert Townsend, Raymond Monroe, James Thomas, Curtis Norman, and Penns himself as they remembered:

- The Kelly brothers, Robert the quarterback and Louis the running back, who coached at his alma mater before building a dynastic program at Lubbock Estacado.
- Never having more than thirty players on the team, because there was a uniform shortage, but enough room on the bus for the entire team.
- Traveling on a Trailways bus to play Corsicana Jackson and the shock from lining up against "running backs as big our linemen," including one who "looked like he had just came out of the cotton fields—he had a goatee!"
- Sitting low in their seats as they left Wichita Falls Washington, dodging a hail of rocks, win or lose.
- Putting gas in the bus but being denied use of the service station restroom, prompting Coach Valentine to order the white attendant, "Shut that pump off! We don't want to fill up here."
- More stories about Valentine's toughness, like the time a player ran through the line, caught a knee to the helmet, and fell to the ground holding his head, telling Valentine how bad it hurt, and Valentine responding, "Drag him out the way. Ain't nothing but men out here."
- Hanging out after games around the corner from Woodson with R&B tunes blasting from the loudspeakers at Larry's Burgers, a drive-in with "the best burgers in Abilene."

Penns explained about Larry's as the others nodded and smiled in agreement: "We assembled there after games, bought burgers, malts, and sodas, sat around on cars like *Happy Days*. That was our *Happy Days*. We loved Woodson, took pride in it. Even today it's a part of us. Every two years, everybody comes home and we celebrate for three days of reunion, to reflect and talk about the days of football and the history of our lives at Woodson."

The evening progressed smoothly as children scurried back and forth through a hallway, their rambunctious, playful sounds echoing off the walls of the otherwise empty sanctuary. The noise did not distract the fellas, who were eager to relive the good ol' days of football, community, friendship, and family, familiar themes among black high school athletes who grew up navigating segregation and the complications of adolescence. And as for football, they all agreed that "Friday night lights, that's white folks." One of the men offered, "We never got bent out of shape about segregation. We were used to it. We just had fun."

Woodson's athletic teams were originally known as the Black Eagles to differentiate them from the Eagles of all-white Abilene High, but Valentine, who had starred at Austin Anderson, changed that when he took over the program in 1956: "We're going to be the Rams." So for every home game, a local white farmer brought an actual ram and parked him in a steel cage near the Woodson sideline.

Amid the laughter and side conversations, each man was eager to take the floor and tell his story. In an orderly progression, each introduced himself as though a starting lineup were being announced:

Billy Gene Thomas, Class of 1959, left halfback, nose guard, linebacker: "You had little kids that looked up to you. One day, I saw some kids playing football, and one of them said, 'I'm Gene Thomas.' I watched him, and he was good. That made me feel good, but it also made me realize I had little kids looking up to me, and I thought of how I had looked up to the football players at Woodson when I was a kid. Woodson was everything. It was where we got everything we needed to learn to grow up. Older dudes would start a team for youngsters, no pads, but they taught the plays and everything so when they got to Woodson they already knew the plays. That's what happened for me. When I got there, I already knew the plays, too! But one time, I got frustrated 'cause I wasn't playing, and quit the team. When I went back out, Coach Valentine talked to me and told me, 'You got five minutes to get dressed, and three of 'em are already gone.' That day, he put me at nose guard, and I took it out on them guys. That's how I made the team."

Robert Townsend, Class of 1963, guard and linebacker: "I'm proud to know I was part of being at Woodson. I tell my kids all the time how things were in the 1950s and 1960s. It was hard times, but they don't believe me. When I was thirteen, I saw a white man slap my stepfather on our front porch about some money he was owed. I had a job, and guys would ask me what I thought about the Abilene High games, and I'd tell them, 'I don't care who wins. I went to an all-black school. I went to Woodson.' I couldn't have gone to school with the whites, there was that much hate. I had seen some things. But in the summer, I played baseball with them, and they were good to me. One boy and his momma would pick me up for practices and games, 'cause I was a good player. I was a shortstop and had a tryout with the Cincinnati Reds, but I came back home because of my girlfriend. We stayed in our area, the whites stayed in theirs. We knew what our territory was. I see streets now that I remember, when I was a kid, we couldn't go that far. But Woodson was a special place in a special time. We were all so close. We see each other now and it's still the same. Nothing's changed between us."

Raymond Monroe, Class of 1962, center and tackle: I was about six-two, 215 pounds, ran the quarter mile and on the 440 relay team. I wanted my daddy to see me the first time I put on a uniform. That meant a lot because he was my best friend. My mom didn't want me to play, but dad would always stand behind the bench, behind the fence, and I'd always look over my shoulder to make sure he was there. I was representing the school. I'd be seen, and folks would know who I was. I was the first one in my family to play football, but I also boxed, and my mom didn't want me to do that, either. She said, 'You silly if you want somebody to hit you upside your head!' I loved school, because that was where the people were, the girls, everything was at school."

James Thomas, Class of 1963, right halfback, linebacker: "I was never interested in football before junior high school, but my brother encouraged me. When I first went out, I didn't make the team, sat on the bench for a year. What changed was that a friend of mine broke his leg. He was a halfback, too. So I filled in, and that was it for him. We had a good winning team, and most of the people who played enjoyed the recognition they got from the girls. Me, too. In fact, I was right in the middle. I might have been one of the worst. I scored a lot of touchdowns, four in one game, one time, and I lettered three years. I was offered several scholarships, but I went into the military. Abilene was prejudiced, sure enough, but we didn't suffer a lot of it.

We'd go to the movies, and the whites would be downstairs, blacks upstairs. We'd throw popcorn and stuff down there, and they'd come up and want to fight. But otherwise, we weren't interested in trying to socialize with them, because we had so much going on for ourselves."

Curtis Norman, Class of 1967, split end, 9.9 sprinter: "If you threw it out there, I'd just go get it. Woodson was fun, it was hard, it was fair, and if you messed up, you got your butt whooped."

Andrew Penns, Class of 1967, guard, center, tackle: "We loved that school, took pride in it, and even today it's a part of us. . . . I told my grandson about the history of Larry's Burgers and how we assembled there after games. It was white-owned, but it was one of the only places we could go and hang out. It catered to whites, blacks, and Spanish, and it was a place that we could feel safe, could hang out, a place that was a part of us because it was in our neighborhood, the black neighborhood. We'd have football pep rallies on Friday mornings. I was a pretty good player, and I played two years with my brother, John, side by side. He was a lineman, too—the Penns brothers. There were so many good players at Woodson: Robert Wilcox, Joe Brown, Aubrey Vaughn, those guys were achievers. Then, E. A. Sims, Charles Sims, the Kelley boys, Delmar Lyons, and others. Gene Thomas was one of the greatest players around here. Curtis Norman was fast—Harold Jefferson, Jimmy Strahan, Ben Jones, myself. A lot of us could have been considered pro material, but we didn't get the opportunities, because of the times."

Louis Kelley was two and a half hours from this scene, ensconced in Lubbock, where he had fashioned a successful coaching career, having learned his lessons as a team captain and two-time all-state running back (1954, 1955) at Woodson while playing for Earvin "Cat" Garnett and Don Grace. Kelley was a fullback at New Mexico State. He began his coaching career in the PVIL in 1970 at Lubbock Dunbar before settling in for a twenty-five-year stay at Lubbock Estacado, where he directed a program that won seventeen district championships, played in four state semifinal games, and contended for the state championship in 1983, losing 30–0 to Bay City. The teams' success brought accolades from all over: *Lubbock Avalanche-Journal* Coach of the Year eight times, induction into the Texas High School Coaches Association Hall of Honor in 1997, the Abilene ISD Hall of Honor in 1988, the New Mexico State University Hall of Fame in 2004, and the Prairie View Interscholastic League Coaches Association in 2014. In 2001, Kelley was named Texas Tech Legendary Coach of the Year. He retired in 2000 with a 240–91–10 record.

Kelley recalled his time at Woodson: "We used to get hand-me-down black-and-gold uniforms from Abilene Eagles, but in 1952 E. F. Green came in to be principal. He was little, short guy, spicy, had the name of the school changed and the team colors to green and white. They had just built a new school, and we got better coaches, with Don Grace the head coach and Earvin Garnett his assistant. They were just out of college, and I was a freshman. I was fortunate to get some good knowledge from them. When they came in, they looked the part, just out of Prairie View, and all the single teachers loved them. I said, I want to be like you guys. They taught some good stuff about football.

"We had good teachers that made you do what you were supposed to do, and good parents that made you do what the teachers told you to do. If a teacher called the house with a complaint, when I got home I got a whipping, first, then it was, 'Now tell me what you did.' If it was bad enough, I got another one. I had an English teacher, Thelma Roberts, feisty. One day in class, she said, 'I know four or five of you guys are getting scholarships to play football somewhere, and some of you will be back home by the first semester. Louis Kelley, you will be one of them.' I thought, why me? So when I was tired or something, I'd think of Mrs. Roberts and buckle down. We were playing in Wichita Falls one year, and I saw her and reminded her of that. She said, 'I challenged you, didn't I?' She did.

"Growing up in Abilene, in the summer, there was baseball—a black team, a white team, a Mexican team, and we all knew each other, but there was going to be a fight after the game. We'd fight for about fifteen minutes, hug each other, see you next week."

As the evening came to a close, there was a distinct sense that especially in this place, Coach Valentine's spirit hovered with a watchful eye. The men began breaking their huddle, but they would never break up or lose an allegiance to Woodson. This attitude was typified by the stance Penns took when integration offered the option to change schools: "When integration came in and we were allowed to go to white schools—Cooper, Abilene High—most of us said no. I said no, and told my mom if they demand we go to Abilene High School, we'd go. But, I said, you're going to have to send me to Wichita Falls, because they still have a black school. I had been at Woodson all these years and was one year from graduating. I wouldn't feel comfortable graduating from Abilene High because that's not my school. Woodson is my school. So I chose to stay there."

## *The Flying Tiger*

The essence of PVIL talent was in the players' speed, and there was plenty of it. Clyde Glosson at San Antonio Wheatley, Reggie Robinson at Wichita Falls Washington, Charlie Frazier at Angleton Marshall, and Leo Taylor at Houston Yates were but a few of the league's football track men, and vice versa. At Beaumont Hebert, football stars Jerry LeVias, Don Bean, Mel Farr, and Jerry Ball were also sprinters who formed a PVIL state-championship sprint relay team.

On a whim, Charles Frazier decided to tag along with his buddies William Gulley and Winston Hill to the Houston Oilers' training facility one summer day in 1962 as a break from summer classes at Texas Southern University. The local professional team, a franchise in the new American Football League, was preparing for its training camp. Gulley, a running back, wanted to gauge the team's interest in him, but Hill, a sophomore lineman, was already on the Oilers' radar, so he could check in with them, as well. Frazier was a track guy, a sprinter in one of the best programs in the country. TSU's legendary coach Stan Wright forbade him from being a two-sport star as he had been in high school at Angleton Marshall.

Frazier grabbed a seat in the foyer. Gulley and Hill were shown to the coaches' offices. Suddenly, a team executive passed through.

"He asked if he could help me, and I explained I was waiting for those guys."

"You play football?"

"No, sir."

"Well, what do you do?

"I run track."

"What kind of times do you run?"

Frazier had an eye-popping career-best 9.2-second split in the 440 relay, so he tossed out that number. The exec's eyes popped, and he offered the only reasonable response: "Do you want to come out for football?"

Yes, he did. The Oilers gained a new wide receiver, barely six feet tall, who made a speedy downfield target for the ageless quarterback George Blanda. Frazier was in the vanguard of track men making an impact on the gridiron, three years before Bob Hayes signed with the Dallas Cowboys and two seasons before his TSU teammate Homer Jones joined the New York Giants. Playing in the upstart AFL, Frazier was overshadowed by both, but he averaged 22 yards a catch as a rookie, and in his best season, 1966, caught 57 passes for 1,100 yards, 20 yards a catch.

In a 1961 US-USSR dual meet in Moscow, he teamed with Paul Drayton, Frank Budd, and Hayes Jones for a world-record 39.1 clocking in the 4 × 100 meter relay, and followed that the next year at the Texas Relays in Austin with a dead-heat 10.6 tie with Longhorn Ralph Alspaugh in the 100 meters.

Frazier's track credentials were impeccable, though he had an awkward start. He first ran not on a track but around the elongated blocks of Angleton, fifteen miles from the Gulf Coast. He recalled how it all started: "Track came into play as a result of our having nothing else to do. So on Friday afternoons after school, we'd get together [and] run around the blocks. When we first started, I couldn't outrun a girl on my block, but as time passed, things got better and better and I started beating the girls *and* the boys. When I went out for track team, one of my coaches, Arthur Alexander, took me over to West Columbia to compete in a meet, and one of the other coaches said, 'We need somebody to run the 200.' Mr. Alexander said, 'Don't put Frazier in there. He can't run.' That kind of ticked me off a little bit, 'cause I felt like I could run a little bit. But after he said that, I got in the race and finished second. When I came off the track, he just looked at me and started laughing. I think he was using psychology, but it really helped, because after that I started to blossom."

Abraham Barrington Marshall High School had three sports, and Frazier competed in each of them: basketball, football, and track. He had to. Given the small student body at Marshall, there wouldn't otherwise have been enough boys to fill out the rosters. His 1957 senior class numbered twelve graduates, and the football roster had fewer than 30 players. "Everybody had to do everything," he said. That included a few kids bused in from area towns like Rosharon and McBeth. In McBeth on August 31, 1923, Nathan Lee, an illiterate black sharecropper, was convicted of fatally shooting his white employer in a dispute over money. Lee's execution was the state's last "legal" public hanging.

Frazier recalled a segregated Angleton where black and white athletes attended each other's games, cheering each other on and maintaining tolerable but distant relationships. Many of the town's black parents worked for white families, and on occasion black kids accompanying their parents to work might cross paths with white children. But a racial status quo generally prevailed. As Frazier recalled it: "I don't recall too many incidents. We stayed to ourselves, they stayed to themselves. At times, I felt like if we could get these teams together, we could really be something down here, because we had quite a bit of speed on our side of the track, and they had the size."

After Sunday church services, black kids gathered at one of several open fields for games of sandlot tackle football or baseball, and young Frazier held his own. When he discovered his speed, he outran everybody. In the spring and summer, he hit and played shortstop well enough to consider a baseball career as a teenager, and tried out for the Houston Buffaloes, the Triple-A affiliate of the St. Louis Cardinals. But summers were more for sweating in arduous jobs in rice fields, on local ranches, or at a cement house, physical labors that young boys welcomed as a way to prepare for the fall football season. As Frazier put it, "Our weight program was working."

A Bishop College grad named W. R. Toles was the Lions' football and track coach. His track teams won state titles in 1959, 1960, and 1961, and later, at Dallas Lincoln, his 1970 team won the UIL state championship, setting a national record in the 440-yard relay (40.2 seconds) and a state record in the 1600-yard relay (3:12.0). His teams included the standout sprinters Gene and Joe Pouncy. In 1963, Toles's quarterback was the future Pro Football Hall of Fame defensive back Emmitt Thomas, who went to Bishop College on a music scholarship to play the clarinet. During Marshall's football season, Thomas would play the first half of games, march with the band at halftime, and return with the football team to play the second half.

Toles first positioned Frazier as a 155-pound running back. That did not go well. Frazier remembered the exact moment it ended: "We played Bay City Hilliard one night, and next to their field there were some cars. And let me tell you, I took a pitchout and tried to get around the corner, and three or four of those big boys hit me and drove me out of bounds under one of those cars. Coach Toles took me out, and that was the end of my running-back career. He moved me to wide receiver. They started to use me more in my junior year. I wondered how I was going to take some of those hits, but I found out they weren't going to kill me."

They couldn't catch him. Frazier was an all-district receiver, but Texas Southern's Stan Wright came calling with a track scholarship. Frazier won at district meets with 9.8 times in the 100-yard dash and 21.8 in the 220, and he anchored Marshall's 4 × 100 relay team. He was a perfect fit for the Flying Tigers, a program that was beginning to dominate major meets around the country—the Texas Relays, the Drake Relays. It also hosted one of the top events, the TSU Relays, which packed Houston's Jeppesen Stadium, a short sprint east on Wheeler Street from the TSU campus. The PVIL teams were always featured at the meet, and the best amateur and college athletes competed there, many of them prepping for the Olympic Games. "Bullet" Bob Hayes, Rod Milburn, Wilma Rudolph, Willie Davenport, TSU's own "Duncan and Hines" duo, sprinters Jim Hines and Clyde Duncan, and Robert Taylor all tested themselves at the most anticipated event of Houston's spring.

In 1966, Wright became the first black head coach of a US national track team. He handled the US team in dual meets against Poland and the Soviet Union. Frazier became another of his prized pupils as an all-American and all-SWAC sprinter. Frazier esteemed the latter honor: "Running in the SWAC was like running in the Olympics. The guys you had to compete against set world records."

In 1966, his best season with the Oilers, Frazier was named an AFL all-star. His buddy Winston Hill also did pretty well for himself. A high school tennis star at Gladewater Weldon, he was named a black-college all-American at TSU. The Baltimore Colts made him the 145th pick (eleventh round) of the 1963 draft, but cut him in training camp. The New York Jets signed him the next day, and he built a fifteen-year career at left tackle, protecting quarterback Joe Namath. He played an integral role in the Jets' Super Bowl III upset of the Colts. Hill set a team record for offensive linemen by playing in 195 consecutive games, and he was a four-time all-star.

Hill was a natural pro-football talent, but Frazier admitted to a steep learning curve before he found success in the league: "I was pretty fortunate to make the Oilers because I hadn't played since high school. I had to learn to run routes and things of that nature. They gave me a playbook, and I was just running downfield like those lines drawn in the book, and I'd run right into the defensive back. The coaches said, 'You can't do that.

You've got to try to avoid the guy.' I got it down pretty good and surprised myself."

Maybe not.

"When I was a kid, I was watching the Oilers one Sunday with my mom, and I went to the television and pointed to a position and told her, 'One day I'm going to be playing right there,' but I didn't have any idea that would come about."

## The Sunnyside Flash

At some point between hot dogs, burgers, and barbecue at the Sheffield Steel annual family picnic, all the boys were summoned to compete to see who was the fastest. They were weighted down from the picnic grub, but that didn't dampen their youthful energy. Boys of all ages and sizes lined up, including nine-year-old Cliff Branch, who was about to discover his need for speed. "I beat everybody!" he recalled.

For the next couple of decades or so, that became the norm. Branch outsprinted everybody in South Houston's Sunnyside community on the track and on the football fields at Crispus Attucks Junior High School, Worthing Senior High School, Wharton Junior College, and the University of Colorado, and finally for the Oakland Raiders. In the built-for-speed PVIL, Branch was the premier, dominant sprinter of his era. At the 1966 state meet on the cinders at Prairie View, he breezed to a state-record 9.3 in the 100-yard dash, the first schoolboy in Texas to record such a time. Every race was a picnic. Branch understood the importance of that win: "I couldn't believe it, but that was the first time I realized I could run fast, and from that I just took off. I started playing touch football in the streets with kids who were older than me, and I could outrun them."

Branch's speed immediately caught the attention of Coach Oliver "Show" Brown when he enrolled at Worthing, at the time a junior-senior high school, grades seven through twelve. The school became Attucks Junior High when a new building opened a mile away for grades ten through twelve. Brown taught physical education and coached football and track at both schools. To know Brown was to like him as a tough but caring mentor and to fear him as a disciplinarian, as a couple of truants once confirmed. Caught by police, the boys were given the option of being taken back to Worthing to face Brown or going to jail. They chose jail.

Brown had been a standout lineman at Texas Southern University, playing for Alex Durley on the school's 1952 black-college national championship team, but became widely known in the Houston area as a brilliant track coach. Branch was his most prized pupil, but he first had to convince the boy's parents that running track was not just a way for their son to get out of his after-school job. Branch explained: "I had a job throwing the *Chronicle*, the afternoon newspaper, every day after school. My dad threw the *Post* in the morning. I'd come home from school, get on my bike, and go through the neighborhood throwing the paper. I wasn't into it, but it was a job, and I was making a little money. But one day at Attucks during gym class, I ran 5.6 in the 50-yard dash, and Coach Brown, who became my mentor, said, 'You need to come out for track!'

'I can't come out for track. I got a job.'

'You come out for track, and I'll talk to your parents.'"

Brown visited the Branch home and convinced the parents to allow their son to join the team, though the elder Branch stipulated, "He's still got to throw his newspapers."

Branch continued his paper route. He began making headlines of his own as a track star who was evolving into a football star. As a B-team quarterback at Attucks, he led an offense that was Branch left, Branch right, Branch touchdown. By the time he had reached tenth grade at Worthing, he was a multisport athlete, excelling in both track and football. But his first love was baseball. Branch had a gifted swing, and his speed made him a terror on the base paths. He played in Pony Leagues during the summer as an outfielder. He admired the Pittsburgh Pirates all-star Roberto Clemente, whom Branch honored by always wearing jersey number 21, in football and baseball.

So what would it be for his athletic career? Branch explained how he arrived at a decision: "I always considered myself a football player, though back then people thought track was number one with me, because I had world-class speed and was so dominant. But football was always number one for me. My goal, my ambition, my dream, was to be the next Charley Taylor. I'd watch the Houston Oilers and Dallas Cowboys on TV, but I was never a Cowboys fan, though I loved Bob Hayes. Charley Taylor and the Washington Redskins were my team. I loved Sonny Jurgensen throwing to Charley and Bobby Mitchell. I admired those guys, and I focused on being a receiver, because of their receiving corps.

"But I liked the Houston Oilers' receiving corps, too. They had Charlie Frazier, then Sid Blanks, and George Blanda was throwing to those guys. Coming out of Texas Southern, Charlie was a sprinter and was so fast. They also had Charlie Hennigan and Bill Groman. Blanda was throwing pretty much every down, so I'd be flipping channels—we only had three back then—but the Oilers would be on one channel, the Cowboys on another, and I always dreamed of one day being a pro receiver."

At Worthing, he was a wingback on some pretty average teams. He and quarterback Karl Douglas clearly stood out as the Colts had their best year, a 6–4 finish in 1965, the first year for both of them at Worthing. Clint Williams was head coach, and Brown was one of his assistants, along with some of the coaches who had worked at Attucks.

Branch was thrilled to start playing at Worthing. There was no B team, just varsity—and much better competition, in both football and track. Surprisingly, he was not the team's premier sprinter. That was Woody Wallace, for as long as it took to match the two in practice. Branch recalled their matchup: "I got to run with him for one season. When we started competing, I dethroned him. But San Antonio Wheatley had Clyde Glosson, and they had the fastest sprint team in the district."

Two years ahead of Branch, Glosson was a split back for the Lions and then an all-American Division II sprint champion at Trinity University in San Antonio. Branch wasn't sorry to see Glosson move on: "I was glad when he graduated and I told him, 'Now, maybe I can win some races!' Particularly in the longer sprint: "He was only a 9.5 guy in the 100, but in the 220 he was 20-point easy. Man, he'd get in that curve, come out and straighten up, and power home. He could tear that curve up, leaning over like he was going to fall."

And he did, right out of the blocks. Branch recalled having the field more or less to himself: "Nobody was close. Leo Taylor at Jack Yates could run, but for sprints I really didn't have any competition, especially after Clyde left."

Branch set the state sprint record as a junior, and in the next spring, 1967, the Houston Independent School District held its first integrated meets. Brown took his charges to Northwest Houston's Dyer Stadium, and Branch was licking his chops: "I definitely wanted to compete against them."

The outcome was no different from those in any of his other races. Branch won the 100-yard dash in 9.5, easing up at the finish line and still winning by five or six yards. The next day's *Chronicle*—his former employer—pictured him breaking the tape. Branch noted the importance of his win: "That was a proud moment for all of us to have competed against white kids and do so well."

He graduated that spring and never got to play football against white teams, a missed opportunity he regretted. He wanted the chance to compete in their stadiums, on their turf, if only because black teams could play only at Jeppesen. Some white schools in the area had their own stadiums.

"Our league was special, but the perception was that [the UIL] was better. We knew it wasn't, because we played some powerhouse schools and the big game every year was Yates and Wheatley in front of thousands of people. Everybody went to that game on Thanksgiving Day at Jeppesen.

"That's where we played our games. [The University of Houston] was playing in the Astrodome back then. They took Jeppesen and all that property, and there's a new stadium there. I drive by there all the time, and I'm just so amazed. I look up there and can still picture this memory of the field, the field house for basketball, the baseball diamond, junior high games, and all the track meets, the TSU Relays.

"Man, there was some good football played there. I'm glad I was part of that. Segregation was going on, but we didn't feel slighted, because our competition was so strong. The only time we thought about the white teams was when we passed Delmar Stadium, where they played. We'd pass by on the bus going to Aldine to play Carver, and I wondered what it would be like to play in that stadium. But we couldn't even go in there.

"We had a league of our own on Wednesday and Thursday nights at Jeppesen. I don't think back then we realized what a special league we had, but we did. We didn't need integration. It was special football, and I'm glad I was part of it."

### The Baby

Branch made his Worthing debut in 1965 when the Colts kicked off their season at Jeppesen Stadium against Beaumont Charlton-Pollard. No one was surprised to see one of the country's top prep sprinters catching and carrying the ball. The quarterback throwing to him was another story. Coach Clint Williams had handpicked Karl Douglas the previous spring, when the quarterback was a fifteen-year-old, five-eight, ninth-grade backup at nearby Crispus Attucks Junior High. Douglas had the foot speed of a turtle crawling through a mud puddle, which was of no concern to Williams, who saw a coachable kid with a lively, strong arm and the ability to make all the throws—with zip, with touch—between the numbers.

Douglas could elevate a mediocre program that had not had much of a history before 1965. The school was only seven years old. Its sports claim to fame was muscular basketball center David Lattin, who led Coach Bennie Roy's 1962 team to the school's only state championship and achieved fame as the best prep player in the nation. In football, the Colts' top athlete had been all-star quarterback Otis Taylor, who was destined for stardom as a receiver on two black-college national championship teams at Prairie View and then as an All-Pro receiver with the Kansas City Chiefs.

Williams was so anxious to get his young phenom down to business at Worthing that he worked him out at Worthing during the spring and then spent the summer pushing him through drills and conditioning work in the sweltering Houston heat every other day. Williams devised a twenty-pound sand-filled inner tube collar and had Douglas wear it while running sprints. Douglas diligently played along, worked hard, and was ready for fall practices. He waited his turn for playing time from the bottom of the depth chart.

Douglas recalled the grueling workouts: "We hit every day. I couldn't outrun our slowest lineman, and I was sore, getting hit by all these guys older than me, so they nicknamed me 'the baby.'"

On opening night, the fresh-faced kid was in the locker room channeling his inner Johnny Unitas and Bart Starr leadership abilities, going from player to player, slapping pads, stoking the fires for the night's contest. Getting little reaction from his veteran teammates, he headed to the next room and rejoined the other backup and special-teams players. Then Williams posted the starting lineups. And as Douglas remembered it, disbelief filled the room: "I figured that was my only part for the night, pumping up everybody for my first high school game, then all of a sudden I heard, 'The baby?!' I'm thinking, 'What about the baby?' I had to ask myself, 'That's me, isn't it?' You could hear a pin drop when I walked back in the room. I didn't know what to say or do. I was too scared to run away. I felt I was ready, but at that point everything just left my mind, my mind was blank. I thought it was a prank. After the kickoff, Coach Williams told me to go on out there. I couldn't show I was frightened, though I was. I didn't know if I could even take the snap. I think I threw two touchdown passes, and we won 13–6. I felt better, because I didn't let Coach Williams down. I knew that was a controversial decision."

Worthing's principal was the powerful A. E. Norton, a very stern, nononsense man with no tolerance for thugs or truants. His student body feared him. His influence was district-wide, earning him the unofficial title "black superintendent." He impressed on Williams his disapproval of the coach starting Douglas in the first game. They had a heated shouting match in Norton's office. For some reason, Douglas just happened to walk in, and he was immediately directed back out. Williams was undeterred. With Douglas starting under center, Worthing had a respectable 6–4 season, and the baby's premature career was off to a healthy start. He gave no thought to the reality that in the mid-1960s, black quarterbacks had no future at that position in nonblack college programs and certainly not in the NFL or AFL. Grambling's James "Shack" Harris wouldn't have his historic NFL debut until 1969 with the Buffalo Bills.

Douglas and Branch thrived at Worthing. The team had a breakthrough win in 1965 when it beat Wheatley for the first time in school history, igniting campus celebration—a "funeral" to bury the ghost of the Wildcats. That was as good as it got during the Douglas-Branch era. Worthing finished its next two seasons 5–5 and 4–5-1, but college recruiters found their way to South Houston because of Branch's speed. Not so much for Douglas's arm.

The recruiting circus frustrated Douglas: "A lot of white coaches came and asked if I could play defense. That got old. Could I catch? I thought about Tennessee State, but those would have been some heavy shoes to fill. Eldridge Dickey was my idol! One white guy came, and they called me, Cliff, and some other guys to the coach's office. And I was thinking, 'Aw, man, not another one.' So, I was just leaning against the wall, and he looked at me and said, 'Karl, we looking for a quarterback.' I looked around, 'You talking to me?'"

Texas A&I head coach Gil Steinke was the only nonblack college coach to visit Worthing and talk to Douglas about playing quarterback.

He promised that Douglas would have a four-year opportunity to play the position. Steinke, who was as sure of Douglas as Williams had been, took a similar approach, inviting Douglas to spring practice in Kingsville. Douglas recalled that things moved fast: "I thought I'd go to watch, but they started outfitting me, and I participated in practices."

Houston Oilers running back and A&I alum Sid Blanks had accompanied Steinke to Worthing. Blanks, an African American, had grown up in the Texas border town of Del Rio and was fluent in Spanish. When the Javelinas were on the road, Blanks was instructed not to speak English when they checked into hotels that did not allow blacks. When desk clerks asked, "What about this guy?" Steinke would respond, "He's Mexican!"

Douglas didn't have that kind of persona to fall back on. He answered his critics by becoming one of the most prolific passers in school and Lone Star Conference history, passing for a school record 5,027 yards. He led A&I to back-to-back NAIA national titles (1969–1970) and four consecutive Lone Star Conference championships. He was the first player to be named most valuable back in the NAIA title game in consecutive years. He was selected to play in the 1971 College All-Star football game. From 1934 to 1976, the game pitted a squad of the top collegians against the reigning NFL champions. The 1971 game matched the Super Bowl V champion Baltimore Colts—ironically, the team that would draft Douglas. He was also honored by getting inducted into the Javelina Hall of Fame in 1979.

One of his favorite targets at A&I was another PVIL product. Eldridge Small was considered the best athlete in the history of Houston Wheatley football. He was also outstanding in baseball and basketball. Small starred on the Wildcats' 1967 football team, which finished the season with seven consecutive victories, including four shutouts. In those seven games, they outscored their opponents by an average of 46–5. He was also an integral part of the 1967 and 1968 championship basketball teams, which marked Wheatley's entry into the UIL. Major League Baseball scouts showed interest in Small, but he accepted a scholarship to A&I. There, he contributed to the 1968–1970 Lone Star Conference championship teams and the NAIA title teams in 1969 and 1970. Small set school records for pass receptions in a game, season, and career. He was an Associated Press Little All-American in 1971, and was named to the All-Texas College and All–Lone Star Conference teams for three seasons. He was selected for the *Houston Chronicle*'s all-college team, which included players from university and college division schools. The New York Giants took Small in the first round of the 1972 draft, but as a defensive back. He retired in 1974 and returned to Houston, teaching and coaching. He took over the Wildcats' football and soccer teams and served as athletic director for fifteen years. He was inducted into the Javelina Hall of Fame at Texas A&I in 1991. Small passed away at age sixty-five in 2015.

From 1971, when Douglas was drafted in the third round by the Colts, to 1984, he had a frustrating pro career. A journeyman, he bounced from NFL training camps to the Canadian Football League to the United States Football League and finally got a brief look by the hometown Oilers. Douglas is candid about the racism that helped thwart his career: "My parents never told me I wasn't good enough or that I wouldn't get to play, but other blacks told me I needed to change positions. I didn't know I couldn't play quarterback, but started hearing the rumors about why blacks can't quarterback in the NFL. I even had a fan at A&I explain to me why black people are not intelligent—because our heads are slanted and it takes away from our brains.

"I was always put in position to fail in the pros. At Baltimore, they really wanted Jim Plunkett, but couldn't trade up, and I was next on the radar. Carroll Rosenbloom told me, 'We put together the best white quarterback to play [Johnny Unitas], now we're working on the best black quarterback, and that's why we got you.'

"I wish it could have been better. Why did I have to be a 'black' quarterback? I'm wishing, if my son gets to play they won't put 'black' in front of his name."

### Charles Green

As a junior and senior, Douglas was in the very capable hands of assistant coach Charles Green, considered by many a brilliant offensive mind. He was on Clint Williams's staff and then an assistant for Coger Coverson.

Douglas recalled working with the innovative coach: "Charlie was one of the best offensive minds around. He'd put us in double tight double wide sets, leave one back in backfield. We ran that offense and had a whole lot of success with it. You could do a lot of stuff off it."

Green liked working with Douglas, but didn't think he had that much to add to his game: "He was good already, a big strong boy, good kid, good arm."

Green had many of the same qualities. He was a product of Pemberton High in Marshall, a town where he never played any position other than quarterback, if kicking doesn't count, even in pickup games. That was how Pemberton coach C. H. Broach discovered him. It was hard to miss a big kid like Green throwing the ball "a long way" during lunch-period games. Upperclassmen began calling Green "Pro," and that seemed to fit. He could execute the Panthers' wide-open offense so well that he called his own plays. That was a glimpse of his future as a coach.

As a player, he had a highlight that isn't likely to be equaled. In a game against Texarkana Dunbar as a senior, he ran ninety-five yards for a touchdown—in the rain, after he fumbled the snap—and passed ninety-six yards for another score.

Green proudly noted: "I don't know of anyone who's done that."

Green got his first letter in 1955 as a freshman kicker. He started at quarterback the next season, and as a junior he led the Panthers to an undefeated, ten-win regular season. He was named all-state. Pemberton lost the district playoff game to Dallas Washington in a game played at the Cotton Bowl.

That same season, right across the street from Pemberton, quarterback Floyd Iglehart was leading Wiley to an 11–0 finish and a SWAC championship. Wiley was among the colleges that Green considered: "Pop Long wanted me to come to Wiley, but I went to Tennessee State and worked for a couple of months and thought I'd go there with Willie Richardson. I came back home and decided to go to Texas Southern. I liked Coach Long, but I wanted to get away from home."

Tennessee State lost both Green and Richardson that summer. Richardson went back to Mississippi and became a four-time black-college all-American receiver at Jackson State. At TSU, Green had the difficult task of following Audrey Ford as quarterback. After a high school career at Emmett Scott in Tyler, Ford led the Tigers to their first black-college national championship, in 1952. Considered the best quarterback in TSU history, he was the first Tiger to win all-American honors (1952), and he did it twice, achieving the distinction again in 1955. He was also the first and only TSU quarterback to pass for 21 touchdowns in a single season—again, twice (1951, 1952).

As a freshman, Green was an immediate starter on a team that included receivers Warren Wells, Homer Jones, and Herman Driver, three PVIL greats. Wells and Jones went on to have pro careers with the Oakland Raiders (Wells) and the New York Giants (Jones).

Green led the Tigers in passing for his four years there, and also set a school record by averaging 42.9 yards a punt. Yet the player his friends called "Pro" never got a call from the NFL, which then had no interest in black quarterbacks. Green was understandably disappointed: "I wanted to be a pro player, but I really didn't have any role models [black quarterbacks]. Choo-Choo [Brackins] had gone to the Packers, but that was about it back then. I didn't get much interest from anybody, just a couple of letters from the Philadelphia Eagles and the Chicago Bears."

He had a brief flirtation in the Canadian Football League and then played semipro for two years, 1966–1967, with the Texas Football League's Pasadena Pistols, before settling into a twenty-four-year coaching and teaching career in Houston. He nonetheless regretted the chance that got away: "I would like to have had the chance to compete and see what I could have done against the big boys. But that's the way things were."

# CHAPTER 3

# Learning and Teaching the Game

*A lot of coaches kind of thought, "They've got some good athletes but we can outcoach them." I think they proved to be sadly mistaken.*

BOB WEST, *Beaumont Journal* columnist, 1967, on integration and the perception of black coaches by white coaches

It doesn't take long to see through to the real meaning of the coded term "outcoach" as used by white coaches in regard to their black peers. In fact, if it takes more than a second to decipher, you are overthinking things. "Outcoach" meant "outthink," meaning that black coaches didn't have the mental capacity to strategize and mentor their young players for success. Nothing could have been further from the truth, as white coaches discovered when they began to match wits with black coaches at the onset of integration.

What most of them found out, or knew but would never publicly admit, was that black coaches knew *X*s, *O*s, and winning. Especially winning. Good and bad coaching crossed color lines, but good black coaches were severely underestimated and unrecognized for their savvy and creativity. Because they had so much talent at their disposal, it was assumed that they just suited up players and told them to score on offense and defend on defense, and then sat back and waited for the outcome, hoping for the best. The reality was they were eager students of the game. For years they were barred from attending coaching clinics open to white coaches only, but they read books about the game, improvised, developed strategy and organization, and learned from the best of their own kind—Pop Long at Wiley, Billy Nicks at Prairie View, Arnett "Ace" Mumford at Southern University, Alex Durley at Texas Southern, Eddie

Robinson at Grambling, and others, great minds whose players, lacking pro football opportunities before the 1960s, returned home to teach and coach at black high schools.

Andrew "Pat" Patterson at Houston Yates, Les Ritcherson at Waco Moore, Walter Day at Corsicana, Willie Ray Smith Sr. at Beaumont Charlton-Pollard and Orange Wallace, Ray T. Sheppard at Galveston Central, Ray Timmons at Austin Anderson, Joe Washington Sr. at Port Arthur Lincoln, Earvin "Cat" Garnett at Wichita Falls Washington, and Raymond Hollie at Dallas Washington were among the top PVIL coaches. Patterson and Ritcherson had dominant programs that won four state championships apiece, and all of Ritcherson's titles were outright. Timmons was the only 3A coach in PVIL history to win back-to-back state championships—1956 and 1957. Timmons-led teams won three of Anderson's four state titles. Hollie coached six Washington teams to the state championship game—in 1948, 1950, 1953, 1956, 1957, and 1958—and won in 1950 and 1958. One of his players was a 150-pound end named Ernie Banks, the future "Mr. Cub" and Major League Baseball Hall of Famer.

"He (Hollie) was one of the best coaches ever in this country—black, white, green, or purple," recalled Bill Blair, a Washington football alum who pitched in the Negro Baseball League, worked as a community activist, and published the weekly *Elite News*. "The football atmosphere was one of discipline. Mr. Hollie made sure you did the things you were supposed to do."

Hollie and his peers at PVIL schools were revered as coaches, admired as leaders, respected as men.

The Texas Longhorns' legendary coach Darrell Royal knew there was something special going on in Austin east of I-35. Royal was a controversial figure in the black community, long chided for his seeming lack of interest in recruiting black players. But during Mack Brown's tenure as the Longhorns' head coach, Royal was pleased to see the diversity of Brown's coaching staff, which included several black coaches, and Royal expressed his respect for black coaches. "I have a lot of great friends who were pioneers as black coaches and could have coached at any level," Royal said. "I remember them well, and I am also really proud that we're reaching the point where the color of a person's skin doesn't make any difference to anybody. I know it never did for me. I grew up appreciating people for who they were, not for what they could do for me. I also think there is a whole lot of positive in being proud of your roots."

Bum Phillips (Houston Oilers, New Orleans Saints), too, was among the few white coaches who had no problem giving black coaches their due: "The coaches I liked I liked because they were good football men. Willie Ray Smith and Joe Washington were good football men. It never occurred to me that they were black and I was white. Hell, they were friends of mine and they were good coaches."

Yet when black high school programs in rural areas first began to form, some of the men in charge of those programs weren't coaches or former athletes at all, but teachers assigned to provide physical education activities, or men who volunteered to supervise extracurricular programs. There was very little teaching of the game, and the coaching staff consisted solely of the head coach, who also had classroom duties and received no extra pay for doubling as a coach.

Johnny Allen, who went to Amarillo's new high school for blacks, George Washington Carver, in 1948, was the entire coaching staff. Allen, who taught math, had been a multisport star at Temple Dunbar and Samuel Huston College in Austin. Perhaps it was fitting that he landed at Carver as a multisport coach with sole responsibility for each of the school's teams: football, boy's and girl's basketball, baseball, and track and field. In 1950 he convinced his wife, Jewelle, to take over the girls basketball team, which was discontinued five years later. Allen coached football and track and field at Carver for nineteen years, but didn't gain an assistant until the late 1950s. His 1952 football team and his 1964 and 1965 track teams were state champions. When the school closed, in 1967, Allen had been its only football coach. He is remembered as Carver's "greatest Dragon ever." Allen coached wide receiver Ron Shanklin and his brother, running back Don, both of whom had NFL careers. Don Shanklin, playing for Kansas State, was named most valuable player in the 1969 Orange Bowl. Ronnie Shanklin was an All-Pro receiver with the Pittsburgh Steelers and a member of their Super Bowl IX championship team.

Allen walked into a humble, hectic career armed only with desire, the common denominator for most of the PVIL coaches who sought entry into careers as makers of men.

*Integration was inevitable, and it was a good thing, but I had mixed emotions. Some black kids were going to be left out in the cold and weren't going to get that kind of teaching you get at all black schools.*

*Black coaches were actually concerned about you. You weren't just
a football player, you were a person to them. After integration,
I couldn't imagine a white coach having as much feeling for his
players in those days as a black coach would have.*
ELLIS HUBBARD, Conroe Washington


## Joe Washington Sr.: Movietone Playbook

Growing up in the German-Polish community of Rosenberg, thirty miles
southwest of Houston, the teenage Joe Washington really didn't know
football, and no one was available to pass on knowledge of the game. So
Washington amused himself on Sundays in the 1940s by taking a bus to
Houston to catch a movie at one of the black theaters. The movie didn't
matter all that much. What Washington really wanted to see, and learn
from, was Stanford's all-American quarterback Frankie Albert, the T formation ball-handling magician, and other college football stars featured
in Movietone newsreels. Washington's teachers at A. W. Jackson High
School were good men, solid in the classroom, but without any athletic
inclinations. In effect, they supervised the activity as a physical education
exercise. So Washington watched and made mental notes about the star
he admired, a player who at five-ten was only a couple of inches taller
than he was.

Washington and his classmates formed the first football program,
such as it was, at Jackson. He shaped the team's offensive system from
his Movietone experiences and from what he had read about the sport
in the school's library books, the *Houston Press*, and magazines such as
*Scholastic Coach*, which included formations and plays. He was a true
student of the game, self-taught. Washington found motivation in his
forays into Houston and from standing behind the end zone to watch
local high school games. Blacks weren't allowed inside the high school
stadium in Richmond, but they could shinny up a tree and find a good
view of the field.

Washington recalled his lack of both experience and guidance when
it came to football: "My only real exposure to football was reading about
it. But when I went to the movies in Houston, the bus would drive down
Main Street and pass by the football field at Rice Institute. I could see
them playing and I'd come back and tell the boys, 'Man, I saw Rice and

Tulane playing!' I was a real fan of Rice, and I did see them play, but I didn't tell them I saw them playing while passing on the bus and looking through the gate.

"But, I was in awe. And because I'd seen Frankie Albert on Movietone, we ran the T formation and I was the quarterback."

At five-eight, 135 pounds, Washington was a self-described "little person," but also the best athlete at the school, excelling in basketball. He walked into the office of Principal Andrew Webster Jackson (so scholarly and influential statewide that they named the school after him while he was still principal) one day in 1945, Washington's junior year, and asked whether the school could have a football team to challenge the black kids up the road in nearby Sugarland and Richmond. The basketball season for Jackson started in September, but that grew old for Washington, who was eager to make football, the neighborhood's sandlot sport, an official school activity. With Principal Jackson's approval, Washington, the de facto head coach, gathered his friends, and the ragtag gridiron games began.

The first order of business was a trip to the local Sears. Washington remembered exactly what he ended up wearing: "My first uniform, I bought a pair of shoes and a surplus tank helmet. A relative of mine had been in the tank corps and played sports in the service. Knowing my love of football, he bought me a uniform and I was the only one at Jackson with full gear. It was all too big for me, but I had a full uniform."

A teammate purchased his uniform at a local hardware store, but his gold pants clashed with Washington's blue pants. No problem. The A. W. Jackson school colors would be blue and gold.

With the players decked out for the first time in their new uniforms, Washington had the first inklings of pursuing a coaching career. The guys were starting to look like a team, but lacked the refinement and proper training that only a coach could bring. Washington yearned for someone like that, but was left to his own devices—newspapers, magazines, Movietone, and games watched while perched on tree branches. He admitted that it was not the best preparation: "I would have been a more refined athlete if I had had a coach."

Despite the lack of formal instruction, Washington did pretty well on his own under crude conditions. The sandlot games were played with cardboard oatmeal canisters. You couldn't do much passing, so running was the thing. The players rejoiced one Christmas when a teammate's aunt gave him a real football. Now the boys could play "set back," a game to show off their arm strength. They took turns throwing the ball as far as they could, and the opponent's throw would be from the spot where the ball was caught. The object was to "set back" the opponent as far as possible from an agreed starting center point. The kicking equivalent was punting: the object was to see who could get the greatest distance and accuracy. You had to kick it straight so that it stayed within the bounds of the street's width. As Washington commented, "That's how you learned."

At the ripe young age of seventeen, the lessons ahead for Washington were many. He had picked up about all he could in Rosenberg's limited environment, so he talked his mother into signing his US Army Air Forces enlistment papers, looking ahead to GI Bill benefits and college. The wide world awaited, and oh, the places he would go to learn about life and football. Hawaii, for instance. World War II had ground to a halt in September 1945, sending the greatest generation home to launch the space age—and for black servicemen, the civil rights movement. A wide-eyed file clerk left the United States in 1946 for Wheeler Army Air Field, Honolulu. The base had squadrons of P-51, P-38, and P-47 fighters, along with an integrated football team that competed against other service teams, from Schofield Barracks and Hickam Field, and local semipro teams.

Some of his white teammates and coaches had played in the National Football League, and some at major colleges. Washington recalled what it was like to be on a team with them: "That was my introduction to organized training. I had skinny little legs, and I was light, but I was quick, had moves and could rip and run, so that wasn't a factor. The drills were new, but I caught on quick. I had a pretty good career over there until I injured my hip. That ended my season overseas."

Several months later, GI Bill in hand, he made a pit stop at Prairie View, got a degree in physical education in three years, and then headed to Bay City, eighty miles southwest of Houston, to begin his coaching career. Conditions at Hilliard High School were lean. There was no gym and no dressing area. The football team, which had fewer than twenty players, had to bus three miles east to Van Vleck's Herman High School for practice. And the program was $1,400 in debt. For games, the team got dressed in a classroom.

None of that scared Washington off, but it took three years before a gym with a small locker room was built. The local Oshman's Sporting

Goods store gave the team a break on equipment and uniforms, so the Panthers "had a well-dressed team." By the time he left Bay City in 1964 for Port Arthur Lincoln, the Hilliard program was in pretty good shape, and popular. One season, 105 kids came out for the team—basically, every boy in school. Washington's twelve-year record was 105–30, including the PVIL 2A state championship in 1959. Washington recalled the support the team got from both black and white fans: "I was one of few schools that had my own stadium and we played on Friday nights when the white school was away, or Saturday night if they were in town. We'd have blacks on one side, whites on the other, but good attendance."

Washington, who saw integration coming, knew that staying in Bay City would mean a demotion. Since he had no interest in becoming an assistant coach, he jumped at the chance to move to Port Arthur. He stayed there thirty years, the last two in administration.

Washington arrived in Port Arthur as a veteran coach well equipped to deal with the transition to integration. He knew about competing against larger schools with better funding. Despite the inequities and coaching disparities, he fielded competitive teams. He did it by being realistic and maximizing his strengths: "If I have the same boots or shoes that you have, I'm going to beat you or at least compete with you, but I'm not going to outswim you if I have a log on my back and you have fins. I realize that white guys do a lot of teaching and coaching, but we did a lot of developing. They're coaching techniques, we're judging talent, human nature. We didn't have that background of techniques, but we had the background of character and determination. We were developers of character and discipline. That's what we did. That's how we survived until we were able to get into the flow of things."

Plus, he had a much larger pool of better players at Lincoln than at Hilliard: "Numbers rule the world. I was scraping the barrel at Bay City, but when I went to Port Arthur the number of athletes I had were not marginal. I was getting the best athletes and the rest of the guys could be in the band or something." And he had at least one budding superstar in his own household—Joe Jr. In Bay City, both Washington boys, Joe and his younger brother by two years, Ken, won jackets in punt, pass, and kick contests. When the big kids came knocking on the Washingtons' door while organizing sandlot football games, they asked for Joe Jr. Joe Sr. was hesitant: "I'd say, 'My boy is too small. He can't play with you guys.' They said, 'He's better than all of us!'"

That didn't convince mom, who wasn't about to let her nine-year-old get roughed up by those bigger boys. In Port Arthur, things started to change. Joe Jr. and Ken were trainers for the Lincoln varsity, mostly carrying towels, but Joe Jr. was also lining up in the backfield with the junior high school team. Dad was so busy with Lincoln's varsity that he hadn't found time to see how his son was doing, but when he finally did, even his jaw dropped. Joe Sr. recalled the occasion: "His coach asked me to come down and look at Joe, who was already 'better than all the kids we have.' I went to one game, they were playing for the championship, and Joe scored about 30 points."

For a game at Aldine, Joe Sr. took all available bodies, freshmen, sophomores, junior varsity, and varsity. It seemed like a good time for Joe Jr. to get added to the depth chart. His junior high coach had told Joe Sr., "He's just too good for us."

The message got through. Joe Jr., a freshman, was allowed to scrimmage with the varsity at midseason, in 1969, as the Bumblebees were struggling toward a 1–9 season. He played wide receiver. His father's assessment: "[He] was pretty good. What did we have to lose?" The next year, he was moved to running back, and he played well. As a junior, "he just blew up," making all-state while playing on a 5–5 team. His highlights included a 200-plus-yard game against Port Arthur Jefferson. In Joe Jr.'s senior year, Lincoln was the hottest team in its district. Joe Jr. started at running back, and Ken, a tenth grader, at quarterback. Joe Sr. credits Lincoln's success to Ken's play: "He was a shade under 5–10, thin, but could throw the ball and was a smart field general. He was something." Lincoln won district in 1971, finishing 11–1. After Lincoln, Ken Washington went to North Texas State and started for Hayden Fry, and then played for two years in Canada.

Joe Sr. saw some of his younger self in Joe Jr.: "He did things that I did half-assed. I was not as good as he. He saw the field better than I did, and where I was just reacting to plays, Joe anticipated. I wasn't a bad back, but not the back that Joe was."

Joe Jr. was one of the most sought-after football players in Texas history. A Parade Magazine High School All-American, he chose to play for Barry Switzer at the University of Oklahoma, where he was all–Big Eight for three consecutive years and was all-American in 1974 and 1975. He was a runner-up for the Heisman Trophy in both those years, and the San Diego Chargers made him the fourth player selected overall in the 1976

NFL draft. Washington also played for the Baltimore Colts, Washington Redskins, and Atlanta Falcons. He was named the Redskins' 1981 team MVP after leading the club in rushing and receiving, the only player in Redskins' history to do so. As a Redskin, he was a member of two Super Bowl teams (XVII and XVIII), with the Redskins winning XVII.

Even so, Joe Sr. considered one of his former running backs, Sam Clark at Hilliard, a better back: "Joe knows that, he saw him play. He was bigger than Joe, 200 pounds, could catch, run punts back, quick as a water bug. He was the best running back I ever had."

Joe Sr. went to great lengths to be able to coach his boys at Lincoln. When Port Arthur's schools integrated, some of the better black players enrolled at either Jefferson High School or Austin. The Washington boys were supposed to attend Austin but never did, thanks to dad. Joe Sr. explained how he did it: "I went against the rules and changed my address for my kids to go to Lincoln. My wife had a relative who lived in town, and we used that address. It was selfish, but I wanted them to go to Lincoln. If a kid is going to help a coach pay his bills, I want my kid to help me pay my bills. Plus, this kid would have died if he hadn't played for his daddy."

## Damon Hill: Cotton Pickin' Football

Prairie View did not have a "president" until 1948. Up to that point, the school had been led by a principal, and W. R. Banks was its seventh. Banks, who considered the students his children, sought to ensure that each had a mission in life. He made himself available to them for guidance and wisdom. He could also be a stern disciplinarian, and was not shy about directing an out-of-line student to go to the highway and grab "the first thing that went by smoking."

Banks counseled Damon Hill after he completed his Depression-era studies for a degree in mechanical arts. Hill, from Houston via Hallettsville, Austin, and Orange, had been passed along from relative to relative after his parents died. He finally settled in Houston's Fourth Ward and graduated in 1932 from Booker T. Washington High School. As a newly minted college graduate, he was unsure what direction his life should take, with the country in such dire economic straits. A good student who had played football—halfback and safety at a light 145 pounds—and run track for the Panthers, coached in both sports by Sam Taylor, Hill turned to Banks for career advice. The principal directed Hill to the highway, but with good intentions. As Hill recalled, "He told me, 'Go west, young man.'"

As president of the Colored Teachers State Association of Texas, Banks was acutely aware of the need for black teachers in the Panhandle, where education for blacks clashed with the big business of cotton picking, the chore that drew black laborers who worked their way from East Texas to the region on migrant "cotton picks."

Hill applied for a job in Lubbock. His hiring increased the faculty total to seven and the athletic staff to one. He taught industrial arts and mathematics, and coached everything. Charles Sedberry had volunteered to get the school's football program started, but Hill was the first coach hired for Paul Laurence Dunbar High School's football team. And its basketball team, track squad, and, later, tennis team. Damon Hill was the foundation of Dunbar's athletics history. Despite a segregationist atmosphere, his teams were allowed to use Lubbock ISD facilities as well as those at Texas Tech University. Dunbar played in hand-me-down uniforms from Tech and Lubbock High School.

The excitement of his new assignment was tempered with great caution about leaving Prairie View: "I sure did hate to come out here. I had a girlfriend on campus and hated to leave her with those cats. But I got off the train and knew I'd stay here. I saw all of those tall buildings and knew I wasn't in the sticks."

Compared with rural, predominantly black Prairie View, Lubbock was a metropolis. Blacks were a minuscule portion (less than 1,000) of the city's population of 30,000 when Hill arrived. Organized education for blacks had been provided only since 1920; classes were first held in servant's quarters, then churches. The school had five tenth-grade graduates in 1928, an eleventh grade was added in 1930, and the growing black population called for the building of a new school structure. That was what greeted Hill, all five rooms of it.

Some of the conditions at the outset were a little grim, as Hill recalled: "I made $850 a year, and that was big money. Charles Sedberry got the football started as a volunteer coach, but it was more a club team with maybe six schoolboys on the team. I don't think they were ready for football when I came out here. There were only 150 students, and to get enough games we had to play each team twice—Amarillo, Abilene,

San Angelo. There were no black teams at the time in Midland-Odessa. It was a hassle.

"But my biggest enemy was the cotton patch. I didn't get full use of my boys."

One of those boys was Tommy Wyatt, whose family picked cotton all the way from Point Blank, on the western shores of Lake Livingston in East Texas, to Lubbock. They made friends along the way and quartered in cotton-field shanties. On Saturday mornings, children would pick until noon. With the five or ten dollars they might have made, they headed to the nearest movie theater that allowed blacks. In the evenings, adults wound down at dance halls. Wyatt's family settled for a while in Stamford, 150 miles southeast of Lubbock, and on Friday nights he would tune into Stamford Bulldogs football games on the radio. That was the extent of his knowledge of the sport. He had never seen a football game, and blacks weren't allowed in the school's stadium in Stamford.

He had heard enough "good block" and "good tackle" descriptions from the radio play-by-play announcer that when he made his first attempt to play for Damon Hill in Lubbock, he boldly stated that tackle was the position he wanted to play. Looking at Wyatt's puny frame, the coach got a nice chuckle out of that, but played along.

Wyatt recalled his initial exposure to football in real life: "I was in ninth grade, and we had just moved to Lubbock. Some of the kids asked me, 'You in football?' I said, 'Oh, yeah. How do you play football?' I was a little runt, weighed about 120 pounds, but I'd grow about a foot by the next season. Coach Hill put me in front of the first-string tackle and guard and told me I had to get through the hole between them, and if I did, he'd let me play tackle. They knocked me on my butt three or four times, and I headed to the showers."

And the next week he headed to the band director: "I told him I wanted to be in the band, so he gave me a trombone, but no instruction how to play it. He said, 'Just blow in it, and when you get a sound to come out of it, you call me.' I never went back."

He did go back to football, the next season, with his added weight and the reluctant approval of his mom, who thought football the craziest thing. Hill, in his final season as head coach, greeted Wyatt, "You back, huh?" He put him through the same drill. Success.

Wyatt and several of his teammates who also were from families that made their living picking cotton balanced football with work in the fields. Hill and his successor, George Scott, ferried players to and from the fields for practice when they could. At times, the players had to walk ten miles back to the fields. The picking season lasted from late September to late December, forcing the kids to start school in January, and then they had to stay six weeks in the summer to keep up with their schoolwork. Wyatt graduated in 1956, had an all-SWAC career at Bishop College in Marshall, and later became publisher of the *Villager* newspaper in East Austin.

Hill rarely had enough kids to hold full scrimmages. And those first few years, some of the "kids" weren't kids, but older outsiders who came to the Dunbar campus only to play football, and even then only sporadically. After his first couple of seasons, he disallowed that kind of participation. He focused on coaching true students, using kicking, passing, and running drills. He determined the players' level of talent personally: "If they were good enough to tackle me, they were good enough to tackle anybody else. I had some pretty good moves." He sometimes drove his Buick onto the field for use as a tackling dummy (!) in a drill called the "Huck-a-Buck."

Scott, his successor, told the *Lubbock Avalanche-Journal*, "He was quite inventive at practice. When he didn't have enough players to make up both the offense and defense, he'd assemble the defense and then with a couple of other players, he'd take them on and they'd run the play."

From 1937 to 1953, Hill coached 150 or more football games without a losing season, took his teams by auto caravans to distant locales such as El Paso and San Angelo, and produced players who went on to have distinguished careers in and out of football. Sam Metters, a standout at Prairie View, became a lieutenant colonel in the army and a highly successful engineer and businessman. Prenis Williams also starred at Prairie View, and in 1974 he was hired by Darrell Royal as the first full-time African American football coach at UT-Austin. Curtis Gipson was later the coach of Dunbar's 1965 PVIL 3A basketball championship team. Jackie Graves became a Philadelphia Eagles scout.

Back injuries from an auto accident forced Hill to step down from coaching in 1953, but he continued winning, guiding several Dunbar industrial arts teams to PVIL state titles. "We were doing a good job educating, getting kids to college," he said. "That was our prime objective."

## *Earvin Garnett: "Cat"*

Earvin Garnett left Abilene Woodson, where he had been an assistant to Don Grace, in 1955 and headed to the Texas-Oklahoma border town of Wichita Falls, where winning high school football championships was the norm. All-white Wichita Falls High School had won three by the time Garnett pulled up, and his new assignment, all-black Washington High School, had two under its belt, thanks to A. Tennyson Miller. It seemed like a pretty good place to settle and maintain a winning tradition. Talent didn't appear to be a problem, and the town had a close-knit, flourishing black community on the city's east side.

It was only a couple hours drive from his hometown, Fort Worth. And it fit into his near-future plans: "I planned to stay a year or so and come back to Fort Worth to coach at Terrell. The principal had told me he'd bring me in. There was a guy who had played at Bishop, and the principal was a Bishop boy, so he brought him in. But he didn't know anything about football. Then he made Jap Jones coach and said he'd make a change and get me. Instead, he got Walter Day, which was all right. I could have gone with Lubbock, but didn't want to go further west, so I stayed in Wichita Falls."

It wasn't a bad decision. "Wichita Falls was always known as a football town," he said. Garnett fell in line with what was expected, taking the Leopards to the state championship game in 1960 and then winning back-to-back PVIL 3A titles in 1965 and 1966. Garnett stayed until 1989, ending his career as assistant superintendent. His teams went 157–41, earned two state titles and seven district titles, and were state finalists three times.

In Fort Worth, Garnett played at I. M. Terrell as a quarterback and kicker for Marion "Bull" Bates's 1940 state championship team, the first official state title game for the PVIL, a 26–0 defeat of Austin Anderson. Bates, an all-American at Prairie View, taught Garnett how to drop-kick extra points and field goals.

His Terrell friends gave him the nickname "Cat" because of his inseparable best friend, nicknamed "Mice." As Garnett put it: "When you saw him, you saw me."

Coming out of Prairie View, Garnett weighed the option of signing a contract with the Los Angeles Rams, but figured it wasn't worth the headache: "If I made it, I'd get a $5,000 salary. But Tank Younger was the first black college player in the NFL in 1948, and Jackie Robinson had just gone into baseball. I didn't want to fool with that, so I decided to go into coaching. You can't tell me I can't get in the end zone. I could get in the end zone, and I could teach and motivate kids, at least I thought that and worked hard at it. I used to tell my running backs, 'Son, don't put my ball on the ground. You hug it like you hug your girlfriend. You don't drop her, so don't drop my ball.'"

He started at Spigner High School in Calvert, east of Temple, a three-year stay resulting in a state track championship in 1951, his second year. Facilities at Calvert were spartan—no locker rooms—so players would take their uniforms home on game days, change, and come back to play. Garnett improvised as best he could: "We had four or five huge coal bins under the school, and my second year there they put in natural gas, so I asked the principal if I could clean up one of those bins and use it for dressing room and equipment. Me and the players cleaned that sucker out. When the principal saw that, he wanted me to clean out the rest of them. I said, nooooo, and told my players, 'I'll kick your butt if I see any of you out there doing it for less than a $1.50 an hour.'"

Next was Abilene Woodson, where he coached with his former Prairie View teammate Don Grace and vied for a state championship with a team having only thirteen players. James Hill, who later became the first black vice president of the University of Texas, was the band director at Woodson. The band would travel on the same bus with the football team, and some of the football players were in the band.

One player who was only fifteen years old somehow had talked his way into the army. After being wounded in Korea, he came back to finish his high school degree.

At Wichita Falls Washington, Garnett won with speed and defense. The Leopards featured Reggie Robinson, a PVIL 2A sprint champion. Quarterback Johnny Davis, who went to Washington State, led the undefeated 1965 state champs. James Harris was an all-around player on the team: split end, safety, kicker, and punt returner. He was named PVIL all-state as a safety. "I knew I was ready," Garnett said. "In 1964 we won our last seven games. They were hungry. Davis was a heck of a quarterback. He ran that sprint out, bootleg. Gordon Wood [the legendary coach at Brownwood] said he was the most dangerous player he ever coached against."

Harris recalled the feeling of that season: "We were not going to let anything stop us from winning. We could not have had a better coach. He was like a father figure and always taught us to be respectful, don't be out here clowning, stealing, drinking, acting a fool. Try to make something of yourself. We grew up as a family, and on the field he just let us play. The year we won state, he told us, 'I coached you all enough. It's up to you guys if you want it.'"

Washington faced a tough Nacogdoches Campbell team in the championship game. The Wichita Falls community showed its support by holding a citywide pep rally at Washington. Wichita Falls High School students came. Harris recognized the importance of the event: "The rally was in the gym. We broke some racial barriers that day. Everyone was cheering, and there were no problems at all. The city really got excited about Booker T. Washington. That opened a lot of doors for us, though we didn't see ourselves in a struggle. We were secure in ourselves and in our own neighborhoods and schools."

After integration in 1967, many doubted the Leopards' ability to compete with white teams. But Garnett had big wins against in-town rival (and state-ranked) Hirschi and Wood's powerful Brownwood team. Integration was nonetheless painful to watch as players whom Garnett had groomed were directed to Wichita Falls High, Rider, and Hirschi. He recalled how it felt to see that happen: "I used to let those little jokers hang around my practices, get on the bus to go to the stadium. I love pecans, so they'd bring me pecans. Ronnie Littleton [the legendary running back] was mine, but he went to Wichita Falls High. For the next four years, all of the quarterbacks at each one of those schools were mine. It hurt."

## Waco Moore High: The Hero, the Football Coach

It was the 1941 Christmas season, and like most servicemen far from home, Doris "Dorie" Miller was perhaps thinking about his family back in Waco. Regardless, he went about his duties on the USS *West Virginia*, at rest in the docks at Pearl Harbor. The burly—more than two hundred pounds on his six-three frame—mess attendant known as the "Raging Bull" when he carried the ball for A. J. Moore High School's Lions was below deck, collecting towels for laundering after breakfast chow. Then the world suddenly changed. The *West Virginia* was hit portside by three torpedoes as the Japanese commenced their surprise attack on the US naval base at Pearl Harbor. When the battleship's general alarm began blaring, Miller darted to his battle station at the antiaircraft battery magazine, an ammunition storage location, but found it already damaged beyond use. He hustled up on deck, where he helped move wounded sailors to safety, including the ship's captain.

In the segregated navy, black sailors held few positions other than menial, noncombat roles. They received no training in handling weapons, which made Miller's next action so extraordinary. With the *West Virginia* sinking fast, Miller took control of a .50-caliber machine gun and began firing at enemy planes, downing one or more—the exact number has long been the subject of debate. Miller humbly described his actions: "It wasn't hard. I just pulled the trigger and she worked fine. I had watched the others with these guns. I guess I fired her for about fifteen minutes . . . They were diving pretty close to us."

In an instant, Doris Miller the Waco Moore football hero became Doris Miller the US Navy war hero. To newspapers, he was an unnamed "heroic Negro messman." The black media rectified that when the *Pittsburgh Courier* sent one of its war correspondents to locate Miller, who otherwise might never have been identified. In April 1942, Miller received the Navy Cross, unprecedented for a black sailor. At the ceremony, held aboard the aircraft carrier USS *Enterprise*, Fleet Admiral Chester W. Nimitz, commander in chief of the Pacific Fleet, pinned the medal to Miller's chest. Nimitz, a fellow Texan from Fredericksburg, remarked: "This marks the first time in this conflict that such high tribute has been made in the Pacific Fleet to a member of his race, and I'm sure that the future will see others similarly honored for brave acts."

Miller and 643 shipmates were killed in action in November 1943 when the aircraft carrier USS *Liscome Bay* was sunk by a Japanese torpedo. Miller was an unlikely hero. The navy hadn't had a black sailor in thirteen years, and when it resumed recruitment, black enlistees were channeled into the Steward's Branch as mess men—a noncombat role. Navy recruiting posters in Waco prompted a sarcastic response from the *Waco Tribune*, which the black weekly *Waco Messenger* rebuked: "Our local daily puts it, presumably . . . in force humor, as giving colored men the opportunity of 'totin' plates instead of cotton sacks . . .' Just think of it! The only way Negroes can die in Uncle Sam's democratic Navy is slinging hash."

Miller was likely the first US hero of World War II, a symbol of black patriotism. His example recalled that of Sam McCullough, who had fought heroically in the Texas Revolution. A free black man, McCullough participated in the Battle of Goliad (1835), and is considered the first Texan casualty of the war. McCullough was born in Abbeville, South Carolina, and came to Texas with his father, who was white. McCullough joined the Matagorda Volunteer Company as a private. He was severely wounded in the right shoulder during the storming of the Mexican officers' quarters, the only Texan wounded in the battle.

———

Another sharecropper's son was just beginning to find his way at Moore High when Miller stepped heroically into the World War II spotlight. Lewis "Les" Ritcherson, the second of three boys, was born in the farming community of Hillsboro, thirty miles north of Waco, but grew up in the larger town with his mother and paternal grandparents after his father died. John and Eugenia Ritcherson stepped in to help ease the hardship caused by their son's death, pledging to raise the boys, whom they cared for through their younger days. Industry was a strict part of their upbringing. They helped raise corn and potatoes, and tended the hogs, which meant gathering garbage from around the neighborhood to use as feed. The boys also found time for football, when a ball was available.

Ritcherson recounted: "One of the things I remember most about my father was we used to play football in the street, and one year I got a ball for Christmas and somehow one day he ran over it and I was standing at the door boo-hooing, crying, yelling, and screaming."

It was likely an unfortunate accident, though Ritcherson remembered that his mother and grandparents didn't want him to play football at Moore, because of a chronic nosebleed problem. Coach R. L. Posey intervened and received permission for their son to join the team, but also took his newest player for a physical. The doctor prescribed exercises—deep knee bends and pushups—and declared Ritcherson ready to suit up. Ritcherson was grateful for the coach's involvement: "That turned out to be a blessing. I never would have been able to go to college otherwise."

Ritcherson played football and basketball at Moore. The school began in 1875 as a response to concerns expressed by Alexander James Moore, a professor at Waco's Paul Quinn College, about the absence of formal education resources provided by the city for young black children. Moore held classes at his home for what was called the First District Negro School. The small groups quickly grew in numbers, necessitating a move in 1881 to a small, four-room frame building, a former hospital, that took the name Second District Negro School. Moore was principal for the next twenty-four years. His first five students graduated in 1886. The building was destroyed by fire in 1921, and a new, brick structure with thirty-five classrooms opened two years later. Named for Moore, who had passed away in 1905, it had the distinction of being the only Waco school district facility named after a person. The *Waco Tribune-Herald* noted that the community chose the name to honor the "selfless legacy" of Moore. The school closed in 1971, leaving a record as the "first and arguably most successful effort for the provision of systematic and quality education for children of all races in Waco."

Moore was one of two PVIL schools in the Waco area. Five miles north of Waco, Carver High School was created in the La Vega Independent School District in 1956 for 500 black students. The school was in operation for fourteen years, closing in 1970 with the advent of integration, but its 1967 marching band appeared in the Montreal World's Fair, Expo 67, and won a $1,000 prize in a musical competition. In 1965, running back Eddie Bell graduated from Carver and then starred at Idaho State as a Big Sky Conference sprint champion in the 220-yard dash and was an all-American wide receiver in 1969. Bell played in the NFL from 1970 to 1976. As a rookie with the New York Jets in 1970, he tied a club record with twelve catches in a game against the Baltimore Colts. He was inducted to the PVIL Hall of Fame in 2016.

At Moore, Ritcherson began his football career as an all-district end. The school played in PVIL District 4, which included San Antonio Wheatley, Corpus Christi Coles, Victoria Gross, and Austin Anderson. Before Moore could join the 4A group, it had to overcome the problem of not having enough students to meet the classification standard. The schools were classified by counting enrollment from tenth through twelfth grades. Moore included grades seven to nine in the same building with the higher grade levels, so the principal, wanting to move up to the league's highest bracket, simply counted all kids enrolled in the school. When Ritcherson started playing, Moore was 3A, but had stepped up to 4A by the time he left, in 1943, for Wiley to play for Pop Long.

In Ritcherson's recollection, Long had one overriding concern: "He wanted us to be the best conditioned team, so we ran before, during, and after practice, up and down the field, with Pop just standing on the sidelines yelling, 'Run, run, run, till I get tired,' end zone to end zone. But I carried that philosophy about conditioning with me when I started coaching."

Ritcherson was named to the *Chicago Defender* sportswriter Fay Young's "Negro All-American Team" in 1945. Wiley finished 10–0 that year, and was named black-college national champion. Wiley handily defeated the great Jake Gaither and his Florida A&M Rattlers 32–6 in the Orange Blossom Classic in Jacksonville, Florida. The OBC, as it was called, was the black colleges' Rose Bowl and unofficial national title game, the signature event for historically black colleges and universities during the 1950s and 1960s. Gaither's dominating teams took on all comers.

"It seems I couldn't miss a pass that year, couldn't do no wrong," Ritcherson recalled of that undefeated season.

Wiley student Velma Joyce Grace, the sister of PVIL coach Don Grace, didn't miss Ritcherson, spotting him at a campus eatery, the Wildcat Inn. Ritcherson described the scene: "She told her friends, 'Oh, yes, there he is,' as soon as I walked in. I didn't know anything about it, but she told them, 'He's mine!'"

They married and headed to West Texas for Ritcherson's first coaching job. In 1947 he guided an undermanned team at Midland Carver. He also briefly played quarterback in his first season there, under an assumed name. Ritcherson was unapologetic about it: "I had always wanted to play quarterback. I didn't have insurance, and we had a youngster on the way, so that ended my brief 'pro' career."

Three years later, the head coaching job at Moore opened up. While the Ritchersons were in Waco for Christmas, the school principal asked Les to apply for the job. He got it, at age twenty-three, and the balance of power in the PVIL soon shifted to Waco. From 1950 to 1965, Ritcherson taught civics, history, and health education. His football program went 132–38, won five district and bi-district titles along with two state championships (1960, 1964) and two cochampionships (1951, 1960).

The Lions played on Wednesdays and Thursdays. After traveling 200–300 miles for the weeknight games, they slept in the gym when they returned to Waco, in order to be on time for the next day's classes. Ritcherson thought the schedule "was cruel."

In an added complication, Ritcherson's first year was shadowed by the team's recent struggles: "When I first got to Moore, I had so many other schools writing me for games. Everybody wanted to play us because it was a sure win for them. I instilled in those young men that if they wanted to be good in life, they had to be good in what they attempted to do. They had to work hard to be successful. I had some good players and good assistants. Vernon Hicks was the first assistant I had."

By adhering to the Pop Long philosophy of "conditioning, conditioning, conditioning," Ritcherson quickly turned things around at Moore. The Lions tied Yates 6–6 in the 1951 state title game, and came back the following year to defeat Corpus Christi Coles 14–0 for the state championship; that was the last of three games his team was forced to play in eight days, because of a three-way district tie. Moore survived the grueling stretch by leaning on its physical training, which became a staple of Ritcherson's teams.

James Jones, a receiver on the 1964 team, saw the benefit of the emphasis on conditioning: "Coach Ritcherson was an absolute disciplinarian. Back in our day, coaches were very physical with us. But we had the best-conditioned team I ever played on. We always knew we were one of the toughest teams, regardless of size."

Moore's 1964 state championship team was the school's last. As integration loomed, so did Moore's closure. Ritcherson departed for the University of Wisconsin in 1966, becoming the Badgers first black assistant coach. He was joined there by his son, Lewis Ritcherson Jr., a quarterback who led Moore's high-powered offense in the title-winning 1964 season after assistant coaches and Lions' players had lobbied for his insertion into the starting lineup.

Lewis Jr. was well prepared for the role: "They told my dad, 'Why don't you go ahead and start him? He's better than the other guy.' I guess he needed that approval to start his son. He didn't want to be accused of favoritism. I would always watch film with him, and learned a lot just listening to him. By the seventh grade, I knew all the varsity plays, formations, where everybody was supposed to block. I had started practicing throwing the ball through a swinging tire when I was in fifth or sixth grade. Don Trull was the quarterback at Baylor, so I started doing the drills he suggested on a film. You had to throw at least a hundred balls a day against a wall and know how it was supposed to come off the wall, how to use your footwork."

It all came together for Lewis Jr. as a senior. Besides guiding the

Lions to the state championship, he was named a Parade Magazine High School All-American. Recruiting offers came from dozens of major programs, including Ohio State, SMU, UCLA, Wisconsin, and the locals at Baylor. He chose Wisconsin, though his dad wanted him to attend UCLA and play for Tommy Prothro. In the end, Coach Ritcherson called their moving to Wisconsin "a package deal."

Wisconsin learned of Ritcherson the coach from his counterpart at Houston Yates, Pat Patterson, who suggested to Badger recruiters visiting Houston that they go see Ritcherson in Waco, telling them, "He's got some good players there."

Described only as "a high school football team" from 1909, the team pictured most likely represented the "Colored High School" located at Hall and Cochran Streets, the only high school in Dallas at the time for African American students (it eventually merged with and relocated to the nearby Booker T. Washington High School in the early 1920s where, incredibly, it remained the city's only high school for black students until Lincoln High School opened in South Dallas in 1939). A 1909 blurb in the *Dallas Morning News* announced that the "football team of the Dallas Colored High School will play the Wylie [*sic*] University team from Marshall at Gaston Park" (November 12, 1909), without question one of the first games played by black high schools in Texas. (Courtesy of the J. L. Patton Collection, Dallas Historical Society. Used by permission.)

For years, legendary Wiley College coach Pop Long was upset that his nephew Darnell Johnson (center) didn't join the Wiley program. Long had said he wanted Johnson because he could "out-run any rabbit in the bushes" and that "in natural talents, neither Jesse Owens nor Harrison Dillard had a thing on Darnell!" Johnson is shown here with other Hopewell High School football athletes, circa 1930. Johnson also competed in Prairie View track meets, and when he arrived at a state meet muddy and disheveled from changing a flat tire in the rain, he and his teammates were derided and gestured at for their motley appearance. However, Hopewell won the championship with first place finishes in five events and two runners even lapped the field ahead of their respective challengers. (Courtesy of PVILCA)

At six-three and over 200 pounds, Doris "Dorie" Miller was called the "Raging Bull" when he carried the ball for A. J. Moore High School. As a mess attendant aboard the USS *West Virginia* at port in Pearl Harbor on the morning of December 7, 1941, the football hero became a war hero, helping move wounded sailors to safety as the Japanese attacked the naval base. Miller also instinctively took control of a .50-caliber machine gun, though he had never been taught to use it because the Navy did not assign African Americans combat positions, and began firing at enemy planes, possibly downing one or more. Miller humbly described his actions: "It wasn't hard. I just pulled the trigger and she worked fine." In April 1942, Miller became the first black sailor to receive the Navy Cross. (Official US Navy photo)

Anderson High School
1942 Football Team
State Champions of 1942

In 1942, Austin had two state championship teams: Anderson in the PVIL and Austin High in the UIL. In the first six seasons of the PVIL's structured playoffs, beginning in 1940, William Pigford led Anderson to the 2A state finals three times, winning in 1942 with an 11-0 squad that trounced Paris Gibbons 40-0. Willie "Zipper" Wells Jr. (son of the Negro League baseball star) caught five touchdown passes and kicked four extra points. (Courtesy of Leroy Bookman)

Marion "Jap" Jones was an athlete at Booker T. Washington High School in Dallas and at Wiley College in Marshall; he was an all-American in both football and track, but also competed in basketball and tennis. He is considered the greatest all-around athlete in Wiley history, earning sixteen varsity letters and the nickname "Mr. Everything." After Wiley, he coached, taught, and served as a high school administrator for thirty-eight years. Drafted into the army in 1942, he and his fellow draftees would frequent Jap Jones Café in Tyler where his buddies began calling him "Jap" because he ate most of the food in the serving line before they could get their fill. Jones was a co-founder of the PVIL Coaches Association. (Courtesy of the Texas Sports Hall of Fame)

In 1952, Galveston Central running back Ray Dohn Dillon became the first African American from the city drafted into the National Football League. Dillon starred at Central and then at Prairie View A&M where he became a *Pittsburgh Courier* all-American in 1950 as a defensive back, and the next year as a fullback, before the Detroit Lions picked him in the thirtieth round of the draft. Dillon later returned to Central as an assistant coach for Ray Sheppard. (Courtesy of the Ray Dohn Dillon family)

Barbara Jordan was a PVIL debate champion at Houston's Phillis Wheatley High School, where she graduated in 1952. In 1966, she was elected the first black Texas state senator since reconstruction and in 1972 was elected to the US House of Representatives, becoming the first black woman from a Southern state to serve in Congress. (*Black Americans in Congress 1870–2007*, US House of Representatives)

The Star Theater was the movie venue for Beaumont's black citizens. Here, Charlton-Pollard football player Eugene Luke and majorette Alice Marie Moore pose in front of the theater's marquee supporting the team. (Tyrrell Historical Library [Beaumont, Texas], the Gilbert Papers, MS 159)

Livingston Dunbar's 1958 team was coached by James "Big Jim" Dewalt, led on the field by quarterback Richard Ryans (no. 13), a talented four-year starter who, it was said, "could hit a stop sign" at fifty yards, and running back John Payton, who would become the all-time leading rusher at Prairie View. It was the school's third state 1A championship, this one clinched with a 26–24 win over Grand Prairie Dalworth and its star running back Charley Taylor. Coach Ross Hardin was at the helm for the other two titles (1953, 1954). Former Livingstone lineman/linebacker Marion Johnson (no. 60) said, "We were pretty feared. . . . We thought we were good; we knew we were good." (Courtesy of Marion Johnson)

From 1960 to 1965, Charles Brown had an incredible run at Conroe Washington, winning five district titles and two 2A state championships (1960, 1965), with both teams finishing with 13–0 records. (Courtesy of PVILCA)

Coach Charles Brown and his wife, Carolyn, who also taught at Conroe Washington, were the guiding force behind the program, Charles as coach, Carolyn as the team's "mom," preparing meals before the games, repairing uniforms, and even serving as laundress. It was not unusual to pass the Brown's home and see freshly washed football uniforms draped across a fence and drying in the breeze. (Courtesy of PVILCA)

A 1960 graduate of Kashmere Gardens High School in north Houston, Marcelite Harris became the first black female general in the air force in 1990. Her great-grandfather, I. M. Terrell, was a noted educator who founded the first school for African Americans in Fort Worth. (US Air Force)

Led by Orsby Crenshaw and Roy Horton, Anderson's 1961 team finished its season with a 20–13 state 4A championship win over no. 1–ranked Houston Yates in the Lions' backyard, Jeppesen Stadium. However, it would be the final title for the Yellow Jackets, who from 1956 to 1961 compiled a 65-7-5 record and five district crowns all coached by Raymond Timmons. (Courtesy of Leroy Bookman)

Playing for his dad, Les Ritcherson Jr. quarterbacked Waco Moore's 1964 champion-ship team, the school's last, as integration led to the school's closure. Les Sr., the head coach, had been hesitant to elevate his son to the starting position and only did so after assistant coaches and Lions' players lobbied him. "They told my dad, 'Why don't you go ahead and start him, he's better than the other guy.' I guess he needed that approval to start his son." Following the 1964 season, Les Jr. was named a *Parade* magazine all-American. (Courtesy of UW–Madison Archives)

At 150 pounds, Andrew Penns was considered "large" for his class, and played guard, center, and tackle at Abilene Woodson, graduating in 1967. Penns recounts how "we assembled at Larry's Burgers after games. It was white-owned, but it was one of the only places we could go and hang out. It catered to whites, blacks, and Spanish, and it was a place that we could feel safe, could hang out, a place that was a part of us because it was in our neighborhood, the black neighborhood." (Courtesy of Andrew L. Penns)

Dan Haskins coached and taught math at Texarkana Dunbar, his high school alma mater. He was a member of the last Tillotson College graduating class in the spring of 1952 and that fall Tillotson and Huston College merged to form Huston-Tillotson College in Austin. As Haskins recalls, "They had school Monday through Friday, no Saturday classes, and the girls stayed out until 9 o'clock." In 1967, Haskins guided Dunbar to its only state championship game appearance, losing a 3A battle to Elmer Redd's Lufkin Dunbar squad, 44–24. (*Texarkana Gazette* obituary)

Leo Taylor graduated in 1967 from Jack Yates High School where he was quarterback for coach Pat Patterson and team MVP. Taylor led the Lions to a state championship in 1965 and was named all-district. At North Texas State University, he was switched to running back for his sophomore season and set a Mean Green single-season rushing record (1,017 yards), was named first-team All-Missouri Valley Conference, and was chosen to the AP and UPI honorable mention all-American teams. With Calgary, in the Canadian Football League, he was a member of the 1971 Grey Cup championship team. (Courtesy of PVILCA)

Eldridge Dickey's star-crossed career began at Houston's Washington High School where his strong arm, leadership, and pocket instinct made him an instant legend, though no official documentation of his stats exists. At Tennessee State, he was a three-time black college all-American with 6,523 passing yards and 67 touchdowns and was dubbed "The Lord's Prayer," leading John Merritt's Tigers in 1966 to their first black-college national championship. However, Dickey's career quickly bottomed after he was selected by the Oakland Raiders in the first round of the 1968 NFL Draft, a first for a black quarterback. Dickey never saw action in a regular season game, was traded to the Kansas City Chiefs, and in four uneventful years, was out of the league. Chiefs Coach Hank Stram would later say, "What happened to Eldridge Dickey has to go down in history as one of the greatest sports crimes ever committed." (Courtesy of Tennessee State University)

Andrew "Pat" Patterson, from Gary, Indiana, was a revered coach at Houston's Jack Yates High School. Before Yates, he was an all-around athlete at Wiley College, then an all-star infielder in the Negro Baseball Leagues. At Yates, from 1938 to 1968, he guided teams to state championships in football, basketball, and baseball. In 1982, Patterson became the first coach from the PVIL elected to the Texas High School Coaches Association Hall of Honor. (Courtesy of PVILCA)

Running back Joe Washington Jr. played for his dad, Port Arthur Lincoln coach Joe Sr., and was one of the most sought after football players in Texas history, eventually playing in two Super Bowl games with the Washington Redskins. In 1981, he was the team MVP after leading the club in rushing and receiving, the only player in Redskins' history to do so. In spite of his son's success, Coach Washington had his misgivings about integration, saying, "They put those kids in situations that were new to them, and some of them were not able to handle it. Yes, we were probably better off educationally, but not as a race. We lost too many people in the shuffle. Coaches and teachers lost jobs, kids dropped out of school." (Courtesy of Beaumont Enterprise)

The Kelley brothers—Robert, the quarterback, and Louis (pictured), the running back—were among the best to come out of Abilene Woodson. Louis was a team captain and two-time all-state running back (1954, 1955), coached by Earvin Garnett and Don Grace. Louis Kelley coached at his alma mater and Lubbock Dunbar before building a dynastic program at Lubbock Estacado that lasted twenty-five years and won seventeen district championships. He was named *Lubbock Avalanche-Journal* Coach of the Year eight times and inducted into numerous halls of fame. He retired in 2000 with a 240–91–10 record. (Courtesy of PVILCA)

The Prairie View Interscholastic League Coaches Association in Houston works to keep the league's history alive through its traveling exhibits of PVIL memorabilia and an annual Hall of Fame and Hall of Honor banquet. (Courtesy of PVILCA)

# CHAPTER 4

# Gold in the Triangle

*My first year at Washington, in Houston, we went to Beaumont Charlton-Pollard, and it was outrageous the way Bubba Smith treated "Sloppy Joe" [quarterback Ural Johnson]. It was muddy and rainy, and [it] looked like Bubba was another coach on the field. How he could tell what we were going to do, I don't know. We ran around end—he was there. Run up the middle—he was right there. He was all over the place, and when he hit Sloppy, he'd get up pushing Sloppy's head down in the mud.*

COACH BO HUMPHREY, Houston Washington

Like the Atlantic Ocean's Bermuda Triangle, the Southeast Texas area known as the Golden Triangle retains a sense of mystery. For the latter, the question is, how do you explain the overabundance of extraordinarily talented black high school football players emanating from the area? With players such as Ernie "Big Cat" Ladd out of Orange, Bubba Smith in Beaumont, and Joe Washington Jr. in Port Arthur, you could put together a formidable team along with reserves who could hold their own against the starting elevens. The Golden Triangle gushes football players like the powerful black geyser of oil that exploded from Spindletop in 1901 and converted the area into a petrochemical center. The region gave birth to Mobil, Gulf, Texaco, and other oil companies. They built fume-spewing refineries and chemical plants from Beaumont to Orange (thirty miles to the east) to Port Arthur (twenty miles to the southwest), and along the twenty-two miles back to Beaumont. Those were the corners of the Golden Triangle, but Baytown, a Houston suburb, and even Galveston were loosely included in the triangle, at least where the PVIL schools were concerned. From Baytown to Orange, a one-hundred-mile petrochemical alley along I-10, a lot of exceptional football players came to prominence.

"Golden" in the name "Golden Triangle" refers to the money made from black gold, but it could just as easily describe the wealth of area black athletes who enriched dozens of collegiate programs.

"They have all of those industrial places, and we used to say it was something in the smoke up there," Leon Bedford suggested, having coached at both Beaumont Hebert and Galveston Central. "You talk about some great people that came out of the Golden Triangle, man, you can't talk about athletes until you talk about the ones that came out of there from Hebert and Charlton-Pollard. The old man—Coach Willie Ray Smith—and his sons, Tody, Bubba, and the best one of them, Willie Ray Jr., at Charlton. And Hebert had a hell of a lot of good football players, too, with Mel and Miller Farr, and so many others.

"There's more football players that came out of the Golden Triangle than anywhere in the state of Texas. You can't go nowhere and find as many good players, not even Houston, that came out of the Triangle. When you played them, you just lined up and got your butt whipped."

Or maybe you got your head squashed into the mud by the most dominant defensive lineman of his era. Golden Triangle football meant several PVIL schools: Hebert and Charlton-Pollard in Beaumont, Wallace in Orange, Lincoln in Port Arthur, and their neighbors to the south near the oil-sheened beaches: Galveston Central and hard-hat Baytown Carver. The center was Beaumont, proclaimed by Hebert's Jerry LeVias to a national television audience in 1968 as the "pro football capital of the world." Beaumont mayor Ken Ritter—nephew of the singing cowboy actor Tex Ritter—seconded the motion, and the Texas State Senate piled on with a proclamation and a senate resolution in 1971. That year, sixteen players from Beaumont could be found on NFL rosters, eleven from the city's two PVIL schools: Bubba Smith, Tody Smith, Jess Phillips, and Wayne Moore from Charlton-Pollard; LeVias, Warren Wells, Mel and Miller Farr, Anthony Guillory, Charles Ford, and Bob Pollard from Hebert.

Hebert's Panthers played on Thursday nights, Charlton-Pollard's Bulldogs on Saturday nights, and when the teams closed their regular-season schedules with the Soul Bowl, Beaumont's black community chose sides. LeVias explained, "No one died or got married that week, and if you were married to someone who went to the other school, you separated for that week. It was a great tradition. When we played each other, guys would bet a month's check from their jobs at the refinery. Barbers would offer free haircuts 'if ya'll beat 'em,' restaurants would say, 'Come by and get a few BBQ sandwiches.' We had great support from whites, too. People were behind us, but that also put a spotlight on you. You had to behave, because you were an example.

"It was a big deal, playing for Hebert or Charlton-Pollard, and a great environment to grow up in, a great environment to have the PVIL, because we had some of the most competitive teams. We had fun playing the game. It was very competitive, spirited, just unbelievable. When you were a kid growing up, you wanted to play football because our coaches would ride in the evenings and throw footballs in the yards of kids in the neighborhoods so we'd have something to play with. And we'd have a big game every Thursday in the park near the public pool.

"Football was everywhere—in vacant lots, in the streets, football was king."

The royal family's surname was Smith, its monarch a charismatic coach named Willie Ray.

## The "Strap System"

*We'd have two-a-days at the school, and some of us would be walking to his [Coach Smith's] house to eat lunch, then walk back to school. He passed us up in that damned Cadillac, listening to Aretha Franklin, and do you think he gave us a ride? Hell, naw! He'd blow the horn and keep going. "I'll see ya'll at the house, okay!"*

WALTER SMITH, all-district center, Charlton-Pollard

In a glowing, and extremely rare, mainstream-media feature story on a black coach, the Sunday edition of the *Orange Leader* on February 13, 1949, lavishly praised Willie Ray Smith Sr. for his corporal discipline: "It's doubtful that the strap system of coaching high school athletic teams ever will become widely popular but it works fine for Coach W. R. Smith of Orange's Wallace high school for Negroes. The strap system, in case you're not familiar with it, is based on the old-fashioned idea that cowhide liberally applied to a boy's bottom is a wonderful aid in helping him to remember lessons in discipline—or in the fine art of sidestepping tacklers on the gridiron.

"Whatever the merits or disadvantages of the strap system, it drew 40 of the 73 boys in Wallace high school out for football last season, although all were well acquainted with the penalty for failure to fulfill an assignment or for breaches of discipline. It also has the full support of parents and fans. A number of players have had the punishment doubled at home for mentioning that they had been on the receiving end of one of coach Smith's lessons in leather."

Willie Ray was indeed a devoted proponent of getting a player's attention by applying a lick or ten to his backside, and the preferred tool for delivering his message varied—a leather strap, a deflated inner tube from a bicycle tire, and the very popular paddle, widely used by coaches throughout the PVIL. One paddle-less coach reportedly became so apoplectic at a player who repeatedly failed to perform his assignment during a scrimmage that he frantically destroyed a nearby wooden hurdle and fashioned one of the remaining parts into a paddle for immediate use. Players expected and accepted the strap system and its associated forms of corporal discipline as part of their training. Charlton-Pollard lineman Walter Smith, and close Smith family friend, explained: "He taught me how to snap the ball for punts. The old man would be sitting there on a stool fifteen yards back, pointing at his [scrotum], and he'd say, 'Hit me right here, and I don't want to reach for it.' If you didn't hit him right there, he was hitting your ass. He had something for you. That paddle was right there. He had one of those paddles they made in wood shop with a grip on it like a fraternity paddle, with holes in it so there was no wind resistance. You got a natural butt whipping."

Bum Phillips, the former Houston Oiler head coach, grew up in Orange. He recalled Willie Ray keeping his team on the field at halftime during a game in which they trailed. Instead of a locker room rah-rah speech, he delivered a motivating lick with his leather strap to each player. "I'll tell you what," Phillips said, "business picked up in the second half."

Willie Ray paddled his way to 235 wins while coaching at Lufkin Dunbar, Orange Wallace, and Charlton-Pollard—an astonishing feat for a man who never played a down of football. Willie Ray grew up in Denton, Texas, with no interest in sports, an amazing fact in and of itself for a male high school student in Texas. He was good-looking and quite the fashion figure, known as the "Denton Doll," always impeccably groomed and dressed to impress the girls.

Willie Ray walked with a limp, and how that came to be delightfully adds to his lore. Young Willie Ray happened to be in downtown Denton on a day when Bonnie Parker and Clyde Barrow decided to display their unhappiness with the local police, who were holding an associate of theirs. The felonious duo fired a hail of bullets at the police station, and one of the strays wounded Willie Ray in his right leg. After five years of treatment in a Dallas hospital, the wound had not healed, and doctors felt that amputation was the solution. Willie Ray resisted, and a new doctor suggested maggot therapy to relieve the infection. It worked, but left Willie Ray with a pronounced limp for the rest of his life. But the disability hardly slowed his career.

He studied at Prairie View, where he met Georgia Oretha Curl, his future wife and "co-coach" of the Smith brood and Charlton-Pollard football. In Beaumont, she sent Willie Ray off to games with a reminder: "Now, Coach, don't you forget our little play," which was called the "Louisiana ride." It was basically a reverse. Georgia had observed that since "everybody was going one way, why can't we go the other way?"

The couple graduated, and Willie Ray, a disabled nonathlete, started his career by talking his way into jobs teaching and coaching football and basketball at Lufkin's Dunbar High School. Georgia taught homemaking. His first big success came in Orange at Emma Wallace High School, where he won eight district titles and two state championships, 1949 (1A) and 1954 (2A). He coached Ernie "Big Cat" Ladd—Smith once lined him up as a receiver—and his uncle, Garland Boyette. At Charlton-Pollard, Willie Ray's son, "Bubba," was a six-eight, 250-pound freshman, eating at every opportunity, but that was nothing compared with the equally large Ladd, whose appetite was legendary, even in high school. The Big Cat agreed to attend Grambling while consuming a huge meal, his fourth of the day, in front of Eddie Robinson at the Tigers' dining hall, announcing, "I like the way you feed here."

Ladd grew to be six-nine, 315 pounds, with a fifty-two-inch chest, thirty-nine-inch waist, twenty-inch biceps, nineteen-inch neck, twenty-inch calves, and size 18D shoes. He was a sophomore on the 1954 Wallace state championship team as well as an all-state basketball player. With the San Diego Chargers of the American Football League, he was a three-time all-AFL player and by far the largest player in the league.

As a Charger, he competed in 1961 in a contest called the Golden West Eating Classic, in which he chowed down against a local tuna fisherman in front of 1,800 fans. Ladd won, polishing off a menu that consisted of lobster tails, tossed green salad with oil and vinegar dressing, spaghetti and meatballs, southern fried chicken, baked Virginia ham, roast prime rib of beef au jus, New York–cut sirloin steaks, assorted vegetables, mashed potatoes, rolls and butter, and a layer cake with ice cream. Plates of hamburgers were on standby to break a tie, if needed. They were not.

Boyette recalled, "Ernie was always a big kid, and on the football field he was as mean as a four-headed rattlesnake. He was my sister's son, and we lived across the street from each other. My sister was a cook, so we always ate well."

Ladd was the big man on campus, and Boyette one of the smallest. Though barely six feet tall, he was still an imposing 217-pound lineman. He gained twenty-two pounds between his sophomore and junior seasons for the Dragons. At his nephew's urging, Boyette followed Ladd to Grambling, where he was all-SWAC and all-American, and then to the pros, playing as a linebacker throughout his thirteen-year career.

At Wallace, most classes had fewer than a dozen pupils. There were forty-one in Boyette's 1958 graduating class. Willie Ray's football squad was so lean that practices were limited to "half line" play—center, guard, tackle, end—but the coach still managed to put together winning teams. Boyette remembered how the coach went about his business: "He coached with the iron hand whacking your butt. He had those fat bicycle tires that he'd cut the tread part out of the middle and make a strap. He coached a lot out of fear and discipline."

Willie Ray was last seen at Wallace being carried over Ladd's shoulder. The player was preventing his coach from punching out the school's principal during a heated clash of egos. Willie Ray relocated to Beaumont, where he would raise three of the PVIL's best-ever players.

### The Pear Orchard

*Bubba hit me in a scrimmage and damned near knocked my pants off. His dad comes up and says, "How you doing, sweetheart?" That's what he used to call everybody. They had smelling salts all over me, trying to wake me up. How am I doing?! Man, I don't even go to this*

*school. He said, "I never saw anybody take a lick like that. You can*
*play for me anytime."*
GEORGE VALLERY, Charlton-Pollard

The 1901 oil boom that Spindletop spawned meant a flood of new jobs
in the Beaumont area. African Americans claimed their share, moving
to the city in large numbers and settling in the south side, spreading
from what is now the Port of Beaumont. The Beaumont Lumber Company and the Beaumont Sawmill were in that part of town, and they too
were hiring blacks. Others worked in nearby rice fields, on ranches, for
railroad and freight businesses. Black workers and their families had
a desire to educate their children. Both Charlton-Pollard and Hebert
were founded with the help of former slaves. Charlton-Pollard, which
predated Spindletop by almost three decades, came to be after a freedman named Charles Charlton made his way to Beaumont in 1870 and
worked with another freedman, Woodson Pipkin, a Methodist minister,
to establish the first school for black children in the city.

The first graduating class numbered all of two students, but enrollment grew as Beaumont's African American population increased 45
percent by 1880. Classes were held in several locations, including Pipkin's AME church, to accommodate more students. The school would
bear Pipkin's name. Two other school structures were erected, one with
Charlton's son, T. J., as principal, and the other guided by Thomas Titus
Pollard, an 1888 graduate of Prairie View. In 1918, the schools merged,
taking the name Charlton-Pollard. In 1926, Pollard was elected president
of the Colored Teachers State Association of Texas, which was instrumental in forming the Texas Interscholastic League of Colored Schools,
the PVIL.

Hebert's meager beginnings were in a four-room facility. Its first
graduates—five students—got their diplomas in 1924 after finishing the
eleventh grade, which was common for most Texas high schools. Hebert
had no twelfth-grade graduates until 1942. Two freedman brothers,
Usan Hebert and Ozan Blanchette, donated two of the seventy-five acres
they owned for construction of the South Park Colored School in an
area called the Potts Addition, which would become known as the Pear
Orchard. Principal John P. Odom and other black citizens requested
a name change, and the Beaumont School Board accepted the name
"Hebert School."

During World War II, competition between blacks and whites for jobs in Beaumont's shipyards was intense. On June 15–16, 1943, a familiar issue ignited two nights of violence: a white woman reported being raped by a black man, though she was unable to identify the suspect being held at the city jail. On the evening of June 15, more than two thousand white workers, plus perhaps another one thousand interested bystanders, marched toward city hall and then dispersed into small bands, which began breaking into stores in Beaumont's black neighborhoods near downtown. With guns, axes, and hammers, they terrorized and assaulted numerous black residents. Several restaurants and stores were pillaged, a number of buildings were burned, and over a hundred homes were ransacked. More than two hundred people were arrested, fifty were injured, and two—one black and one white—were killed. Another black man died several months later of injuries received during the riot, adding Beaumont to the list of US cities that experienced violent race riots that summer, including Detroit, New York, and Los Angeles.

Three miles separated Charlton-Pollard and Hebert, but young football players in both neighborhoods had no problem gathering in the Pear Orchard for two-hand-touch sandlot games that could have gotten sponsorship as a series of college all-star games. The Saturday-afternoon off-season games included Jerry LeVias, the Farr brothers, Don Bean, Rufus Cormier Jr., Warren Wells Jr., Wayne Moore, and the Smith brothers— Bubba, Tody, and running back Willie Ray Jr., considered by many the best of the Smith brothers. He became a roommate of the "Kansas Comet," Gale Sayers, who felt that Willie Ray Jr. was the better back before a nagging injury hampered his career. Willie Ray Jr. brought Sayers home with him, and Tody brought his Southern Cal teammate O. J. Simpson. "It was a beautiful day in the neighborhood," Walter Smith said.

Tody grew to six-five, 250 pounds. As a defensive end, he started his collegiate career at Michigan State, but transferred after two years to Southern Cal, where he teamed with Al Cowlings in the third-ranked Trojans' "Wild Bunch" defense. Tody was the Dallas Cowboys' first-round pick in 1971 and a member of their Super Bowl VI championship team. In his six-year career, he also played for the Houston Oilers (1973–1976) and the Buffalo Bills (1976).

Willie Ray Jr.'s star-crossed career began to crumble during a game in his senior year. His right knee buckled after a late hit in a game against Marshall Pemberton. It was another late hit in a contest of questionable defensive play against Willie Ray Jr. by Pemberton's players, and there were no whistles from the officials, prompting Georgia to race onto the field and hit an official on the head with a chair. But the damage to Willie Ray Jr.'s career was done. Up to that point, he had been sensational, drawing over one hundred college scholarship offers. He was idolized by his younger brother Bubba, who considered Willie Ray Jr. the best football player he had ever seen. Bubba dreamed of joining his brother in a college program and blocking for him. Willie Ray Jr., for vague, strange reasons, thwarted that idea after starting his collegiate career, suggesting that Bubba not join him at Iowa, and the two became estranged for years.

Willie Ray Jr. picked up the nickname "Beaver" because of the shape and alignment of his front teeth, though others said the name resulted from his hard work and ability to "chew up those yards, like a beaver gnawing on trees." In 1961, both Kansas and Iowa recruited Willie Ray Jr. and Sayers, from Omaha, Nebraska, envisioning a dream backfield. "Beav" chose Iowa, Sayers Kansas. Despite the injury, Willie Ray Jr. led Iowa in rushing as a sophomore, but left the program in 1963 for Kansas, joining Sayers in what should have been one of the most exciting backfields in college football history. A *Lawrence Journal-World* sports column hailed him as "all the way," an "affable Negro," a jovial, confident player who loved to talk and was as brash as Cassius Clay. Beav, a "home run threat," warned his friend Sayers in the local press, "Better get all the headlines you can this year, Gale, baby. Next year they may be doing most of the reading about Willie Ray." He was a bit faster than Sayers—9.6 to Sayers's 9.7 in the 100-yard dash—but more knee problems limited his play and essentially ended his career. Sayers ended up a two-time all-American and then had a Hall of Fame career with the Chicago Bears. Beav never played a down in the NFL, though Sayers and Bubba got him tryouts with the Bears and the Baltimore Colts. But his knees were too damaged. He was nothing like the dazzling running back who had thrilled PVIL fans and had had college scouts envisioning him leading their teams to conference and national championships. He returned to Beaumont and disappeared, despondent over a football career that never was. He continues to shun the public.

In a 1999 interview with the *Dallas Morning News*, he reflected on the legends surrounding his abilities. "In your youth," he said, "strength is everything. Football at that time was the measuring stick of who you were and what you were . . . Yeah, it was difficult. But time brings you to different realizations. At this point, I'm just grateful to have experienced those few good years. Gale was something to behold. I was pretty good, I guess. But I would never in a million years try to diminish who he is, or what he's done.

"Sometimes guys kind of exaggerate."

Sadly, as of 2016, he is the remaining survivor of a magnetic family that elevated the profile of Beaumont, the PVIL, and Texas football. Willie Ray Sr. passed from cancer in 1992, Tody in 1999 (at age fifty), Oretha in 2005, and Bubba in 2011.

## Ozen: Larger than Life

Down the way at rival Hebert, Clifton Ozen shared Willie Ray Sr.'s belief in using the paddle, but at six-six, 285 pounds, the sheer sight of an upset Ozen should have been more than enough to scare a player straight. He came home to Beaumont and his alma mater (Class of 1941) in 1958 to begin a twenty-five-year career as coach, teacher, and principal, one year after Willie Ray Sr. first set foot on the Charlton-Pollard campus. Both men became synonymous with Beaumont high school football as they shrewdly managed their rosters of wildly talented athletes.

"If you had any kind of ability, those guys were able to utilize you," Coach Joe Washington Sr. said. "Willie Ray, Ozen, when you have a good product and you can harvest it, you have a good crop, and those guys harvested and had good crops."

Year in and year out, bumper crops of exceptional football players seemed to sprout from all corners of Beaumont, from every street in the Pear Orchard neighborhood. Carl Zenn, Russell and Warren Wells, Rufus Cormier Jr., Anthony Guillory, and Jerry LeVias were among the dozens of star-quality players who helped Ozen reap 147 wins in 181 games in sixteen years as the Panthers' head coach. His 1959 and 1966 teams were PVIL 3A and 4A state champions. Whereas Willie Ray Sr. had shown little interest in athletics as a student and then was limited by a disabled leg, Ozen was a "monster" on the field as a lineman at Hebert and then at Texas College, where his teammates included the future PVIL coaches Bo Humphrey and Charles Brown. After one of his dominant performances, Ozen exclaimed, "Bishop 15, Ozen 24."

LeVias recalled the coach: "I had been around Coach Ozen all my life, and basically I was scared of him. He was the big demon, a big man who chewed Red Man tobacco. He was the man. Like he used to say, he was 'rough as the Gulf.' He'd stand in the middle of the field with that board, and if you were last in sprints, you got whipped. If you weren't far enough ahead, you got whipped. What he did to us—these days you'd have him in court for child protective services. But he was a great coach, mentor. He and Enous Minix checked grades every week, attendance, and there was none of that stuff that you could play football but not go to school. There was no misbehaving. If you misbehaved in class you got some sprints and whippings when you got to practice.

"We had no pass no play before they started it, because of Coach Ozen, Mr. Jackson, the principal, Coach Minix, Coach Sonnier. They were all very good disciplinarians and mentors. If you were going to play football for Hebert, there was no thuggishness tolerated."

In 1995, the Texas House of Representatives passed House Resolution 347, which recognized Ozen a month after he died: "More important than the victories he accrued were the students whose lives were changed by his guidance and inspiration, and in his 36 years in the field of education, Clifton J. Ozen undoubtedly made a profound impact on countless students and players; his dedication and leadership can never be replaced, but his unique spirit will live on in the hearts of the many people whose lives he touched."

Ozen coached two of Hebert's three state championship teams (1959, 1966), both in the PVIL era. A decade later, in 1976, Hebert became the first former PVIL team to win a UIL state championship when the Panthers rolled over Gainesville 35–7, for the Class 3A crown. The defensive coordinator for that Hebert team was the PVIL legend Leon Bedford, and one of his defensive backs was his son, Vance, who built his own career as a collegiate defensive coordinator at Texas, Louisville, and Oklahoma State.

In 1997, the Beaumont Independent School District opened a new magnet high school named in Ozen's honor.

With so much talent, it is surprising the Beaumont schools didn't win more state championships, though in a sense that deficit is a testament to the overall talent in the area's PVIL schools. LeVias offered this explanation: "By the time you got through with Wheatley, Yates, Kashmere, Lincoln, and Central, you were beat up. It was so competitive, from head to toe."

## "Baby Sticks"

*Jim Brown came and talked to us one day at Charlton-Pollard
about playing ball and having an impact on life, and he said to
always make an impact with your first move. I thought about that
when I went to the University of Corpus Christi, now Texas A&M–
Corpus Christi. It was after the summer, and I was late for training.
So they put me on the line to do some pass blocking. This big ol'
white boy was across from me with his elbows bleeding, blood on
his wrists. He was growling and carrying on. I thought, I don't have
but one choice. It's the first time I have a legal chance to hit a white
man, so I jumped offside and hit him right across the forehead and
knocked him out. The coach ran over and asked what I was doing.
I told him, 'Coach, my count was off.' I figured that's what Jim
Brown meant: have an impact right off. I got there on a Tuesday,
and I started the game that Friday night.*

GEORGE VALLERY

His legs were frail and weak from polio, and for a short while he could
not walk. Jerry LeVias would become the most celebrated running back
in Beaumont history with his explosive speed and quick, darting moves.
But at age seven, the biggest hope for LeVias was that his life would not
be cut short by the dreaded disease, which killed thousands of children
in the United States. In the segregated Beaumont of the 1950s, blacks
weren't afforded the best of care, and to make matters worse, the black
population was served by only a handful of overworked black physicians.
LeVias was fitted for braces, and his school attendance suffered, though
he was a bright, promising student. Luckily, he had a set of guardian
angels in his older cousins Mel and Miller Farr, sons of LeVias's paternal
aunt in Beaumont's other famous football family, counterparts to coach
Willie Ray Smith Sr. and his brood of athletes across town.

While LeVias struggled to get around awkwardly in the braces that
supported his legs, Mel and Miller remained his companions and idols.
He could only watch and admire as they dominated the regular, spirited
Thursday after-school games in the Pear Orchard. A decided football
heredity in Beaumont's black neighborhoods forecast the fates of its
young boys early in life, and LeVias was no different.

Nobody had an explanation why LeVias, after two years, suddenly began to gain strength in his legs. He had recovered enough by sixth grade to be able to join the flag football team. He played in pickup games with his Farr cousins, who chose their little cousin as a teammate to be sure he got to participate. Then it became, "We got Jerry!" "No, we got Jerry!" As LeVias himself recalled: "Everyone wanted me to play. It was two-hand touch in those days, and I could run, catch, and outrun all of the big boys. I didn't have a problem getting into the games after that."

Beaumont's south side was getting its first looks at the boy wonder running back with "baby sticks" legs, a description coined by Coach Clifton Ozen at Hebert. LeVias was always smaller than the kids his age, and though he had survived a life-threatening illness, his parents ruled that flag football would be the extent of his gridiron career. Ozen, on the other hand, saw greatness in the making, no matter his star pupil's size. He nurtured LeVias every step of the way, first by recruiting him as his personal water boy.

The LeVias family lived across the street from Hebert, and its football practice field afforded LeVias a convenient view of the practices. He quietly cheered for his cousins and dreamed of the day he would get to wear the Panthers' blue and gold. Ozen, meanwhile, began noticing the youngster across the street. LeVias had vivid memories of his first exposure to Hebert football: "I got into football by being a water boy. I just wanted to be around the team so much. I lived about three houses from the field. And it would be hot, but the team didn't get water breaks. One day, Coach Ozen called me over and told me to get him some water. I was about ten or eleven years old. I started doing that for him, and later I became the trainer. I didn't know anything about taping ankles or anything like that, but my job was cleaning up the locker room, washing jocks, shining shoes for guys like Warren Wells and his brothers. The guys only had one pair of cleats, and they wanted their shoes to look clean for the games. I'd get ten cents a pair."

That began the LeVias-Ozen relationship, which took off like a LeVias touchdown sprint once the coach saw LeVias dazzling his friends in touch football games. Ozen asked the ninth grader why he was not playing for the junior high team. LeVias echoed his parents, telling Ozen he was too small. But he decided that he was ready to take a chance. All he had to do was step on the scales and prove he could meet the 121-pound weight requirement.

Ozen and one of his assistants, Enous Minix, were standing by, charting each would-be player's weight. LeVias didn't quite make it: "I got on the scale, and I weighed 115. I told the coaches the scales were wrong."

They were not, and a heartbroken LeVias slowly walked away, his football dream seemingly ended. But he didn't give up that easily. Slipping outside the building and out of the coaches' sight, he picked up a paper bag, filled it with gravel, and stuffed it inside his pants. He approached Ozen and Minix again: "I told the coach that scale was wrong, and I wanted to get weighed again. I got on the scale, stomped my feet and the bag broke, rocks all over the place. Mr. Minix told coach Ozen, 'If anybody wants to play football that bad, we gotta give him a chance.'"

Hebert's latest and youngest sensation was finally on board, but LeVias noted that not everything changed: "I still had to clean up after practice."

That didn't last much longer. Seeing how advanced his youngest charge already was, Ozen decided there was nothing he could learn on the B team. He promoted him to the varsity. In a span of six years, Jerry LeVias had been transformed from a crippled child in braces to the most exciting runner in Panthers' football history—and one of the best in Texas high school football history. His parents could not have been more proud, once they discovered his secret. Despite all the fuss and mentoring from Ozen, and the encouragement from Miller and Mel, LeVias thought it best not to inform his parents that their smallish son with the "baby sticks" was taking tackle football by storm. Even his sister, a member of the band, kept quiet and vouched for his extended stays after school to work with the team as its "trainer."

Something like that could not stay a secret for long in high-school-football-crazed Beaumont. His parents were among the very few in town who paid no attention to the sport. LeVias explained how they discovered the truth: "They didn't find out I was playing until somebody in the grocery store told them, 'Your son sure did play good last night!'"

Yes, thank you, they replied, assuming the kudos were in reference to his skills as the team's water boy, which they were quite pleased about, secure in the knowledge their son had adhered to their restriction of no tackle football. The grocery store exchange continued until it became clear that Jerry was not exactly the trainer any more, which made for an interesting discussion back home. LeVias remembered direct guidance being given: "Oh yeah, they prayed for me. They, you could say, put their hands on me. But dad said, "If you're willing to disobey me and you really want to play, go ahead. But if you play, you can't quit."

With their blessings, and a sore backside, LeVias had a green light to excel without looking over his shoulder. He played "everything," from running back to quarterback to wide receiver. LeVias recalled one way of choosing which position to play: "If your brother or cousin played running back or quarterback, that's what you were. And if you ran the 100-yard dash in under ten seconds you were a quarterback."

Hebert had plenty of guys who could do that. They proved it in the spring track season, winning the PVIL state 440-relay championship with LeVias, Jerry Ball, Don Bean, and Mel Farr clocking times in the 42-second range, blazing fast in those days, especially since they ran on cinders and sometimes dirt.

With only a year of organized football under his belt, LeVias began receiving recruiting offers, which for Hebert and Charlton-Pollard players was practically a given. LeVias and his friends enjoyed the recruiting circus: "I felt it could happen for me if I kept doing what I did. Miller did it, Mel did it, Bubba. We were going to go to college, but I didn't know I was going to be that good, that people would want me and the doors would open like that. I had scholarship offers from everywhere in the country, but not from black colleges, because I was too small. At that time, the SWAC had their choice."

Hebert linebacker Anthony Guillory went to Nebraska and then back to Beaumont's Lamar University as the school began recruiting black players. Miller Farr went to Wichita State as a defensive back, a switch from the quarterback position he played at Hebert. Running back Mel Farr accepted an offer from UCLA. LeVias noticed the uptick in recruiting visits: "People started discovering Beaumont, and the next thing you know coaches were coming from UCLA, Michigan State, everywhere. They just made a trail there."

At first, the coaches came to see other players, but a speedy little underclassman kept catching everyone's eye.

## Cormier: Laying Down the Law

*In my senior year, we were making a goal-line stand against Beaumont Hebert. Rufus Cormier was in the backfield for Hebert,*

*and he was about forty-six inches in the chest. Our defensive
coordinator, Leon Bedford, had been teaching, "When we're in goal
line, you have to hit the runner in the chest to stop his penetration."
So Hebert runs a play, and a hole opened up the middle. Cormier
has a head of steam, and our linebacker Leonard Fields, "Tough
Dude," comes up to stop him. When the smoke had cleared, he had
stopped Cormier, but Fields came to the sideline looking out the ear
hole of his helmet. We started trying to get his stuff back on straight,
and Coach Bedford was yelling for the backup linebacker, Johnny
Blount, to get in the game, but Blount was watching Fields walk by
with that crooked helmet. Hebert calls the same play, and here comes
Cormier again. Blount hit him around the ankles, and Cormier rolls
in for six. Bedford met Blount before he could get off the field and
was raking him over the coals, "Man, what's wrong with you? You
know you supposed to hit the man in the chest on a goal-line stand!"
Blount didn't say a word till he got down there on the bench by us.
"Man, did ya'll see Tough Dude's helmet? I wasn't about to put my
head in there."*

DAVID O'NEAL, Galveston Central

LeVias was an immediate sensation at Hebert as a ninth grader. By his
junior year everybody in Beaumont—actually, everybody in the state and
plenty of college coaches around the country, too—knew who he was and
his value to the team. On the other hand, outside of the Hebert band,
Rufus Cormier Jr. was far from being a household name. With that in
mind, and playing outside linebacker, he decided during his first varsity
scrimmage to introduce himself.

It did not go well.

Cormier gave the details: "We ran a play where Jerry got the ball and
ran kind of a sweep on my side. As fast as he was, he ran by me, but I
continued to chase him, with the space between us increasing. He scored
and turned around, and that's when I got there and laid him out. I had it
in my mind if I was going to play football, I had to get somebody's attention. I quickly learned that was not the way to get it.

"Coach Ozen sprinted down there and asked what was wrong with
me and was I absolutely crazy. He told me what I could do and what that
boy could do and instructed me that when LeVias ran the ball, if I was
anywhere near him I was to touch him with a finger on his shoulder pad.

And if I ever hit him like that again, he was going to kill me. And then he got his board and gave me a few licks. That almost sent me back to the band."

Almost. Not only did Cormier stick around the football program, he became an integral part of the offense as a hard-nosed fullback and lead blocker for LeVias, whom he would follow to Southern Methodist University as the second black athlete to receive a scholarship to play for the Mustangs, though he shifted from fullback to undersized defensive lineman. Both were honor students, and LeVias was named an Academic All-American. The beauty of their classroom success was that it derailed the notion that black high schools were inferior academically, that their students, especially athletes, entered previously all-white schools unprepared for rigorous study. That line of thought was also applied to the academic competence of students and professors at historically black colleges.

Cormier and LeVias were as ready for classroom work as they were ready for Coach Hayden Fry's strenuous drills on the football field. Hebert and the other PVIL schools may have lacked resources such as up-to-date textbooks and educational aids, but they had built-in support systems from teachers—often, graduates of black colleges—who had keen eyes for gifted students such as Cormier.

He was well aware of the value of the education he got at Hebert: "I knew I could be competitive academically as long as I did my work. I was not intimidated, though SMU was more intense than high school. The teachers at Hebert were incredibly supportive. And I didn't sense the degree of our lack of resources at home, because nobody had very much. I had no idea how little money my father made until I applied to law school and he had to fill out an earnings statement.

"At Hebert, I had taken precollege courses, calculus, physics, and didn't know what to expect. But I was prepped to spend all of my non-football hours with my schoolwork, and that first semester I studied really hard and did very well. It was clear to me that it was just a question of doing the work. My father had only gone to eighth grade, but he had a real appreciation for education."

That was one motivating factor for Cormier. The family, headed by the Reverend Rufus Cormier Sr., owned a fifty-foot-by-hundred-foot urban farm with chickens and ducks roaming in the backyard, a garden, and fruit trees. The younger Cormiers—Rufus Jr., Henry, and Katie—were expected to feed the chickens, till the garden, and pick the fruit, chores Rufus "hated with a passion." He could do those chores after school, or he could stay at school and study. He chose the latter: "My dad told me that as long as I had school-related activities, I didn't have to do that. So I got involved in every school activity there was, and if it wasn't dark by the time those were over, I went to the chemistry lab until it got dark."

And then there was the band, which Cormier initially preferred over football. He had the desire to one day become a director. Band had been his favorite activity since sixth grade, but in ninth grade he hit a growth spurt, and the Hebert coaching staff took notice, encouraging him to trade his band uniform for football togs. Ho-hum. Wrong tune. He wasn't interested. The tuba made him reconsider.

Hebert had a program that required band members to purchase their instrument of choice once they had gained proficiency. The Cormier family's finances didn't allow for that, so when Rufus learned an instrument, he moved on to another one, from trumpet to saxophone to baritone sax. By eighth grade, he was told of a way to avoid the instrument roulette and never have to purchase an instrument: pick up the tuba. Cormier did not blow the big brass for long: "So I started to play the tuba, which lead to a demise in my interest in music."

Given his growth spurt, football was a natural step, perhaps even more than putting the shot for Hebert's track team, which he was very good at. Rufus Sr. was a preacher, but also the head cook at Beaumont's Ridgewood Resort. On weekends, he would take young Rufus with him to help clean the buffet area. Rufus Jr. recalled the feasting that resulted: "They had lots of things I'd never heard of—chateaubriand, crabmeat imperial, and those sorts of things. When they broke down the buffet at nine thirty, employees were able to eat all they wanted to, and I would eat until I couldn't walk. That was the best food I'd ever seen or heard of, so between my eighth- and ninth-grade years, I gained about twenty-five pounds, primarily from eating at that restaurant."

Football came to seem inevitable. After all, in Beaumont's South End the lure of neighborhood sandlot games was strong. Playing in the regular Saturday-afternoon games of tackle, Cormier held his own in the rough-and-tumble contests. He went from five-ten, 180 pounds to six feet, 215 pounds by the time he as a senior. He enjoyed the game as a fullback. Ozen had first looked at the shot-putter as a quarterback. He had a pretty good arm, but didn't like the position. He played well at fullback, leading the way for LeVias, who really didn't need much blocking. But as defenses began to key on LeVias, Cormier could gain yards and get noticed by recruiters.

Offers came from the Big Ten and Big Eight, but the only southern schools interested were the University of Houston and SMU. Michigan State was a possibility; Bubba Smith had been there, and Jess Phillips was headed there. But in the bitterly cold Midwest winters, Cormier feared fumbling every time "someone looked at me." The Mustangs won his services, but eliminated his opportunity to join LeVias in pro ball. Cormier explained what happened: "I went from being a big running back to a small lineman, and that greatly curtailed my chances of doing well in the pros. I accepted that pretty readily, but I was happy with my career at SMU."

His career after SMU was pretty good, too. Incredible, in fact. He graduated from Yale Law School, worked with Hillary Rodham as counsel to the House Judiciary Committee during the Nixon impeachment investigation, and in 1974 joined the Houston law office of Baker Botts. In 1981, he became the first African American lawyer to make partner at a large Houston law firm and the first to be partner at a large corporate law firm in the state of Texas. He was given the 2014 Leon Jaworski Award and named one of the best lawyers in America. *Texas Monthly* deemed him a "Texas Super Lawyer."

Good thing that way back when, he adhered to Ozen's hands-off-LeVias policy. And much as Ozen knew LeVias was headed for greatness, he saw something in Cormier beyond football. Cormier recalled a time when the coach made that clear: "Coach Ozen very much believed in requiring sprints as punishment if you weren't practicing well or played poorly, and sometimes we'd run until it was dark. But there were some little trenches along the practice field at Hebert. And sometimes when he was running our tongues out, some of the players would lie in the trench and hide in the dark to skip a sprint or two. I never tried that, but as a senior, one day he was really running us to death, so I thought I'd try that and skip a sprint.

"Coach Ozen came down and got me, took me to the other end of the field, and told me I was one of the few that was going to have an opportunity that otherwise might not have been available, and how disappointed he was in me for doing that. Then he got his board and gave me about ten licks.

"I was a little upset, but afterward I thought about what he had in mind, and I appreciated him more for that."

## Gene Washington's Great Migration

LeVias and Cormier were among the first black players in the Southwest Conference. Before that, PVIL schools were forced to send players out of state if they wanted exposure in major-college programs. Hebert and Charlton-Pollard players led the way to Big Ten and Pacific Eight programs. None of the players seemed to embrace the concept more than the Baytown receiver Gene Washington.

Black folks in La Porte would gather around their television sets on the Saturday afternoons when Michigan State football games were broadcast, eager to cheer on Washington, their native son and a wide receiver for the Spartans. He was one of several black Southeast Texas PVIL stars lured out of state and away from segregation to more accommodating football programs in the Midwest. For Washington, it was almost a given that he would bolt from the Lone Star State as fast as he could and as far away as possible. The thirteen hundred miles to East Lansing, Michigan, suited him just fine.

The eyes of family and friends were intensely fixed on the TV screens. Their ears waited for any mention of Washington's name, and there was plenty of that every game. But there was something off about the way announcers acknowledged him, that he was from Baytown, thirty miles east of Houston on an I-10 stretch increasingly dotted with refineries and other hard-hat installations on the eastern side of the Houston Ship Channel. On the western side is La Porte, and yes, that was really (maybe) Washington's hometown.

Washington explained the confusion: "They'd say, 'Gene Washington, from George Washington Carver High School in Baytown, Texas.' Some people in La Porte would say, 'He's not from Baytown. He's from La Porte!' I'd have to remind them that nobody wanted me to go to school in La Porte, so I went to school in Baytown."

Baytown Carver was "home" for Washington because La Porte never had a black high school. That void slapped him in the face and fueled his desire to compete and succeed in an integrated environment. If Washington had even the slightest measure of endearment for segregation, it was because of the busing arrangement and the relationships that it could produce. Washington had one relationship particularly in mind: "My wife and I met at Carver in ninth grade. She lived in McNair, about five miles north of Baytown, so she was bused to Carver, too. We met because of segregation, because of busing."

La Porte had DeWalt Elementary School for black students. But for secondary school, they had to be bused ten miles, most of it underneath the Houston Ship Channel via the Baytown Tunnel, to Carver. The school was built on six acres of land donated by Humble Oil and Refining, which had been founded by Ross Sterling, a businessman and future Texas governor, in 1917 after a major oil strike in Goose Creek and construction of the state's first offshore drilling operation. Blacks had been provided education in the Baytown area as early as the 1920s. In 1948, the towns of Pelly, Goose Creek, and East Baytown consolidated under the name "Baytown." The next year, George Washington Carver High School opened as a school for surrounding communities, such as La Porte, that did not provide secondary education for blacks.

In Carver's relatively short, meteoric existence, from 1949 to 1967, the school won eight PVIL championships, three in football with Coach Johnny Peoples and five in track—the first, in 1954, with Peoples, and the others with Coach Roy Hutchins. There were also nine state band titles. The football championships came in 1955, 1958, and 1961. The Buccaneer team that won the last title included Washington and quarterback Leon Carr. Those state football championships remain the only ones in the city's history, though Baytown's white school, Robert E. Lee, lost consecutive state title games in 1951 and 1952. Peoples was aided by two assistants, Hutchins and Robert Strayhan, who had been a teammate of Peoples at both Yates High School and Wiley College. The two were members of Wiley's undefeated 1945 black-college national championship team.

Peoples, who was at Carver for the school's eighteen-year duration, finished there with a 136–75–2 football record. His memories of that time were nothing but positive: "Baytown was the best job I ever had. It was the kids and the families, both black and white. The response of the white families to our team was tremendous. Lee played on Friday nights, and we played on Saturday nights. When we played, the white families would pack up and go to the games right with the black families. To the out-of-town games, too.

"All the people in Baytown supported us, the whites and the blacks. That wasn't the case in every town back in those times. The *Baytown Sun,* I remember, was very liberal. They gave us good coverage compared to the coverage black schools in other towns got. I always appreciated that. Baytown is a good town . . . It's a town that likes its football, black or white."

For Peoples, Carver was the first stop in a career that would span forty years. He started out as an all-district PVIL halfback and multisport star at Yates and Wiley, where he is lauded as one of the school's all-time best. The school buses taking Carver students back to La Porte departed midafternoon, and no other transport home was available for Washington and other students involved in extracurricular activities. Because of that, he and Peoples bonded during early-evening drives in which the coach delivered his pupil home to La Porte. The talk meandered from subject to subject: Washington's progress in school, the team's approach to the next opponent, citizenship. Washington had a similar arrangement with his track, baseball, and basketball coaches: "We had an outstanding relationship. There was a lot of coaching and counseling. How many kids got a ride every day home by their coach? I was from a church background—my dad was a deacon, mom was in the choir—and [had] coaches driving me home everyday. With all of that, there was no way in hell, for those five days a week, I could get in trouble."

But he could be a handful for 3A PVIL opponents in Beaumont, La Marque, Settegast, and Port Arthur, among others. For years after their PVIL days, Washington would cross paths with Beaumont Hebert's Mel Farr and happily remind him of their face-offs in baseball, Farr pitching, Washington hitting and connecting with a Farr fastball. Washington still joked about it years later: "By the time I rounded the bases, they were still trying to find it. Every time I saw him, I'd tell him that ball was still going."

They met on the football field, too. At a wiry six-three, 180 pounds, Washington was not hard to find. Besides, Peoples employed him at several positions—sprint-out quarterback, wide receiver, safety, punt returner. Washington, a junior on the 1961 team, was already attracting attention from college football recruiters as well as for his prominence as a PVIL state-champion hurdler. They loved what they saw in the speedy receiver with great hands, but he was becoming increasingly disillusioned about life in a southern state that heaped slights and restrictions on black people—sitting in designated balconies at movie theaters, barred from hotels and restaurants, and a disrespectful lack of media attention for Carver athletics.

Washington made his reasons clear, and unlike Peoples, didn't see fair coverage in the local or statewide media: "Baytown, the state of Texas, had no record of what I was doing. We were never in the paper in our hometown. We were playing in [an] all-segregated situation, but you look at the PVIL competition, playing against the same guys, and they were all good. I was running track, undefeated, against guys like Roy Hicks at Corpus Christi Coles; he was good, too. But I definitely wanted to get out of that situation, out of Baytown, out of the Houston area. In those days, the Southwest Conference schools were on TV, but you couldn't go there, so why watch them? But, Duffy [Daugherty, the head coach of Michigan State] came down to put on coaching clinics, and he and Willie Ray Smith at Charlton-Pollard became very good friends. Duffy did a great job recruiting like that.

"He was recruiting Bubba Smith, and Bubba told him, 'I want Gene to come up with me.'"

Those two players alone made a pretty good recruiting haul for Daugherty's "underground railroad." He used it to raid southern black high schools and bring talented players to Michigan State, including another Washington teammate, quarterback Jimmy Raye, from Fayetteville, North Carolina. Raye became the first black quarterback from the South to win a national championship. Daugherty's efforts facilitated Washington's great escape, and Texas became just a smear in his rearview mirror that he could ignore. Moving forward, he was immediately impressed by the different culture and attitude on campus and in East Lansing, taken aback by the acceptance, or at least tolerance, of black students.

Washington recalled that compared to La Porte, East Lansing was a racial paradise: "It was an integrated situation, and everybody was so much nicer. It was refreshing to feel that people respected you regardless of your background, and the color of your skin. Michigan State was a whole new world, and I wanted to prove to the Texas segregation supporters, and especially to myself, that I would be successful."

His good friend Bubba Smith—"kill, Bubba, kill"—was the big man on campus, and the Spartan fans' favorite. But Washington quietly, and for a change, noticeably, went about his business of becoming a world-class hurdler. He won the NCAA indoor 60-yard high hurdles in 1965, even though he had never run indoors in Texas, and certainly not against white kids. He treated those as motivators rather than hindrances: "After all that segregation, I damn sure didn't want to lose, and I never did."

He won six Big Ten hurdling championships—three indoor and three outdoor. As a senior, he set school football records by snagging 27 receptions for 677 yards and seven touchdowns, averaging 25.1 yards per catch. The Minnesota Vikings made him the number eight overall pick in the 1967 draft. He was an All-Pro in 1969, but the Vikings were on the losing end against the Kansas City Chiefs in Super Bowl IV, which featured another former PVIL receiver, Otis Taylor, who hauled down a spectacular forty-six-yard catch and ran it in for a touchdown. Washington ended the game with one catch for nine yards.

Washington the student was just as driven as Washington the athlete—perhaps more so. Fall football and winter and spring track were mixed with a full load of classes every quarter. Every summer he rode the encouragement, work ethic, and high academic expectations instilled by Peoples and the Carver faculty. The payoff: graduating in four years, the first MSU athlete to do so, with a degree in physical education. In the NFL off-seasons, he went back and earned a master's degree in student personnel administration. In forty-three years with the 3M Company, he worked as a diversity recruiter, developing the business's first minority college relations recruitment program. During his All-Pro football career, he worked at 3M in the morning and with the Vikings in the afternoon.

He was grateful for the training he got in Texas, but just as happy to leave the state: "I was always looking ahead, but I felt prepared. The teachers at Carver made it a challenge, so when I went to Michigan State, I was ready. One of the things driving me in sports and academics was that I wanted to perform well in an integrated situation. I didn't want to go back to Texas, and the people were so welcoming up there. All I had to do was keep up with my studies. Michigan State gave me an opportunity.

"The majority of my black football teammates were from the South. We had to make this opportunity work because we had nothing to return to in the South."

## Making History on Bearcat Island

Galveston is the birthplace of black history in Texas—the place where the Emancipation Proclamation was first announced in the state—and Central High School is part of that legacy as possibly the state's first black high school. Brenham boasts of opening what would become A. R. Pickard High School in 1875.

Galveston also has the distinction of being home to the first high school football team in Texas, at Ball High in 1892. Central first took to the gridiron with the arrival in 1931 of Paul Quinn College legend Ray T. Sheppard, and the school claimed a state championship three years later after a 10–0 season. That came six years before the PVIL was officially organized into districts to determine state champions. Sheppard claimed one of the official titles in 1946, and his successor and former student, Ed Mitchell, won one in 1963.

Central was eighty miles southwest of the Golden Triangle, but Galveston shared the triangle's petroleum industry imprint. It was the entry point, through Galveston Bay, for the Houston Ship Channel. Oil refineries and offshore drilling operations dotted the area. And like the PVIL schools in Beaumont, Orange, and Port Arthur, Central had a wealth of athletic and coaching talent, winning the city's only state championships in football, baseball (1962, coached by Floyd Iglehart), track (1964, Kermit Courville), and basketball (1944, Wilbur Byrd). Central's teams looked good getting off the bus, according to the *Houston Forward Times*, which named the Bearcats the best-dressed team in the state.

First baseman David O'Neal was a .444 hitter and all-state baseball player at Central. In 1966, he should have become the first black player at the University of Houston. Cougars' coach Lovette Hill sent recruiting letters, but when O'Neal showed up, Hill rejected him when he saw that the player he had been interested in was black. O'Neal, at five-seven, 120 pounds, was deemed too light for football, so he became the Bearcats' team manager and statistician. He still got to dress as snappily as the players: "The booster clubs bought us navy blue blazers with 'Bearcat' on the crest, gray slacks, and Roscoe's Shine Parlor made sure your shoes were shined if you couldn't do it, white shirt, dark ties, blue bags with 'Central Bearcats' on the side with your jersey number. It was very impressive to see all these young men, thirty-five guys, and six coaches

wearing the same outfits. Coach Mitchell started that, and Coach Iglehart came in with some of the ideas after he had played for the Chicago
Bears. It made you work even harder to become one of the guys that wore
those blazers, because you got recognition all around the community,
and with the girls. They knew you were part of the show, too, and that
was pretty cool."

Ray Sheppard built a football program that became the pride of the
island's black community, which sustained its own businesses and supported Central academics and athletics. "Growing up here, all the kids
wanted to do was become a Bearcat, because there was a tradition," said
Rochon Chatman, a defensive back on the 1963 championship team.
"I'm proud to say I'm a Bearcat. Graduating from junior high and going
to Central was like going to a big university. Central was like a family.
Everybody knew everybody and the whole community gathered around
the school."

In a thirty-eight-year career, Sheppard became revered at Central.
He had landed there after a brief stop in the Negro Baseball League as a
shortstop and after an illustrious career at Wiley, where he was named, in
1925, as a halfback on the "All Negro American" team by the noted *Crisis*
magazine. Paul W. L. Jones, a reporter for *Spalding's Official Foot Ball
Guide*, had this to say: "Sheppard is the greatest Negro back in the game
today. He is the most accurate punter in foot ball [*sic*]. A great open field
runner, he can twist and squirm, dodge and duck and stiff arm as can
few players. His punting brought his team out conqueror in many contests. Opponents of Paul Quinn start worrying whenever the Quinnites
get within thirty-five or forty yards of the goal posts, for Sheppard's toe
seldom fails to send the ball straight through the uprights. His field goal
record is one of the most remarkable in foot ball history." In 1937, Jones
included Sheppard as a halfback on the "All-Time Negro Football Team."

At Central, Sheppard groomed several all-star players, including Ray
Dohn Dillon, Kermit Courville, Charles Ferguson, and Ed Mitchell. Ferguson, his sandy-colored red hair earning him the nickname "Chockey
Red," was all-state in track, basketball, and football. He was also the first
Galveston native to play professional football (Cleveland, Minnesota,
and Buffalo, 1963–1969) as a tight end. He was a member of the Bills'
1964 and 1965 AFL championship teams.

But the name that still reverberates in Galveston is Dillon's. He was a
Pittsburgh Courier Black College All-American at Prairie View in 1950

as a defensive back, and the next season as a fullback. Dillon was the first black player from Galveston drafted into the NFL, in 1952 by the Detroit Lions. The team released him as one of the final cuts before the regular season, but helped him catch on with the Hamilton Tiger-Cats in the Canadian Football League. Dillon played four seasons in Canada and was a part of Hamilton's 1953 Grey Cup CFL championship. He returned to Central as an assistant to Sheppard, coaching defensive backs and running backs. Dillon saw this homecoming as a fulfillment: "I got an opportunity to teach at my high school. That was always my ambition, to one day come back and teach. I always wanted to teach and coach at Central. I wanted to be a Bearcat."

Charles "Poppa Charlie" Brooks recalled Dillon warmly: "[He] remains a dedicated Central man. He loves him some Central and you can't meet a finer guy. I asked him once if he wanted me to help him make sure everybody was in at ten o'clock, and he said, 'No, you be in too!' He was outta sight. Mr. Dillon is a legend, the best to come out of Central. He was big and could run. Just mention his name in Galveston, and everybody knows who you talking about."

Central consolidated with Ball High in 1968 and gave that school's athletic program an immediate lift. Ball won its first state championship, in track. Central's Courville had made the transfer the year before to begin building the program, accompanied by some former Central athletes. Central's final football season sent the program out in grand fashion, holding the PVIL banner high with a 10–1 record and a district championship in its first and only UIL campaign. "My brother was captain of that team," O'Neal said. "They were picked to come in last, but they buzz-sawed through that district, it wasn't even close."

CHAPTER 5

# Yates versus Wheatley

*At E. O. Smith Junior High School, I thought I'd play in the band
'cause my sisters were real musical. We had a piano in the house,
so I said, "I'm gon' follow music," so I started singing in the glee
club. There were about 200 or so people in there singing. One day,
the woman playing the piano stopped and said, "Something's not
sounding right, and its coming from over in this area." She said,
"Sing one at a time," and when she got to me, she said, "You're
the one! Go find you another class for fifth period." So I went out
for football.*

GODWIN TURK, Houston Wheatley

In 1970, the University of Houston bought a piece of Houston's black
history, gave it a couple of facelifts, and forty-two years later wiped
it from the face of the earth. The school bought Jeppesen from the
Houston Independent School District for $6.8 million and changed the
name in 1980 to honor the oilman and UH regent Corbin Robertson,
who funded the facility's renovation. In 2012, the stadium was razed
and bulldozed into piles of concrete and rebar rubble. When the dust
cleared, the Cougars had a shiny new $128 million den befitting the
wave of gentrification engulfing Third Ward, Houston's Harlem. Jeppesen was long gone, and as gentrification often dictates, so was a lot of
black history from a neighborhood that had served as a vibrant cultural,
educational, and entertainment hub for all of black Houston. None of
that was acknowledged during the stadium's metamorphosis. While UH
held the legal claim, Jeppesen spiritually belonged to the black community and the Prairie View Interscholastic League, which for more than

four decades staged its Wednesday- and Thursday-night football games there, its basketball games in the field house, the nationally recognized Texas Southern Relays every spring, and HISD's most popular, highest-revenue-producing event, the annual Wheatley-Yates Thanksgiving Day football game—the Turkey Day Classic. All were huge events for the city's black community.

Several decades later, the pain lingers. "That was our stadium," lamented Coger Coverson, former Yates lineman and later head coach at Worthing. "When they tore it down, they had all the UH people out there, passing the ball from yard line to yard line. Jeppesen Stadium was important to the black community, and it really hurt to see it go away. I was extremely disappointed when they sold it, and more disappointed when they stopped the Thanksgiving game."

The University of Houston took away the stadium, but integration and the PVIL merger with the UIL killed the Thanksgiving game because of scheduling, bringing an end to the most popular game in PVIL history, a holiday extravaganza rivaling the Texas–Texas A&M and Texas-Oklahoma games, and the largest high school sports event in the United States. The Jeppesen stands filled early, and those who couldn't get seats gladly stood on the cinder track that encircled the field. Others, by the hundreds, milled around outside the arena, following the game through the loudspeakers' play-by-play and socializing, greeting family and old friends hoping to somehow squeeze inside for the second half. From 1947 to 1966, Yates and Wheatley teed it up on Thanksgiving Day for black Houston's Super Bowl, the social event of the season. Education for the blacks who streamed into the city after emancipation was rooted in three schools: Colored High in Freedman Town (Fourth Ward) in 1893, Jack Yates in Third Ward in 1926, and the next year Phillis Wheatley in Fifth Ward. Colored High was renamed Booker T. Washington High School in 1928, and for two decades its football team was coached by the legendary Ben Stevenson of Tuskegee, the greatest player in black-college football history. Stevenson, a versatile back and defender, was a seven-time all-American for Cleve Abbott's multinational championship teams in the 1920s.

Despite rampant overcrowding, there wasn't another high school for black kids in Houston until Kashmere Gardens opened in 1957 in North Houston, and then Sunnyside's Evan E. Worthing in 1958. Most black families reared in Houston probably had a grandmother, uncle, aunt, or parents who attended one of those schools. All of black Houston had a stake in the game that began on a rotational basis among the first three schools. The intracity rivalry was played on Armistice Day and Thanksgiving. "It was *the* event, people were sharp, in zoot suits, big hats broke down on the side," Washington alum and coach Bo Humphrey recalled. "People would come from Louisiana just for the game. A lot of them didn't know a thing about football, especially the women, but the Thanksgiving game was the place to be."

Yates and Wheatley played their first game in 1927, in Independence Heights at Barr's Field, in the Washington Eagles' backyard, but not on Thanksgiving. Three years later, Wheatley beat Washington 7–6 at Buffalo Stadium in Third Ward, home of the Minor League Houston Buffaloes, and the holiday tradition was begun. As the rotation evolved, the Yates-Wheatley game was always the biggest draw, so Washington was nudged out after the 1945 game. The 1946 Lions-Wildcats match was the first official Turkey Day Classic. It drew overflow crowds of more than thirty thousand—an estimated forty thousand in 1961—and generated enough revenue to cover HISD's yearly athletics budget. There were parades down Dowling Street in Third Ward for Yates, and the same thing for Wheatley fans on Lyons Avenue. There were alumni breakfasts, along with pre- and postgame turkey dinners. Besides the excitement of the game, fans were eager to see the outrageous halftime band shows and pageantry, as when Miss Yates and her court arrived in 1958 in a helicopter that landed on the fifty-yard line to a deafening roar from the crowd. The stunt is still talked about, mostly at Yates.

Yates's coach Pat Patterson and Wheatley's Frank Walker would take their teams away from the madness the night before the big game. Wheatley went to a YMCA camp.

Yates's Coger Coverson recalled, "The year before Kennedy was killed, he [Patterson] took us out to Ellington Air Force Base, and they'd feed us real good. We slept in the barracks. The next year, they closed all the bases, so we went to Prairie View. We came back the next morning and had a big ol' breakfast, watched the parade—it was a very big deal. When we were at Prairie View, I saw pictures, and how big some of those guys were. And I said I'm not going to PV, but I got to TSU and it was the same thing!"

The PVIL sponsored other Thanksgiving rivalries: Austin Anderson versus San Antonio Wheatley; Beaumont Hebert versus Beaumont

Charlton-Pollard, which began in 1934 and was called the Soul Bowl; Dallas Lincoln versus Dallas Madison in the South Dallas Super Bowl; the Chocolate Bowl in Corsicana, where Jackson High took on various opponents; and in Fort Worth, I. M. Terrell versus Dunbar. Two Texarkana teams had an annual Turkey Day interstate rivalry—Dunbar High on the Texas side, Washington High on the Arkansas side. All had their traditions and devoted followers, but none had the fame of Yates-Wheatley and the mesmerizing atmosphere of the day, the week.

Thurman Robins, author of *Requiem for a Classic: Thanksgiving Turkey Day Classic,* said of the game: "The Yates vs. Wheatley Thanksgiving Day Classic was an event which grew to glorious heights during the period of segregation. The Classic was a social as well as an athletic contest which engulfed the entire Houston Black community. It was a celebration, a significant prideful 'happening' created and nourished not only by the schools and alumni, but by the majority of Houston's black citizens, and during the height of its glory, by the many white sports fans who attended as well . . . Fans came dressed to kill to witness the game and the glorious halftime activities."

The white fans who attended the games included a large contingent of high school coaches who, according to Walker's daughter Etta Frances, took notes on Patterson's and Walker's strategies: "There was a section reserved for whites in the middle, at the 50-yard line, and it would fill up before the rest of the stadium. There would be two or three hundred of them, mostly coaches, copying some of the things black coaches were doing rather than give them credit. They had notepads writing down plays. There were fresh ideas being generated by the Houston black schools, so this was fertile territory, like professional development for them."

———

Yates and Wheatley were community anchors with strong leaders at their schools and in their communities. William Holland at Yates and John Codwell at Wheatley were head coaches of their school's football teams for the first Yates-Wheatley matchup. Holland, a Hoosier from Terre Haute and a graduate of Indiana State, came to Houston in 1927 as a football coach, though he had excelled in baseball, earning the nickname "Babe." Credited with a TILCS state football championship in 1930 and several track championships, he became principal in 1941 and held the position for seventeen years. During his tenure, Holland repeatedly drew the ire of HISD and city officials. He campaigned for new textbooks and other materials already available at white schools. And then there was the annual Houston Rodeo Parade. The three black schools all marched in the parade behind the livestock, forcing band members to step over, around, and sometimes in the animals' droppings. When Holland led the other principals in a threatened boycott of the event, parade organizers relented, placing the bands in front of the livestock. Where the Turkey Day game was concerned, Holland is also credited with ensuring that Yates and Wheatley received a bigger, more equitable share of revenue from the game.

Holland's constant criticism of the district for its neglect of the black community resulted in a perceived act of retribution by HISD. In 1958, he was demoted to principal at Ryan Junior High just as a new Yates facility opened with labs, industrial workshops, and other upgrades that Holland had wanted. Students, alumni, and Third Ward supporters protested, to no avail, and were quelled by Holland. The community felt it had been slapped in the face by more than Holland's demotion: his successor was John Codwell, a Wheatley man who brought several of his staff and teachers to replace Yates personnel.

The school was never the same. It lost a large measure of its spirit and traditions in a transition that cast a pall over Third Ward. The Reverend Donald Dickson, a Turkey Day Hall of Famer from Yates, bemoaned the effects of the move: "Yates did not have that decorum that they always had. They didn't have the faces of teachers. It had a negative impact on the neighborhood and on the community. The morale and character of the school began to degrade, began to go down because we were hurt."

In Codwell, Yates was getting a seasoned, widely published scholar. John Elihue Codwell Sr. was born in Houston in 1905 to a migrant schoolteacher, James Marshall Codwell, and his wife, Pearl E. Cooper. James Codwell became editor of the black weekly *Western Star*—"Hitch your wagon to the stars; Wisdom mounts her zenith with them," read the paper's credo—and raised John, an outstanding student and athlete at Fourth Ward's Colored High School. After graduating in 1923, he enrolled at Howard University, in Washington, DC, and participated in baseball and football. He returned to Houston after earning a physical science degree at Howard. Texas helped maintain segregation by paying for black graduate students to attend college out of state. In 1936, Codwell took advantage of that program to begin a series of summer courses in Ann Arbor at the University of Michigan. He earned a master's degree and, in 1948, a PhD, becoming the first HISD administrator to do so. His son, John Jr., in 1951 became the Wolverines' first black basketball player. Civic-minded, Codwell became a tireless worker with numerous Houston organizations, including the Houston YMCA, the Boy Scouts of America, and the United Negro College Fund. Codwell was Wheatley's first athletic coach, leading the football, basketball, and track squads, and in 1945 he became Wheatley's second principal following the death of E. O. Smith.

Codwell was at Yates for only six years.

———

The Turkey Day Classic produced dozens of great football players, but Yates and Wheatley boast numerous distinguished alumni in other areas as well. Yates students included Debbie Allen and her sister, Phylicia (Rashad); Texas state representative Garnet Coleman; Judge Andrew L. Jefferson Jr.; the saxophonist and orchestra leader Conrad O. Johnson; and the journalist Roland S. Martin. Wheatley's star-studded walk of fame includes the political figures Barbara Jordan and Mickey Leland; in music, the Crusaders jazz group and the saxophonist Arnett Cobb; in art, the sculptor Melvin Edwards; in the civil rights arena, Otis King; and in education, Ruth Simmons, the first black president of an Ivy League school (Brown).

The Classic went away, but Yates stayed strong in football, and Wheatley in basketball. The 1985 Yates team is considered one of the best teams in Texas high school football history. It went 16–0 and became the first former PVIL school to win the UIL Class 5A state title, easily defeating Odessa Permian—of *Friday Night Lights* fame—37–0. Wheatley dominated on the court, winning twelve PVIL titles, including six straight (1950–1955), and UIL titles in 1968, 1969, 1970, 1973, and 1978.

TURKEY DAY CLASSIC RESULTS

Note: Armistice Day (now Veterans Day) was observed on November 11; Christmas Day is always December 25; the date of Thanksgiving varies. If the date of a game is not given, it cannot be determined from existing records.

1927—Yates 20, Wheatley 6

1927—Washington 19, Wheatley 12 (Thanksgiving Day, November 24)

1928—Wheatley 14, Yates 0 (December 15)

1929—Wheatley 7, Yates 0 (Armistice Day)

1930—Wheatley 7, Washington 6 (Thanksgiving Day, November 27)

1930—Yates 16, Washington 0 (Christmas Day)

1930—Yates 6, Wheatley 0 (November 11)

1931—Wheatley 14, Yates 0 (Armistice Day)

1931—Washington 7, Yates 6 (Christmas Day)

1932—Wheatley 30, Washington 7 (Thanksgiving Day, November 24)

1933—Yates 2, Wheatley 6 (Armistice Day)

1933—Wheatley 20, Washington 2 (Thanksgiving Day, November 30)

1934—Yates 7, Washington 0 (city championship, December 6)

1934—Washington 7, Wheatley 0

1934—Yates 32, Wheatley 7 (Saturday, November 24)

1935—Wheatley 13, Washington 8

1935—Washington 18, Yates 12 (Thanksgiving Day, November 28)

1935—Yates 20, Wheatley 14 (Thursday, November 21)

1936—Yates 6, Washington 0

1936—Wheatley 14, Washington 6 (Thanksgiving Day, November 26)

1936—Wheatley 30, Yates 6

1937—Wheatley 19, Washington 0 (Armistice Day)

1937—Wheatley 8, Yates 7

1938—Wheatley 9, Yates 6 (Thanksgiving Day, November 24)

1939—Wheatley 6, Yates 2 (Thanksgiving Day, November 23)

1940—Washington 6, Yates 0

1940—Washington 6, Wheatley 0

1940—Yates 12, Wheatley 9 (Thanksgiving Day, November 21)

1941—Yates 12, Washington 7

1941—Wheatley 7, Yates 0 (Thanksgiving Day, November 20)

1942—Yates 28, Washington 0

1942—Wheatley 36, Washington 0

1942—Yates 12, Wheatley 7 (Thanksgiving Day, November 26)

1943—Yates 25, Washington 0

1943—Wheatley 20, Washington 0

1943—Yates 21, Wheatley 0 (Thanksgiving Day, November 25)

1944—Wheatley 42, Washington 0

1944—Yates 0, Washington 0 (Friday, October 27)

1944—Wheatley 6, Yates 0 (Thanksgiving Day, November 23)
1945—Yates 12, Washington 0 (Thanksgiving Day, November 22)
1945—Yates 26, Wheatley 0 (Thursday, December 6)
1946—Yates 12, Wheatley 6 (Thanksgiving Day, November 28)
1947—Yates 12, Wheatley 6 (Thanksgiving Day, November 27)
1948—Yates 0, Wheatley 0 (Thanksgiving Day, November 25)
1949—Wheatley 7, Yates 6 (Thanksgiving Day, November 24)
1950—Yates 23, Wheatley 6 (Thanksgiving Day, November 23)
1951—Yates 26, Wheatley 19 (Thanksgiving Day, November 22)
1952—Wheatley 12, Yates 0 (Thanksgiving Day, November 27)
1953—Yates 22, Wheatley 16 (Thanksgiving Day, November 26)
1954—Yates 15, Wheatley 14 (Thanksgiving Day, November 25)
1955—Yates 0, Wheatley 0 (Thanksgiving Day, November 24)
1956—Wheatley 21, Yates 18 (Thanksgiving Day, November 22)
1957—Yates 12, Wheatley 6 (Thanksgiving Day, November 28)
1958—Wheatley 20, Yates 8 (Thanksgiving Day, November 27)
1959—Wheatley 28, Yates 0 (Thanksgiving Day, November 26)
1960—Wheatley 3, Yates 0 (Thanksgiving Day, November 24)
1961—Yates 21, Wheatley 15 (Thanksgiving Day, November 23)
1962—Yates 32, Wheatley 12 (Thanksgiving Day, November 22)
1963—Yates 21, Wheatley 14 (Thanksgiving Day, November 28)
1964—Yates 25, Wheatley 0 (Thanksgiving Day, November 26)
1965—Yates 7, Wheatley 6 (Thanksgiving Day, November 25)
1966—Yates 6, Wheatley 3 (Thanksgiving Day, November 24)

*Source*: *Requiem for a Classic: Thanksgiving Turkey Day Classic*,
Thurman W. Robins

## Andrew "Pat" Patterson: The Lion of Third Ward

*Yates's program builds champions—that was our thing. You could
come to Yates and be a champion, or you could go somewhere and
just play football.*

MAURICE MCGOWAN, former Yates head coach

There is a certain well-earned arrogance across the board regarding athletics at Yates, in what was the PVIL's largest market, Houston. Named for Jack Yates, a former slave and community leader, the school became a perennial force in the league and was synonymous with its loyal Third Ward base, which for decades provided Yates with hundreds of eager, talented athletes looking to wear the crimson-and-gold uniforms of the Lions' program. All the PVIL schools, like most high schools, displayed pride in their institutions and sports programs, but Yates was unabashed about its swagger, taking that pride to a higher level. Winning can have that effect. The man who made it possible at Yates was a native of Gary, Indiana, the best all-around athlete in Wiley College history, an outstanding pitcher in the Negro Leagues, and a coaching genius.

Andrew "Pat" Patterson laid the foundation for excellence at Yates beginning in 1938, when he arrived on campus to lead the baseball and basketball teams and serve as an assistant football coach under Holland. Patterson became head coach in 1940. While playing for Pop Long at Wiley, Patterson quarterbacked the Wildcats to a black-college national championship in 1932. In his second season as basketball coach, Yates won the first of his four PVIL state titles. Barely into his coaching career, Patterson made a lasting impact on the league when he modernized the PVIL's playoff format to formally determine a state champion. Before Patterson devised the system—which was successfully promoted by Yates principal Holland at the league's annual meeting in 1939—any football team in any part of the state that had had a successful season could claim a state championship. Patterson organized the league's teams into districts that fed into a playoff system leading to a state championship game. The system was used for the league's other sports as well.

Patterson coached teams that won three consecutive state titles in baseball—1956–1958—in addition to his football and basketball hardware. He was the only coach to win PVIL state championships in football, baseball, and basketball. His calling card was football. He won three of the six state-title games in which his teams appeared, including four games in the 1960s. His record in the Turkey Day game was 14–7–2.

Leon Bedford played on teams at Wheatley: "One year when we played them, he put [a wide receiver] at quarterback, went to the split T, and beat us to death. The whole season, until Thanksgiving Day, he was running the wing T, but for that game, he took a receiver, put him at quarterback, and ran the split T option, and ran us out of the park. That was the most embarrassing thing I ever saw. It was the first time he'd done it that season, and he installed it in a week.

"Pat was smarter than anybody else. Just that simple. He beat everybody."

Or, more succinctly, "He was the best high school coach in the nation," according to Coger Coverson, who played for Patterson and became a coaching disciple, implementing Patterson's practice methods, offensive and defensive schemes, and other coaching philosophies.

In twenty-one seasons, Patterson put together a 169–62–12 record. His players included Johnny Peoples, who would have a distinguished PVIL coaching career; receiver Bo Farrington, who played for the Chicago Bears and died in an auto accident with Bear great Willie Galimore; Canadian Football League all-star tight end Rhome Nixon; quarterbacks Leo Taylor and Sylvester Armstrong; Grady Caveness; and Major Stevenson, the son of Houston Washington coach Ben Stevenson.

At Grambling, Alphonse Dotson was one of several Yates players who had the distinction of playing for two coaching icons, Patterson and Grambling's Eddie Robinson. He recalled their similar styles: "Coach Patterson said this to all of us, 'Whatever I ask you to do, before you say, "I can't do it," let's try it for two weeks. If after two weeks you can't really accomplish this, then we'll move on and let you try something else, but you must try it for two weeks before you give up.' That said a lot to me, and a hell of a lot today, because today and even back then, everyone wanted immediate gratification for what he or she wanted to accomplish. Coach Patterson installed mentally and physically that you've got to let your brain adjust and your body adjust to what your brain is telling you, and it doesn't always come as rapidly to everybody else or someone else. But two weeks is the time you give yourself to adjust to what he's asking. I applied that not only to football but other things in life.

"He and Coach Rob were parallels. You had to get your books. Coach Rob, the first thing he said to my mom when he and Tom Williams came to recruit me was, 'He's going to get his education.' With Coach Patterson, if we got a D, we got a lick [with the paddle], and the same thing if you didn't have any character about yourself and how you handled yourself at school. You had to be above and beyond reproach. You couldn't be thuggish playing for coach. You couldn't be typical, that's for sure. He pushed not only on the football field, but the lessons he pushed were everyday lessons that carried you through life.

"The first thing Coach Rob said to me when we started working out was, 'Hell, you been coached.'"

One master acknowledging another.

Patterson stepped down at Yates in 1968, and HISD made him assistant supervisor at Jeppesen Stadium, where he would control the venue's activities and visit schools to inspect their facilities. There was also a mentoring aspect for young coaches. "I will not like this job as well as I like coaching, but I am growing older every day and I feel the loss of that strong urge a man needs in the coaching profession," he told the *Informer and Texas Freeman*, a black newspaper in Houston. "Now this job keeps me in contact with sports and I will not be cooped up in some office looking at bills. This job will keep me outdoors enough to not miss coaching too much and I will be making a number of visits to the junior and senior high schools in my district. I am sure I will enjoy this contact and fellowship with the coaches."

Patterson wanted to keep his hand in the game. He delighted in getting out of the office in the afternoon and working with young coaches around Houston as part of his new job. He also visited with former colleagues from the PVIL, most of who, after integration, had moved on to non-PVIL schools.

It was also a time for some to step back and appreciate the man's genius. "I hated Pat Patterson's guts, couldn't stand the man," Bo Humphrey said with a wry smile. "Most of the time, Yates had more material than we had [at Houston's Booker T. Washington], so he was playing a platoon system because he had so much talent. And we'd be playing Yates, and an official would call something against them, and Pat would call time-out. He was an official, so he knew the rules, and would call the official over, they'd talk, then the call would be reversed. They didn't know the rules like Pat, so they couldn't argue."

Humphrey, who was named all-city guard as a senior, discovered years later that Patterson had been responsible for the selection. As their relationship developed (slowly), Patterson became a mentor to the young coach. His new position allowed him to build that same type of relationship with other young coaches around Houston. Humphrey recounted Patterson's routine: "He'd roam around, and when he came to my school in Fourth Ward, Lincoln, I told my coaches when Coach Pat comes I want him to have the run of the practice. I could see the greatness in the man. But when he'd go to white schools, after he left, the white coaches would tell their principal Pat was trying to tell them how to coach, and the principal would call Joe Tusa, the HISD athletic director, and he would tell Pat just don't go out there. That's the way they were. They were just jealous. The man knew so much football. They didn't want to admit a black coach could be that smart.

"But when he came and talked at my practice field, I just felt like I didn't know football."

Patterson had that effect on lots of coaches—on his players, and on his players who became coaches—including Coger Coverson, who grew up in the Cuney Homes projects, a gritty Third Ward neighborhood sandwiched between Yates and Texas Southern. From age six, Coverson eagerly anticipated playing football at Yates and being coached by Patterson. "I used to go over there when I was in elementary school to watch Yates practice. Coach Patterson was the man. Everybody in my neighborhood wanted to play for him. I had a whole lot of respect for him. He was hard, but he was fair. I learned a lot of fundamental football from him. He was a strong man who worked real hard and demanded that you had some discipline. I kind of feared him because I knew if you didn't do what you were supposed to do, you wouldn't be on that team. He threw a lot of outstanding athletes off the team because they wouldn't conform to what he wanted."

Patterson was innovative as a game strategist, but he also brought new training techniques to his team, such as weightlifting. He made the weights by filling empty coffee cans with cement and plunging an iron bar in the mixture to dry: instant barbells. His highly organized practices consisted of almost four hours of exercise, fundamentals, group periods, and a team period.

Yates has always had a deep talent pool, and Patterson refined his players' talents and created an environment of early recruitment through access. On game days, players making the short walk along Wheeler Avenue to Jeppesen would allow kids to carry the equipment bags, which also allowed them to get in the games for free. And they got to see, up close and personal, great players who inspired them to become Lions— Eddie Hughes, Rhome Nixon, Thurman Thomas, Sylvester "Chubby Checker" Armstrong, Leo Taylor, Otis Pointer, and Major Stevenson.

By tenth grade, Coverson had grown to six feet, 180 pounds, a good size for a tenth grader back then. He played on the 1962 state championship team that beat Fort Worth Dunbar 18–15: "We thought we could win state every year. We were heroes at school. We couldn't do any wrong. The teachers loved us, the administration loved us. If you played football at Yates, you were really something. I was captain my senior year, and class president. When you played for Yates, it meant something, and I could see it when I worked at the other schools. We didn't think anybody could beat us."

Coverson hoped to bring that Yates swagger and Patterson's success to his own career. At his first assignment, Aldine Carver, he invited his former coach to observe practices for a week and offer his advice: "He had retired, but I wanted him to come out and consult. He watched, but didn't say a thing. Afterward, he said, 'Look here, man, I can't tell you anything. You got it going on.' Coming from him, boy, I stuck my chest out. 'The man' told me that!"

### Vintage Lion

Coverson's pride in Patterson's acknowledgment is reflected in dozens, hundreds, of young black boys in Third Ward who sought the coach's mentorship at an early age. The prospect of playing for Patterson made easy, for Alphonse Dotson, the decision to attend Yates: "I finished growing up in Third Ward, but I started growing up in Studewood Heights in Houston's North Main Street area. My last days of elementary school were in Third Ward. So I knew families in all of those sections, so I could go back and forth without getting my ass kicked. I wanted to play for Coach Patterson, I wanted to play for Yates. My dad wanted me to go to Booker T., but I said no, I'm going to Yates."

In his years with the Lions, 1958–1961, an off year meant being either runner-up or only district champ. Bad years produced only six wins. From the 1950s, Yates won state championships in track and baseball, district championships in football. Dotson's son, Santana, was a lineman on the powerful, undefeated 1985 Yates team and then an all-American at Baylor. Alphonse flirted with attending Michigan, and had the good grades to get in, but a low tolerance for cold weather. That worked to Eddie Robinson's advantage, as did his imposing squad. Dotson recalled the details of the Tigers' size: "I knew after watching Grambling play. They put their third team on the field against Texas Southern in the second half, and they were averaging six-six, 270 across the line, with a fullback that was 200 pounds. I said, 'That's where I'm going.'

My teammates said, 'They too big.' I said they couldn't do anything but make me or break me, and I don't think they can break me. I was taught not to run from hard work, and that was Patterson again: 'You don't run from hard work. You attack hard work. You learn to do what nobody else wants to do, but do it well.'"

Dotson started his football career at Miller Junior High School, on the western fringe of Third Ward, brushing against downtown Houston. At Miller, he played defensive end and tight end, but once he got to Yates, he lined up wherever there were few players on the depth chart. At six-two, 185 pounds, he began working as a defensive tackle, though Patterson gave him a brief look at tight end. Dotson started at tackle and then settled in at guard, defensive end, nose guard, and, for a change of pace as a senior, fullback in the single wing, and at times quarterback in the Wing-T, and blocking back in the same backfield as Ben Stevenson Jr.

Dotson recalled some of the guys he played with and against: "Otis Taylor and I went to junior high school [together]. I was upset when Worthing came in, because we would have won state at Yates, but he went to Worthing with Horace Chandler. And Kashmere just coming to be, so Wheatley would have been stronger, too. They had Sidney Williams. [The PVIL] had some tough teams. Me and Roland Rogers would battle. They had us put gloves on once and box each other. Round one, we both sparred; round two, we knocked each other down at the same time. That was the end of my official boxing career."

Dotson had a street toughness that often surfaced in situations where he acted, as he called it, "man-ish." That reputation followed him to Grambling, where Coach Rob gave his seventeen-year-old freshman a firm lecture: "I don't normally recruit guys from the city. I go to little rural country towns. It's come to my attention you're doing some things off the field I don't care for, and there are some things you're doing on the field that I'm not content with. Let's get an understanding: as long as you make me need you, Alphonse, I'll go to hell and back with you, but the moment you don't make me need you, you can go to hell by yourself."

Dotson heard him loud and clear. Robinson gave Dotson a mental focus that revealed itself on the field. He started as a fullback, bulking up physically with the help of his teammate Garland Boyette, Ernie Ladd's uncle and a future pro player as one of the first black middle linebackers. Boyette, with his Charles Atlas routine, helped Dotson get stronger, but he put on extra weight at the dining hall too. His role at fullback diminished so much that Robinson moved him to the defensive line—third team, sending Dotson into a season-long funk.

He worked his way back in shape. As a junior, he started at left defensive tackle, opposite Buck Buchanan. He later recalled that he worked even harder the next year: "Everything was live my senior year. I strived to push myself to be better today than I was yesterday. I set out to be the first player to make an all-American team that nobody else from a small school had made. I challenged myself each week and told myself, I needed to make no less than twelve tackles a game."

The payoff came at the end of the 1964 season. Grambling met Bishop College in New Orleans for the Sugar Cup Classic. Grambling won 42-6, and afterward, in the Tigers' locker room, Dotson was fielding media questions when he was asked, "How does it feel?"

"What do you mean?"

"You don't know? You're the first player from a small school to make a major all-American team, UPI, NEA. You're on an all-American team with Dick Butkus, Gale Sayers, and Roger Staubach."

Speechless, he could only say to himself, "Yeah, I did it."

Growing up, he hadn't been sure what his future would hold or what he would become. He first spent five years in the AFL and NFL with the Kansas City Chiefs, Miami Dolphins, and Oakland Raiders. What to do afterward? He had a degree in art education and special education, and a minor in mathematics. He painted with charcoals and oils and taught art in New Orleans. One off-season, he worked successfully with a special education class that had "run off four teachers" during the fall. He counts that as one of the greatest accomplishments of his life. It was well after his football career that he found his station in life, as a winemaker in Central Texas.

Dotson considered a range of possible careers: "I watched the educators around me, so schoolteacher maybe, but not necessarily. Postman, maybe. I did know that football was a way to get a scholarship and education, because we didn't have the money for that. I had watched the old men in the neighborhood complaining about retiring and not having anything to do, but I knew, subconsciously, that I was not going to do my life the same way. I chose to retire at thirty-five or forty and then go back to work, but I wasn't sure what I was going to do."

His postcareer journey took many directions, including sports agent, in which he negotiated the NFL contract that his son signed with the Green Bay Packers—ironically, the same team that had drafted him in 1965, though he chose to join the Chiefs. But his soul was guided by lessons from two exceptional grandfathers. Hezekiah Dotson, his paternal grandfather, a quiet man, was a shop foreman for the Southern Pacific Railroad who performed maintenance and repaired bridges. Dotson recalled his impression of the man: "If I have to count the words I heard him say, it might not be more than a thousand. But whenever he spoke, everybody in the house got quiet." Hezekiah taught his grandson to be on time and to know the value of your word.

"There was a store downtown on Main Street called Bond's. One day my grandmother told me to go there and pick up some things for school. I'm thinking, they'll give me the money, tell me what I can get. My grandfather tells me to go downtown to Bond's and 'tell them I sent you.' I knew not to question him. I go to Bond's, I'm looking around, fellow comes up to me, and I tell him, 'I'm here to get a couple pair of jeans, slacks, shirts, shoes, socks.'

'Anything else?'

'No, that's it, sir. I'm supposed to tell you my grandfather Hezekiah Dotson sent me.' Case closed. When you can go downtown, a black kid, into a major white store and just tell anybody in there Hezekiah Dotson sent you, then I knew the value of your word. That was in the 1950s."

On the other side, his maternal grandfather, Alphonse Certenberg, who had been an AFL-CIO president at Sheffield Steel, taught him to grow grapes, in what is now Kashmere Gardens, adjacent to Fifth Ward in northeast Houston. Behind his house were mules, chicken pens, rabbit pens, a garden with corn and other vegetables, three fifty-five-gallon barrels with Evinrude outboard motors, and two fishing boats parked under a carport made of an arbor of grapes. Dotson was amazed: "You can grow grapes in Houston?! He just looked at me and smiled. That was the best week I had on a vacation as a kid."

It caught up with him in Acapulco, where he had been directed by his teammate and friend Warren McVea. Dotson lived there for fifteen years, mostly playing chess daily in his four-story cliffside villa overlooking the bay, a location he secured through a real estate agent named Martha Cervantes, who become his wife and business partner. Back in the States, a trip to Napa Valley nurtured the seed that Alphonse Certenberg had planted. Today, Certenberg Vineyards, in Voca, Texas, and Dotson-Cervantes Winery in Pontotoc, near Llano, flourish 120 miles northwest of Austin, off Texas Highway 71—Dotson's former jersey number.

Sitting in the scraggly shade of a small tree on a typical hot summer day, Dotson is comfortable and surprisingly cool in a floppy cowboy hat and a denim jacket over a long-sleeved T-shirt. An affable man with a brilliant smile, he speaks with thoughtful, measured words as he reflects on his life's journey and the role played by Jack Yates High School: "It was a good experience—the teachers, coaches, students—an excellent experience. I've been different places around the world, and I've enjoyed it, but the experience of going to Jack Yates and competing with athletes across the city and state, the camaraderie, was unbelievable."

## Frank Walker

Pat Patterson and Frank Walker shared a mutual respect, and Walker acknowledged his onetime rival as a great man, a good role model, and an excellent coach. Holland and Codwell were said to be close friends, but the fierce nature of the Yates-Wheatley football rivalry prevented Patterson and Walker from having much contact. Although overshadowed by Patterson, Walker put together an impressive career at Wheatley. He is thought to be the first high school coach in Texas to win 100 games. The Walker family was one of the first to settle in Fifth Ward, and Franklin Pierce Walker Jr. played quarterback for the Wildcats under Codwell and graduated in 1936. At Southern University, in Baton Rouge, he quarterbacked for Ace Mumford and led the Jaguars to a co-SWAC title in 1938. He returned to Southern to finish work on an agricultural education degree after serving in the army's engineering corps and attaining the rank of captain, a rarity at the time for African Americans. Walker was part of a long line of Wheatley players who played at Southern, beginning with Mumford's reign.

Eddie Robinson and Grambling grabbed the black-college football spotlight in Louisiana and everywhere else. It became a revered, iconic program guided by a coach who retired with more wins than any other in all of college football history. Robinson's rise to prominence greatly overshadowed the success of Arnett "Ace" Mumford, the coach whom Robinson admired and wanted to play for after graduating from McKinley

High School in Baton Rouge. Robinson, an aspiring quarterback, spent ten days at Southern, though Mumford had not recruited him. Feeling unwanted, he left for Leland College in nearby Baker. Mumford asked Robinson to return, but he declined. The two parted ways. Robinson's future lay in northern Louisiana, building Grambling football; Mumford had already positioned the Jags as a dominant force in black-college football circles. During his twenty-five years as Southern's head coach, Mumford had only three losing seasons and won five of the six head-to-head meetings with Robinson. Robinson recalled what that was like: "He beat me so much, I thought I had stolen something. I wanted to play for Coach Mumford, but he had quite a few good quarterbacks, so I went to Leland. He was one of the finest coaches in football, a smart man who did a lot of research. He was a gentleman and good at everything he touched."

Mumford grew up in Buckhannon, West Virginia, but his first coaching job out of Wilberforce College, in Ohio, was in East Texas at Jarvis Christian College, in Hawkins. He then went to Bishop College in Marshall, followed by Texas College in Tyler, where he won a black-college national championship in 1935. He settled in at Southern in 1936. In his thirty-six-year career, Mumford won eleven SWAC titles and six black-college national championships. And he created a pipeline to Houston Wheatley because of the coaching clinics he often held in Houston. Large numbers of blacks had migrated from Louisiana to Texas and settled in Fifth Ward, which became a fertile recruiting area for Southern. And early on, Wheatley had played well against schools in Louisiana, likely attracting Mumford's attention to what Codwell was doing with Wheatley football. When Walker became head coach, Mumford visited frequently and became his mentor. Walker became Mumford's proposed successor at Southern and was twice offered the job, but felt obligated by his family to remain at Wheatley.

Walker has the distinction of having coached state championship football teams in both Louisiana and Texas. He guided Southern University's affiliated secondary prep school, Southern Lab High School, to a title in 1939, and was head coach for Wheatley's 1954 3A PVIL championship. Walker was backfield coach in 1947 at Texas Southern, but the position he relished was coaching the Wildcats. He got that opportunity in 1954 when he succeeded Rutherford Countee after serving as his assistant. Wheatley was his only high school coaching job in Texas, and he stayed at the school until 1971, coaching and teaching history and physical education, winning 145 games and losing only 52. Among the players he coached were Donnie Davis, Sidney Williams, Leon Bedford, Aaron Jackson, Cyrus Lancaster, Elliott Harvey, Harold Trahan, Lester Hayes (Oakland Raiders), Godwin Turk (Denver Broncos), George Balthazar (Baltimore Colts and Pittsburg Steelers), Eldridge Small (New York Giants), and Charlie Thomas (Kansas City Chiefs). Bedford, Balthazar, Harvey, and Trahan also became members of his coaching staff.

Former Wildcats' linebacker Godwin Turk played on the Denver Broncos' Super Bowl XII team. He remembers Walker and the environment at Wheatley, which helped him get a degree in physical education at Southern and a master's degree in communications: "I had heard a lot about Coach Walker. You knew those men didn't take no static. They'd bust your behind. He'd have us doing 100-yard belly flops, the coaches' way of finding out who really wanted to be out there. But they also wanted us to be something, to make something of our lives, and they set examples for us by coming to school dressed like they were going to church.

"There was a stigma against athletes, that we were just brawn and no brains, that if it wasn't for sports we couldn't do nothing else. I was going to show people who thought like that I was not going to be a failure."

Upon retirement, Walker retreated, to a large degree, to his rural domicile in Dayton, Texas, his mother's birthplace, about thirty-five miles east of Houston in Liberty County. Throughout his tenure at Wheatley, Walker spent his own money to provide for his teams what HISD would not, including practice equipment, but also reached into his pockets to ensure that his graduating players had the means to get to college. His daughter Etta recalled how it often wreaked havoc on the family budget: "They didn't want to put that stuff at Wheatley. Half the equipment was marked 'Lamar High School.' When they got new stuff, they'd send the old stuff to Wheatley, but his position was, 'I will not be beaten because I don't have the things to work with. If you're going to beat me, you're going to have to outthink me.' So he'd buy stuff out of pocket that they needed for practice, and it was always confusing in our house because of the budget. He was spending a lot of money on Wheatley and for his players—bus tickets, clothes, pocket money. It was more than just a coaching job for people at the black high schools; it was like a godfather kind of mentoring situation. A lot of those kids wouldn't have gotten to college if people hadn't given them a way to get there."

Despite all the support he gave the school and his players, he also managed to send Etta to the New Mexico Institute of Mining and Technology in 1965 for a degree in physics and then to Stanford for a PhD in biophysics. She taught at Texas Southern for many years. Her academic success and that of so many others from the school stood in stark contrast to the area's reputation as the crime-ridden "Bloody Fifth." One year, *Texas Monthly* called it "Texas' Toughest, Proudest, Baddest Ghetto."

The heavyweight champion George Foreman emerged from that atmosphere. Godwin Turk grew up with Foreman: "He was tough. I knew him a little. I was a year behind him, and he dropped out in eighth grade. I didn't hear from him again until he started boxing. George is a good guy. You never know which way God gon' take ya. He quit school and now is a multimillionaire. How about that? He made it. He made it with his fists because he had that talent. One night he was on the corner preaching, North Wayside in Settegast. I passed by and started talking to him, going over the old days. He was real mean when he was growing up, but he had to be because he didn't have a daddy. He had to be tough, had to fight going and coming from school in the Bottom. I didn't have to do that, but he remembered me."

———

When Wheatley opened a new building in 1949, it was hailed by the *Houston Chronicle* as "the finest Negro high school in the South." Amid the edginess of Lyons and Gregg Avenues, Wheatley was an academic hotbed that graduated future iconic figures.

Etta Walker recalled a close-knit neighborhood that pushed kids to succeed. "People talk about the violence, but I never saw that around me. I saw a community of nuclear families that were very strong, and in many cases both the father and mother were there. People worked together. The church and neighborhood would help families with clothes, school supplies. We couldn't have been doing all of this violent stuff if we were doing all of this good stuff. In the sixties, we had a number of people who went to Ivy League schools. There was a big push to get black kids to schools like Harvard, Berkeley, and you had all of these families, even the ones who didn't know what college was all about, never thought about going, but somehow the message got into Fifth Ward and people who were able to live a little bit above marginal levels knew that's what their children needed to be doing. There was a big push for education, more than I've seen at any other time in the history of black folks in this country. Whether they had two cents above carfare or not, they were wanting their kids to go to college. Nobody knew anything about financial aid. They just found a way to save money to send them."

Walker taught physics at TSU and then set up the science program at Houston Community College, where she created the math and science curricula in the 1970s. Academics was her comfort zone. She reminisced about what it felt like to be the coach's daughter: "It was difficult because I was on stage all the time, and I was like my daddy, I didn't like being in the limelight."

In retirement, Frank Walker continued his hobby, gardening. In Dayton he raised vegetables and maintained a small herd of registered Charolais cattle. He passed away on February 9, 1987. Etta considered what her father's life had meant: "His degree was in agriculture, and he liked to grow things. His legacy is in his performance as a player and a coach, winning, creating a good image for the school. From the time he played until he finished coaching were the glory years, the golden years at Wheatley, and the school has not come back up to that level. We want it to come back up again, but the next golden era won't be in the same vein. It might be more soccer than football, but that's okay. We want it to come up with something. Wheatley needs to be known for something."

## The Turk

Like Frank Walker, his former coach, Godwin Lee Turk retreated to a bucolic East Texas setting. The farming-and-ranching freedmen-founded community of Mount Union in Jasper County, 130 miles northeast of Fifth Ward and light-years from the madness of the inner city. Raising cattle at the Lazy T Ranch, the 1969 Wheatley grad stepped away from a football career during which he was a teammate of Joe Namath, Emerson Boozer, and John Riggins on the New York Jets, and of John Elway on the Denver Broncos. With the Broncos, Turk became the first former Wheatley player to earn a Super Bowl ring. He is regarded as one of the best ever to don the purple and white. Turk, a six-three, 220-pound defensive lineman and offensive tackle at Wheatley, was described by Walker as "one of the best athletes that I ever coached."

The pure joy of playing football captured Turk: "Every year I played at

Wheatley, tenth through twelfth grade, I was making all-city, all-district, that kind of stuff. I was gifted with that talent, but at the time, I was just playing because there was nothing else to do. I was just having fun, but the more I played the better I got. They had the 'bull ring' in practice, with you in the middle of a circle and guys coming in there trying to knock your head off. I hit them, get off, go to the next man. I loved that. I was in seventh grade knocking upperclassmen down. I had to earn respect."

Turk spent his youth in Clinton Park, a black neighborhood whose teens were bused to E. O. Smith Junior High School and Wheatley, passing "two or three white schools." As a team captain, he had the distinction of playing in the last Wheatley-Yates Turkey Day Classic, in 1966. As a junior, he was the only member of the 1967 team to be named first-team all-district in the newly integrated UIL. That team finished 7–3 and allowed only 87 points in what would be the last winning season for Walker, who retired at the end of the 1970 season.

Turk recalled that the transition to integrated play came with plenty of tension: "We jumped up on top of [the white teams] early, and they'd say, 'We gon' beat these niggers,' and we'd say, 'Yeah, these niggers gon' kick your butts.' They called us 'niggers,' but wasn't no big deal." He was all-city at defensive end as a senior.

Turk excelled in academics as much as athletics, and was president of his junior class. Elite academic schools came calling, and he accepted a scholarship from Cal-Berkeley head coach Ray Willsey, as did Turk's 1968 teammate O. Z. White, a defensive lineman. Turk and White were named most outstanding freshmen in successive years, Turk tying for the honor with wide receiver Isaac Curtis. Turk transferred after one season to Southern University, which through the years had developed quite a pipeline from Wheatley. Seemingly destined for greatness with the Golden Bears, he didn't miss a beat with the Jaguars. He was named a black-college all-American linebacker and earned both a bachelor's degree in communications and a master's in education.

Some of the most valuable lessons were ones he learned outside the classroom or practice field: "When I left for college, my daddy said, 'Don't take no wooden nickels.' I would ask for money, but he would hardly send it, and when he did, it would take two or three months, and when it got there, it was only twenty dollars. That made me mad, but it also taught me how to hustle, not with dope, just working hard, learning how to work. And I made sure I got my paper. They were not going to use me for four or five years, punish my body—and brother, they punish you in college, but I wasn't going to let that happen and not get a degree. I was going to make it in life."

Godwin was a third-round pick by the Jets in 1974, but suffered a shoulder injury during the preseason and missed his rookie year. Later, knee injuries also required surgery. Speed had been a large part of his game, but the injuries took that away, and Turk retired in 1978. His post-NFL career began as a longshoreman at the Port of Houston, and he rose to the level of terminal superintendent in Orange, overseeing operations at the Port of Orange and subsequently at the Port of Beaumont.

The Turkey Day Classic, the Super Bowl win, and the injury-shortened NFL career quickly became distant memories, all but forgotten. Turk had no regrets: "I used to whip a lot of butt and had a lot of fun doing it, but I didn't keep clips. I'm not that type of guy. There's nothing in my house that represents football. I'm no better than the next person. Football was only for a little while. I want to stay low-key. That's why I'm living up in the country, making good clean money. All I want to do is get into heaven. That's the team I want to make."

### *Accounting for Defense*

Leon Bedford was minding his own business, issuing payroll checks from the accounting department at Texas Southern University, when his career path was unexpectedly redirected by John Codwell. The encounter was happenstance, but the two men were well acquainted from Bedford's days as a Wheatley student and football player when Codwell was the school's principal and a former head coach. Bedford thought that with a business degree from Southern University, he would become a certified public accountant and lead a stable life caring for his wife and young son. He wasn't interested in the unpredictability and chaotic life of a football coach, with the late-night film study, game planning with the coaching staff, and travel.

Codwell remembered Bedford and his stellar career at Wheatley as an undersized center and linebacker, and his success for Ace Mumford at Southern.

Bedford recalled their conversation: "Codwell walked in and said, 'What you doing in here, boy?'

'Man, I'm trying to make a living. I got a wife and a baby, and I'm working in my degree field.'

'How much money you making?'"

Bedford was ashamed to admit to the $2,500 annual salary, and Codwell likely sensed that. "You want to coach?"

Coach? Not only was entering that profession the furthest thing from Bedford's mind, but coaching also meant teaching, and he had never taken an education course or thought about teaching, either.

"Don't worry about that, boy. You want to coach? Tell you what, the starting salary for teachers with a degree is $4,800 for nine months."

At that, Bedford the CPA crunched the numbers for Bedford the coach and teacher, and one of Wheatley's finest was practically headed back home to the sidelines to begin building a career in which he would be acknowledged as one of the most respected defensive coaches in the country, high school or college. Codwell drew out the necessary path, advising Bedford on how to get teaching credentials by taking summer education classes at TSU. He offered to arrange for Bedford to have a summer job as a swimming instructor in order to make a little extra money.

"Can you swim, boy?" Well, yes, he could.

"You been in the army, right boy?" Well, yes, he had.

The figures kept adding up. Taking classes meant he could also get a GI Bill check. Finally, Codwell got Bedford assigned to Wheatley's business department. By late summer, when the Wildcats began preparing for the fall football season, Bedford knew right away that he had found his true calling.

He could recall that feeling precisely: "I started coaching not because I wanted to coach but because of the money. But the first time I walked on the field at Wheatley and started working with those kids, I thought, 'This ain't half bad.' It was a challenge working with them, because all they knew was knocking heads."

He meant the physical, unrefined play on the field, but could have been talking about the general demeanor on the mean streets of Fifth Ward, which could indeed be perilous. Despite that reputation, Fifth Ward originated thousands of success stories. For example, it was home to a thriving music scene, most prominently represented by Don Robey's Peacock Records. A decade before Motown artists hit the charts, Robey founded Peacock in Fifth Ward to develop the Texas blues and gospel scenes, likely the first such business in the country run by an African American. Robey produced dozens of blues and gospel artists, including Bobby "Blue" Bland, Clarence "Gatemouth" Brown, Memphis Slim, Willie Mae "Big Mama" Thornton, the Dixie Hummingbirds, and the Mighty Clouds of Joy.

Freedmen were the first inhabitants of the area east of downtown Houston that took the name Fifth Ward in 1866. Like Third and Fourth Wards, it became a hub for black businesses and professionals. When Wheatley opened in 1927, it was one of largest black high schools in the United States, with an enrollment of 2,600 students. Bedford graduated from Wheatley in 1950, the last class at "old" Wheatley before the school moved into a new building. He headed to Southern University, the first in his family to attend college. He was fully vested as an athlete, despite a surreptitious beginning.

Bedford recalled the story in detail: "I lived around the corner from Wheatley, but my parents didn't want me to play. They were from the country and didn't know anything about football. But I had an uncle who told me to bring the permission papers to him and he'd sign them. So I started playing football, using the excuse to my parents that I was doing something after school for my uncle's little convenience store—so I could practice and play in the games. We didn't have a TV, but they'd listen to the Wheatley games on the radio. One evening, we went to play Galveston, and the radio guy kept calling my name: 'Bedford made the tackle' then 'Bedford made that tackle.' When I got home, they were up, and I got my ass whipped, one of the worst whippings I ever got in my life. They were going to make me quit, but my uncle came over and talked to my grandparents, who raised me, and they talked for a long time.

"He told my grandmother, 'This is the first somebody in our family who has a chance to go to college on a scholarship.' They finally said okay, but they never saw me play until my senior year in the Thanksgiving game against Yates. My grandfather came, and I was cocaptain and had one of the best games I'd played in long time. And he was up there hollering, 'Get off my son! Don't hurt my son!'"

That was not a problem. Bedford was a hitter with disdain for the passivity of playing offense. He developed a knack for reading and anticipating plays. He would study film with the coaches, and he understood that at under six feet tall, he could have an edge on bigger players—practically everyone he lined up against—if he could be smarter. It worked so well that he got a scholarship offer from Kentucky State. He had his bags packed to leave for Frankfort, and then Codwell found out.

Bedford explained what happened next: "If I had a mentor, it was John Codwell. He got on the phone to Mumford, and the next day I was on my way to Southern. That's how they did things back then." It wouldn't be the last time Codwell went to bat for Bedford. While playing for the Jaguars, he was a two-year teammate of quarterback Billie Matthews. Their friendship later altered Bedford's relationship with Codwell.

He had gladly helped Bedford start his coaching career, but did not take kindly to the young coach departing for a job on the staff of Matthews, his friend, former Southern teammate, and fellow Wheatley alum. They would be coaching at the new black high school in north Houston, Kashmere Gardens. The estrangement from Codwell was not pleasant for Bedford: "Billie was head coach at E. O. Smith Junior High School and asked me to be defensive coordinator [at Kashmere]. I told Codwell I was going to Kashmere, thinking I was doing the right thing. He didn't speak to me. I was teaching accounting and typing, and he called me down to the office. I sat there all day—he never came out. Next day, same thing. I asked what was going on. Frank Walker came in and said, 'I'd rather be a janitor at Wheatley than principal at Kashmere Gardens.' I said, 'That's you, man.' That's how me and Billie got together."

Matthews had been two years ahead of Bedford at both Wheatley and Southern. He graduated from Wheatley in 1948 as an all-around athletic star—football, basketball, and baseball—and at the top of his class academically. His diploma, with honors, from Southern was in architectural engineering. On the football field, Mumford started him right away. Matthews and Odie Posey, a prized running back sensation from San Antonio Wheatley, lead the Jags to an undefeated season (12–0) in 1948–1949 and the first of three consecutive black-college national championships. With Matthews under center, the Jags went 37–4–2 in 1948–1951. Southern didn't lose a game in Matthews's first three seasons. He accepted the Kashmere job in 1959. In 1981, he picked up a Super Bowl ring as running backs coach for the San Francisco 49ers. Matthews coached in the NFL for twenty-five years, preceded by collegiate stops at Kansas and UCLA on the staff of Coach Pepper Rodgers. Throughout his career, he worked with some of the game's best runners—O. J. Simpson, Barry Sanders, Wendell Tyler, Freeman McNeil, Theotis Brown, James McAlister, and Kermit Johnson—but his first superstar runner came out of Kashmere. Delvin Williams was one of the most decorated and coveted running backs in Texas high school history.

Bedford and Matthews got Kashmere's program off the ground, but not right away. In consecutive weeks of their first season, the Rams lost to Galveston Central 60–0, gave up 72 points to Yates, and ceded 75 points to Walker's Wheatley squad, much to Walker's delight. It didn't take long, however, to turn the Rams around. The next year, Kashmere beat Wheatley 20–0, and Yates too, and went on to win several district and regional championships with Matthews as head coach. Matthews passed away in 2001.

Bedford recalled the early days at Kashmere: "We just started getting some football players. The kids we had weren't being coached. Billie and I both played under Mumford at Southern, and those people coached us. They didn't scream and holler, they broke us down into groups and taught this and that, and we didn't scrimmage a lot. We did a lot of individual work. That's what Billie and I were used to. We had Oliver Ross and Tillman Henderson, and we just built a good football team—that's all."

Bedford left Kashmere for Galveston Central as Ed Mitchell's defensive coordinator. The Bearcats won the 1963 3A state title, a 34–14 victory over the home team, Dallas Madison, coached by Don Grace, a Wheatley alum. It was a bone-stinging, bitter-cold night with snow flurries at Cobb Stadium. An adult ticket cost the princely sum of one dollar and permitted the holder to sit, heavily bundled against the cold, and witness the 10–1 Bearcats go up against the undefeated, twelve-point-favorite Trojans. During the game, Central players broke up their benches and started a campfire on the sidelines in an effort to keep warm. A "slim" crowd saw Bedford's defense pick off three passes—one returned seventy-nine yards by Rochon Chatman to set up the game's first score—and recover two fumbles. With the upset, Central won the second state championship in school history.

When Galveston schools integrated in 1967, Central students were sent to Galveston Ball, whose football team had never won a state championship. Mitchell was named principal. At the new school, Bedford worked first as an assistant coach before becoming a defensive coordinator again the next season. He and some others from Central rained complaints on deaf ears about Mitchell having to leave the sidelines: "There was nothing right about it at all. Things were bad. He had won a state championship and went to the playoffs the next year and probably would have gone again, but we integrated. Ball had never won anything."

The Tornadoes had had only one winning season, 1966, in the seven before integration. In the first two seasons with the addition of players from Central, Ball was a combined 22–3, twice winning its district. The team's success eased the transition blues, and Bedford settled in to the very different routine of working at a white school. He noted the much more relaxed atmosphere there: "It was kind of funny. The whole time I was at black schools, I had taught five classes and had one off period. When I got to Ball, I had three classes, one was business math at seven in the morning, nobody showed up, then two accounting classes, and I was through at twelve. I was defensive coordinator, so I didn't have any classes after twelve o'clock, so I'd work on game plans. But when it wasn't football season, I was playing golf with the principal. We had some good times at Ball, and I really got into a coaching background."

That was brought about by the trips to Oklahoma to meet with and observe Chuck Fairbanks and his Sooners coaching staff. Bedford was the UIL's only black coordinator, and at Texas High School Coaches Association meetings he endured white coaches' conversations about how he had gotten a good job. But it wasn't all pleasantries, as he recalled: "[They would talk] like I wasn't there—'nigger' this and 'nigger' that, and I was sitting right there. But I wasn't considered a nigger because I had a good job. I was the only black in the meeting, so there was nothing I could say or do about it."

He had the chance to become head coach at Ball in 1970, and he had support from the Ball players and some whites in Galveston. When Joe Woolley got the job instead, the players boycotted. Bedford quieted the situation. He had met earlier with district officials, and he knew the decision had nothing to do with his coaching ability: "They brought me downtown. President of the board was also on the board at Moody National Bank. He told me, 'Leon, you're the best man for the job, and you should have the job, but we're just not ready to have a black head football coach.' Just like that. It was because I couldn't go to the Rotary Club, and the head coach had his own radio show, making good money, and they didn't see me doing that. They wanted me to come back and help the team, but I said, 'I can't do that, I helped the other man. I'll find another job.'"

That summer, he landed a job on Clifton Ozen's staff at Beaumont Hebert. It was a chance to pair with his son, Vance, who was on a path to follow in his father's coaching footsteps. Playing for his dad, Vance became an all-district defensive back on the first former PVIL school to win a UIL state title. Hebert, under head coach Alex Durley, was 15–0 that season and allowed only 124 points. Vance, undersized like Leon, displayed every bit as much fight as his dad. And that pugnacity would be a problem.

"The first time we got into it, Vance was five-eleven, 175 pounds, playing in a five-man front on the JV at defensive end—coming off the edge, sacking people. So for his junior year, I moved him to corner, and he didn't speak to me for a week. I told him, 'Look, man, let me tell you something. You got the grades and athletic ability, but there's no place in college for a 175-pound defensive end.' He anchored the 4 × 400 relay team, ran a 49.0 open quarter, scratched 4 × 100, ran 9.7 in the 100, 44.5 in the 400, so I moved him to defensive back. And he made all-district, all-this, and all-that. We were playing Gainesville for the state championship in Austin, an all-black team against an all-white team, and he showed out.

"We played a lot of man-to-man defense, which people didn't do in high school when I came through. They didn't believe you could do it. But I never believed in the zone, and we won state. I wanted him to go to Oklahoma because I knew everybody there. He didn't go to a SWAC school, my school, Southern, where I'm in the Hall of Honor, because, they told me, 'We can't offer him a scholarship. He's too little.' I thought he might go to Oklahoma or UCLA; Billie [Matthews] was there. But he said he was going Texas.

'Man, they don't want you up there. They're still segregated.' Texas was the last team in the SWC to get blacks on their football team."

Vance responded, "You don't know nobody at Texas."

"What?"

"You don't know nobody at Texas. You know everybody at Oklahoma, at UCLA. You don't know anybody at Texas. I'm your son. I want to go somewhere nobody knows you."

Vance wanted to make a name for himself without his father's help. So Texas it was, and he started as a freshman. Coaching opportunities at the major-college level were few in Leon Bedford's era, but Vance's coaching career was white hot, with stops as a defensive backs coach at

Florida and Michigan, both of which had national championship teams in 2008 and 1997. At Michigan, he was the position coach for Heisman Trophy–winning defensive back Charles Woodson. He was a defensive coordinator at Oklahoma State and Louisville before returning to Texas to take charge of the Longhorns' defense during head coach Charlie Strong's three-year tenure.

Leon was not surprised by his son's success: "He has a knack for defense. When he was a kid, I'd bring film home at night, studying, and he'd be in my lap. And we'd stay up half the night. He can pick up tendencies in a hurry. I never had the ability to play politics to be a head coach. Everybody says I'm too brash, but I say what's on my mind, and my son is the same. He'll tell you what's on his mind, and he don't care if you like it or lump it. And that's the way I've always been."

# CHAPTER 6

# Integration

## *The Good, the Bad, the End*

*I didn't want integration. I had always said I want equal facilities,
books, equipment, and we'll make it. But things don't always come
in the form you want, so you have to be careful what you pray for.
It was good for those who were going to make it, bad for those who
needed a little bit more nurturing. We lost a generation of kids.
I kept a lot of kids on the team that weren't really capable of playing,
but they were still part of something.*

COACH EARVIN GARNETT, Wichita Falls Washington

The mind-numbing, hand-wringing conversations about the
unthinkable began in 1955. The UIL's State Executive Committee had been thrown into a tizzy when the El Paso school board,
having voted to desegregate its schools, inquired about what that decision would mean for its participation in UIL competitions. El Paso
was the first district in Texas to comply with the US Supreme Court's
ruling in *Brown v. Board of Education*, which deemed segregation in
public schools unconstitutional. The rest of the state, though, took its
time making the change, and did so grudgingly, to say the least. It took
two and a half years for Texas slaves to learn of their emancipation, and
it was a decade or more, in some cases, after the court's decision before
black students and white students sat together in the same classrooms
in Texas. The initial push for that came courtesy of a 1930 PVIL-school
grad, Heman Sweatt of Houston's Jack Yates High School.

In 1946, Sweatt challenged the University of Texas Law School's
policy of segregation when he was refused admission because of his race.
His rejection provided just the opportunity the NAACP and Houston

activists had been looking for to challenge and dismantle school seg-regation. They knew that desegregation would have to start at the top of the educational pyramid, with graduate or professional schools, and work its way down to primary schools. The strategy was to win small victories and build on them. With help from Thurgood Marshall and the NAACP, Sweatt sued the school, in a case styled *Sweatt v. Painter* (Theophilus S. Painter was the UT president). On June 5, 1950, the US Supreme Court ruled in favor of Sweatt, overturning the "separate but equal" precedent established in *Plessy v. Ferguson* (1896). Sweatt's vic-tory opened the way for the court's 1954 *Brown v. Board of Education* decision, which declared unconstitutional state laws creating separate schools for black and white students. Sweatt did not immediately enroll at UT, and two days later, an eager graduate student from Annapolis, Maryland, who had been waiting in the wings quickly jumped at the opportunity. John Chase enrolled in UT's School of Architecture, be-coming the first black student at a major southern university, a fact generally overshadowed by Sweatt's fame. Sweatt did not enroll at UT until the fall of 1950.

The *Sweatt* decision paved the way for *Brown*, which set the stage, via El Paso, for all hell breaking loose at UIL headquarters in Austin.

In putting the motion to desegregate before the El Paso school board, Ted Andress, an attorney and board member, said: "The School Board members have taken notice of the recent Supreme Court decision on compulsory segregation. I think it is time that this board makes the prompt and reasonable start toward integration that should be made. I move that we comply with all rulings of the Supreme Court and that segregation on a compulsory or involuntary basis shall not be enforced in the El Paso Public Schools."

The El Paso board's immediate compliance with *Brown* forced the UIL not only to reconsider for the first time the semantics of its 1910 charter, which specified that membership was open only to any "white public school," but also to envision the decision's most dreaded ramifica-tion—integration. The very thought of race mixing was a castor-oil-bitter prospect whose very mention among whites could carry lethal conse-quences. It revived an attitude that had surfaced in 1865 with the news of emancipation. An editorial in the Galveston *Daily News* saw it like this: "Their freedom can never make them the equals of the white race . . . God himself has made a marked distinction between the white and black races, which no human laws, nor all the abolitionists in the world, can ever obliterate."

White Texans wanted nothing to do with living among unfettered black people. Integration was the next step up—or down, depending on one's racial persuasion—from basic coexistence. It would be a gigantic step: living, working, and learning side by side. The reality was quickly, and not so quietly, approaching. The UIL's State Executive Committee and the UT Board of Regents grappled with how best to respond to El Paso. When they did, it was with surprising quickness and a deft editor's touch. The regents voted to admit the school's first black undergraduates to the 40 Acres (a longtime nickname for the UT-Austin campus) in the 1956 fall semester. The UIL amended its policy thus: "Be it resolved that the State Executive Committee of the Interscholastic League interpret the language "public white school" as not excluding any public school in Texas which has previously limited its enrollment to white students but which has modified its rules so as to admit students of the Negro race."

Problem solved.

Frederick Douglass High School was El Paso's only PVIL school, and its students now had the option to attend Bowie or El Paso High School. It was not that simple in towns where white school districts had no serious plans or thoughts of integrating and refused to play teams that included a black player. A year after *Brown*, the Supreme Court heard arguments from several states, including Texas, seeking relief in regard to desegregation and how to carry it out. In what became known as *Brown II*, the court handed desegregation decisions back to district courts, though ordered that desegregation occur "with all deliberate speed."

Texas school districts apparently interpreted "with all deliberate speed" to mean "take as much time as you like." There was no mass rush to comply with the ruling, and downright defiance was the order of the day in Mansfield, thirty-five miles southwest of Dallas. Mansfield was the embodiment of white fears of the transition to integration. In 1956, it became the first school district in Texas federally ordered to integrate when the US Fifth Circuit Court of Appeals ruled the district could not deny enrollment to three black students seeking to attend Mansfield High. The school board drew up plans to abide by the ruling. At the time, Mansfield's black high school students were forced to commute by commercial bus—Continental Trailways—twenty miles northwest to

Fort Worth's all-black I. M. Terrell High School, a PVIL member. The bus dropped the students off at its station in downtown Fort Worth, a twenty-block walk to the school.

While the Mansfield board had moved to integrate, Mayor Bud Halbert and C. G. Harwell, the police chief, were determined not to comply. They were agitated over the local NAACP chapter's suit against the board on behalf of the three students. On August 30 and 31, 1956, the black students attempted to enroll at Mansfield High. They were greeted by an angry mob of four hundred white students and residents, who hung the three black students in effigy. Reporters and sympathizers were attacked, and stores closed in a show of support. One of the black students, Floyd Moody, recalled years later in a *Fort Worth Star-Telegram* story how the Mansfield superintendent, R. L. Huffman, was very direct in voicing his opposition when he met with the three students. "I can remember the conversation was very short," Moody said. "It didn't take very long for this man sitting across at the end of that table with those thick eyebrows saying, 'You will never enter this school.' Those were the words."

One year after the events in Mansfield, the Texas Legislature passed laws that encouraged school districts to resist federally ordered integration. Mansfield stood fast for another ten years, integrating in 1965 under threat of losing its federal funding after passage of the Civil Rights Act of 1964, and a year after Alabama governor George Wallace declared in his inaugural address, "Segregation now, segregation tomorrow, segregation forever."

Wallace voiced a long-standing, ingrained mantra of southern whites, but as the civil rights movement charged forward, blacks could see a change coming. Integration around the state was mostly quiet, even if not smooth, and there were no violent clashes in Texas making national headlines or leading the network evening news. In Houston, for example, downtown businesses quietly integrated in 1960 after a string of lunch counter sit-ins and other protests by the Texas Southern University Progressive Youth Association, whose organizers and leaders included Eldrewey Stearns, Otis King, Curtis Graves, and Holly Hogrobrooks, all of whom were passionately active in the civil rights movement.

The downtown businesses calmly capitulated because of their desire to avoid the kind of violence seen on TV in civil rights protests in other cities. But some of them may also have remembered a hot, drizzly August evening in 1917 when black soldiers from the Twenty-fourth Infantry marched on Houston, hell-bent on revenge after being knocked around by Houston police and taunted by racist white citizens for a month after their arrival from New Mexico to guard construction of Camp Logan Army Training Post in support of World War I. The Camp Logan mutiny is noted as the only race riot in US history in which more whites (seventeen) than blacks (four) were killed. Nobody wanted to see a repeat of that kind of violence, and businessmen had no trouble imagining that civil rights protests could eventually lead to physical confrontations. Before integrating that summer, the businesses brokered a well-orchestrated and controversial ten-day blackout with Houston media. The businesses would open their lunch counters—seventy of them downtown—to black diners on August 25, 1960, if there was no media coverage of the event. The Houston media was later chided by national outlets, but the *Houston Chronicle*'s publisher, John T. Jones, and his counterparts, Oveta Culp Hobby at the *Houston Post* and George Carmack of the *Houston Press* were all in.

If you blinked, you missed integration in Houston.

"There was a grocery and drug store across from Miller Junior High School on Almeda," Alphonse Dotson recalled, "and one day I was in there, 1956 or 1957. I had gotten to school early for training or something like that, and I was hungry. So I went over there for a hamburger and sat down in the middle of the counter. I didn't think about it. I asked the white lady behind the counter if I could have a hamburger, 'please.' She stopped and looked at me. And I think [because of] the way I asked, not aggressive, but respectful, she said 'Okay,' after pausing. She knew I wasn't there because of a protest. I was a kid just wanting to eat. That taught me, then and there, even though we were directed to the back of the bus, there were those who, depending on how you carried yourself, you could get what you wanted and not be Tom-ish about it, but respectful. But the negative. I remember a couple of incidents after I got into college, but still living in Houston. I had just been drafted by the Chiefs, and they had sent me a 1965 Starfire. Carol Wilkinson, Miss Yates, lived across from me. I was home from college and asked her to go with me to an NFL event at the Shamrock Hotel. We were just friends. We hopped into this new car, went to the event, then heading home, just past the Warwick Hotel, and the lights went on. White officers pulled me over and asked, 'Where'd you get this car from?'

"It's a gift from the Kansas City Chiefs."

"Well, you know you don't have Texas license plates."

"Well, it just got here."

"That was basically the back of the bus and the negative. But based on how blacks were being treated elsewhere, in Houston we were ahead of our time."

————

El Paso knocked over the first domino in the process of integrating Texas schools. A few others followed suit in towns where black populations were small compared with larger Hispanic populations, including San Antonio, Corpus Christi, San Angelo, and Austin. Others fell in slow motion. Most Texas school boards ignored the law, drew up plans that sat idle for years, delayed, and fretted in a segregated business-as-usual atmosphere. The UIL was, relatively speaking, an exception. It had seen the future, and like it or not, the league was moving quietly and decisively toward embracing the reality of opening its membership to integrated schools.

## The Merger

Texans rang in 1964 with, what else, a football game. And a really big game at that: undefeated, number 1 Texas against number 2, one-loss Navy. Both the Longhorns and the Midshipmen featured nationally celebrated players—Navy quarterback Roger Staubach had been awarded the Heisman Trophy, and Texas defensive tackle Scott Appleton the Outland Trophy, given to college football's top lineman. On New Year's Day, a capacity crowd of 75,000 crammed into the Cotton Bowl in Dallas to witness the Longhorns' defense frustrate the scrambling-prone Staubach, the future Dallas Cowboy star, who spent the day on the run from Appleton and sophomore linebacker Tommy Nobis. The Horns solidified their claim to the first of four national championships for head coach Darrell Royal.

The game helped lift a pall that still hung over Dallas less than two months after an assassin's bullet killed President John F. Kennedy as his motorcade wound through downtown and past the Texas Schoolbook Depository.

It was a joyful start to a year when the eyes of Texas and the rest of the nation would focus on scenes of upheaval, demonstration, and change at home, and when more young men would die in Southeast Asia as US combat involvement in Vietnam increased. A loudmouthed, brash, new heavyweight champ shocked the world when he battered into a seventh-round submission an opponent, Sonny Liston, thought to be the most menacing human on the planet. The next day, the champ announced he had taken a new name, Muhammad Ali, and a new religion, Islam. On a Philadelphia, Mississippi, farm, the tortured, murdered bodies of three civil rights workers were uncovered in an earthen dam. On July 2, the president of the United States, a former Texas schoolteacher, signed the Civil Rights Act of 1964. In addressing the nation, Lyndon Johnson said, "We have talked long enough in this country about equal rights. We have talked for one hundred years or more. It is time now to write the next chapter, and to write it in the books of law."

In Austin, the UIL was poised to do just that for its book of laws. However, the PVIL had to start preparing to close its books, permanently. Integration was the final chapter for the PVIL's proud history, and a radical new one for the UIL. Neither was an easy read—and for the fading PVIL, it was downright painful—but the unfolding plots were intriguing. How would the groups handle their transitions? The UIL could be a linchpin for successful integration statewide, beyond athletics. If it could work in the schools and in the athletic arena, with black and white students teaming and competing together, led by black or white coaches, with support from black and white fans, maybe that relative harmony could spill over into other aspects of community. After all, white fans had already proved to be loyal fans of PVIL teams—from an up-close, limited distance—and in some cases showed more loyalty, by traveling to the black teams' road games, for instance, than black supporters. Of course, there was no reciprocity, and the relationship was confined to whites seated and cheering on one side of the field, blacks on the other. With segregation, blacks were generally not allowed inside white high school stadiums, and after football games everybody went back to their respective corners.

Athletics, football in particular, could change that status quo and maybe more, or at least make the process palatable. A former UIL director thought so at the time: "There's no doubt in my mind that the UIL activities did more to make integration come about smoothly than anything else," Bailey Marshall recalled years later. "I never will forget, we had just integrated. It was, like, our second ball game. And I walked down toward the field house, and they were getting taped for the game, and there on a little table sat a black kid and a white kid, and they were punching one another and laughing and going on, and I thought, 'Well, we were right. This is going to work out fine.'"

The merger was really a takeover by the UIL. There had been some thought among its Legislative Advisory Council members that the state would benefit from having two strong leagues; some white schools would move over to the PVIL, and both leagues would receive equal financial support and the backing of school administrators. None of that was ever going to happen. The UIL had agreed to "let the coloreds in," as a later director, Rhea Williams, said. The union would be an absorption, not a partnership, and the PVIL never pushed for the latter arrangement. The UIL was much bigger and had many more resources, including all the tools the PVIL programs needed—better facilities, a better organization, a sympathetic ear from state legislators for funding, and aggressive media coverage. Absorption was logical, though social and logistic elements made it disturbingly one-sided. The PVIL lost more than it gained.

At a May 1964 meeting, the UIL's State Executive Committee unanimously approved Howard Calkins's motion that the time had come to remove the word "white" as a stipulation for league membership, and he urged the UIL's Legislative Advisory Council to make the change. The request was repeated five months later, at which point the council assembled a "Membership Committee" to assess the advantages and pitfalls of the move. The following January, Rodney Kidd led a group of UIL officials who met with the PVIL director, C. D. Yancy, to make him aware that the UIL was moving toward integrating its membership. The contingent suggested that he pass along the word to PVIL officials, gauge their concerns, and report back.

On March 29, 1965, the membership committee met again and recommended that the word "white" be removed from the constitution. The full Legislative Advisory Council, without dissent, approved on May 8, and on June 9 the State Executive Committee followed suit. Because of scheduling commitments, black schools would first participate in UIL football and basketball two years later, beginning in the fall semester of the 1967–1968 school year.

Just like that, after a half century of regulated divisiveness, the UIL tossed out a welcome mat and swung its doors wide open to the PVIL.

Greeted by integration, a resigned PVIL stepped inside.

And died.

## Integration and Winning in East Texas

In the fall of 1967, the UIL and its member schools were in a much better place than before, no matter the adjustments. They inherited talented young black students and athletes, many of them the best and brightest at their PVIL schools. They helped raise the profiles of their new schools and rejuvenated moribund football programs.

East Texas UIL schools had had a prolonged, three-decade drought of football state championships. Tyler won in 1930, and Longview seven years later. Fast-forward to the 1950s. Livingston Dunbar, a PVIL school that had the best program in East Texas during that decade, brought home three state 1A championships, two by Coach Ross Hardin—1953, 1954—and one by "Big Jim" Dewalt, 1958. The Leopards lost 42–12 to West Dunbar in the 1959 title game. The four Livingston teams that made it to the state finals had a combined record of 73–2.

"We were pretty feared," recalled Marion Johnson, who played at Livingston Dunbar, graduating in 1960. "Sometimes, we beat teams so bad, we'd be dressed and changed at halftime. We'd score 60, 70, 90 points. It started when Ross came to Livingston in 1951. We had guys like [running back] John Payton, and Richard Ryans was a quarterback who was ahead of his time. He was a four-year starter.

"We would have beat the crap out of Livingston High. We thought we were good, we knew we were good, and I wanted to be part of that tradition. In 1958, we beat Grand Prairie Dalworth for state. They had Charley Taylor, but we went up there and beat them 26–24."

In the waning years of the PVIL, Lufkin Dunbar, fifty miles north of Livingston, played three times for the PVIL 3A crown, winning in 1964 and 1967 and losing to Wichita Falls Washington 14–7 in 1966. Livingston Dunbar closed in 1968, and Lufkin Dunbar merged with previously all-white Lufkin High School two years later. Throughout Texas, black athletes began to migrate to schools they had previously been barred from attending. They were marginally welcomed, at best.

Yet black athletes, in many cases, immediately changed the fortunes of previously all-white programs. What happened with East Texas schools was a good example, as documented in a 2011 *Marshall News Messenger* newspaper story headlined "Why the Region Has Won 46 State Championships since 1964 after Winning Only Two before Then":

> Daingerfield won its first of an East Texas-leading six state championships in 1968, a 3A title. Five years later, John Tyler won a 4A state title on the legs of Earl Campbell, Troup brought home the 1A championship, and Big Sandy and Lovie Smith won the first of three consecutive Class B crowns to make 1973 East Texas' first multi-title football season.
>
> The UIL and PVIL completed their merger with the PVIL's disbandment at the end of the 1969–70 school year. Since that occasion, Greater East Texas has won 44 football state championships. It seems the UIL-PVIL merger is no coincidence when scanning the timeline . . . The merger—or more importantly, integration—gave schools an entire population base from which to find players.

Left floundering in the wake of that kind of success were the depleted PVIL schools, including a few that held out for another three years, to the league's very end, though all the black schools were quickly on their way to becoming distant memories of a time few wanted to talk about. That was then, this is now. All was better.

Not really.

Public school integration in Texas led to the closing and demolition of black high schools, and to the downsizing of others to junior high schools, middle schools, elementary schools, and alternative schools. An even bigger toll was taken on black coaches and teachers, many of whom lost their jobs. White parents disrespectfully preferred not to have their children taught by blacks, and previously successful black head coaches were demoted to assistant coaching positions at their new assignments. Some moved into school administrative positions, whereas others left coaching and teaching altogether rather than suffer the indignities put on them in the transition.

In Texarkana, the school district declared "freedom of choice," giving black students the option of attending either Dunbar or Texas High. Dunbar head coach Dan Haskins met with his counterpart at Texas

High, legendary coach Watty Myers, in 1967 and their puzzling conversation was indicative of things to come. In Haskins's recollection:
"I lost two players. Ruben Aikens, a good kid. He went over there and
was all-district and most valuable player in the district. Charlie Curry
also went. That's all I lost. But Watty came over and tried to get me to
send him my best players. That was an insult to my intelligence. If I'm
going to maintain my program, I'm going to send you my best players?
I thought, 'Either you're crazy or think I'm crazy.' I just looked at him.
I didn't think I was hearing what I was hearing. You want me to send you
my best players so I can fail?

"The white coaches wanted black players, I'll say that anywhere. They
showed that. They wanted your superstar."

Myers was trying to jump the gun, but black superstars were about
to fall in the laps of white coaches because of integration. Black head
coaches were throw-ins to help bridge the cultural divide, to serve as
conduits for communication between black players and their new white
coaches, if they were to continue their careers.

## *To Coach or Not to Coach*

Haskins was a member of the last Tillotson College graduating class, in
the spring of 1952. That fall, Tillotson and Huston College merged to
form Huston-Tillotson College in Austin. He took his first coaching job
later that year at Harris High School in Belton, an eight-year stay that was
followed by five at Mount Pleasant Washington before his former coach,
W. R. Pollard, recommended Haskins as his successor at Texarkana Dunbar. Haskins was a 180-pound tackle and senior team captain for the
Buffaloes before heading to Austin. He had good reasons for choosing
Tillotson: "I was an athlete, and a football scholarship was the only way
I could go to college, because my family didn't have the monetary means.
I chose to go to Austin, because I'd never been there, but a friend of
mine had and told me about it. They had school Monday through Friday,
no Saturday classes, and the girls stayed out until nine o'clock."

He returned to a Texarkana careening toward integration and still
recovering from the white mob violence that occurred in 1956 when two
black students enrolled at the local junior college. Jessalyn Yvonne Gray
and Laura Ellis passed aptitude tests and were admitted to the school,

setting off a chain of violent protests and community-wide death threats against blacks by local white racists. A black-owned service station was blasted with shotgun fire, two crosses were burned, and a black man was hanged in effigy hours after the thirty-year-old segregation policy was struck down.

Haskins was well aware of all this. He had endured the realities of segregation while growing up in the city's Rose Hill neighborhood, one of ten boys and two girls guided by a father who worked at the creosote plant, loaded railroad crossties onto boxcars, and raised hogs, and a mother who washed, cooked, and cleaned for white families. He sat in the rear of buses, entered public places through back doors, and, as a youngster, heard the word "nigger" so much he thought it was his name, though he would never respond to the expression. Neither parent had gone beyond ninth grade, or even that far, but they worked hard, gathered their family to attend church services, and insisted that their children pursue education. They didn't have much, but neither did their friends and neighbors. Nobody spoke of it. Everybody shared.

Like many, Haskins had a variety of experiences with segregation: "You learned the value of friendship, and you accepted the times. We had no other choice. You had good white people, some bad, but many times they did things because they accepted you as a person. But it was not popular for the whites to accept blacks on an equal basis, because they would have been categorized as nigger lovers. That was the way it was, but privately, some white people would do anything for you.

"I never had a new book in my whole high school career, always had hand-me-downs. They'd get a new book, put their name in there, but whenever we got a book, there was a series of names in there. When I started working with white coaches at Texas High, I told them, 'I know you better than you know me. I know all of your names because I got your old textbooks.'"

Coming back to Dunbar was a dream come true for Haskins. Not only was his coaching mentor there, but A. E. Alton was still principal, and many of the same teachers from when he was a student were still around. All were supportive of Haskins, who also taught math. His challenge was to reverse the fortunes of a losing program whose players had sagging morale: "We'd go somewhere to play, and when we came back, the question was how much did you lose by, not whether or not you won. That was the attitude among the student body, so I had to change the mind-set.

We were going to outwork and outplay some teams, and we had to convince people, but we were going to do that. And I had to have my players buy in to that."

The Buffaloes struggled in Haskins's first year, but the team slowly improved. In 1967, they split with a tough Marshall Pemberton squad, and beat Tyler Scott and Longview Womack twice, winning their 3A district title. They earned a bi-district win over Corsicana Jackson, but in the school's only state championship game appearance, lost to Coach Elmer Redd and Lufkin Dunbar 44–24.

Haskins turned the Dunbar program around. It was a grand note on which to end the program and send Haskins and his underclassmen to Texas High in 1968, where Haskins would be an assistant coach. He looked back on the time with ambivalence: "Integration was the best thing for us and the worst thing—that's my take on it. A lot of people thought I should be head coach, but I didn't think so. Watty had been there twenty-five years. He should have been the head coach. He was a good coach and had been successful."

Myers won twelve district championships, the last two with integrated squads following back-to-back three-win seasons. Haskins, the only black coach on his staff, could see he had no future there as a head coach: "My desire to stay in coaching became minimal. That was the end of my journey. I was really concerned about my players. The white coaches wanted every black boy to be a superstar, but every black boy is not a superstar. My conditions were, if you could tolerate your average white athlete, I want you to tolerate mine."

In 1970, Haskins took a position as the school's assistant principal. Several other former black coaches around the state had done the same, taking roles as peacemakers and, again, conduits, assisting with the incorporation of blacks into their new environment. In Haskins's case, that environment comprised a student body of 1,700 students and 100 teachers. In 1973, he was promoted to principal, the first black to hold such a position at a UIL 5A school. His transition was eased by the rapport he had built with some white parents and students in two seasons on the coaching staff. He was still subjected to surprised looks on the faces of whites in meetings where their expressions said, "What's he doing here?" Some folks who asked to see the principal and were directed into his office stopped in their tracks. Haskins recalled what would happen next: "They'd say, 'I want to speak to the principal.' Well, come on in, I'm he.

As principal, Haskins aimed for inclusion and fairness: "When I went to an administrative role, I told them point-blank, I'm not here to take care of black kids. I'm here to take care of all kids. I did what I thought was right. I took some flak from blacks, and that's okay. If I think I'm doing what's right, that's my guide, and I have to be consistent. Those where dark days. I had some relatives who quit speaking to me because they wanted me to side with them just because they were black. But I made the fairest decision I could make and moved on. At least I knew I had treated everybody the same."

He became an iconic community leader, recognized for helping make Texarkana's evolution to integration peaceful. The city named a street after him, Dan Haskins Way, and on the Texas High campus is the Dan Haskins Student Center.

———

Dan Haskins, Earvin Garnett, and the black teachers and coaches like them were revered in African American communities for providing leadership and nurturing environments for black students. There was confidence and trust between teachers and parents because so many black teachers and coaches had gone away to black colleges and returned to their hometowns to work at the local black schools. They were strict disciplinarians, with paddles at the ready and parents' permission—encouragement!—to use them. Especially in small towns, parents may have been childhood friends of the teachers, or grandparents who watched them grow up and knew their families.

"I knew all the mommas and poppas," Joe Washington Sr. recalled from his days as head coach at Bay City's Hilliard High School and Port Arthur Lincoln. "I was a small-town boy [from Rosenberg, Texas], and I understood small-town mothers. They used to tell me, 'Coach Washington, take him and do what you have to do—just don't kill him.'"

The sting of integration and the closing of PVIL schools took those kinds of dynamics away from black communities. Parents began to send their children to schools they did not know, to coaches and teachers they did not trust, and to neighborhoods where they were not wanted. To be sure, white parents wanted nothing to do with black teachers and coaches, either, or their brand of discipline. No black teacher was going to paddle a disruptive white student, and black coaches lost that kind of discipline and "motivating" tactic on the football practice field.

Civil rights battles had been hard fought, but in victory most African Americans looked back and immediately noted the conflicting results. Integration was both a good thing and a bad thing, bringing more opportunities and resources, but at the stiff price of fractured communities and a loss of culture. "Here's one guy who wanted to cry when integration set in," Washington admitted. "I'm from the old school. I wanted separate but equal, and I still wanted it after integration, which I didn't want because I enjoyed my black culture and black teachers. I thought those people were tough. They made me want to be something. I came from a poor background. My dad could hardly read and write, but he could work and had good common sense—my mother, too. I probably would have wallowed in that if it had not been for those black teachers I had. And that's what I wanted to be to the kids I was over, just like my principal was to me. I wanted to motivate them to want to go from point A to point B, and when I saw those black coaches, I thought those guys were the epitome of coaching."

There was much work to do on many fronts in making the transition. Much to be learned by all. White coaches loved the exciting new dimensions that black athletes brought to the field, but had no real sense of black culture beyond the racist stereotypes they had grown up with in divided communities. In rare instances before integration, black kids and white kids might have interacted in sandlot football games or summer-league baseball games, but the order of the day was that blacks didn't risk venturing to the other side of the tracks, and whites returned the favor. Besides, it was the law.

Small towns, however, could be different.

"I grew up in Leggett, outside of Livingston, about a seven-mile ride by bus," recounts Marion Johnson. "Most of the kids were rural, and in Leggett there wasn't too much segregation. But there was in Livingston. The only thing segregated in Leggett was the school, but the people were really nice. The population was about 500 and most people were rural, worked in the sawmills. Just working people. There were never any racial problems.

"I'd play with white kids growing up, and we rode the same school bus. Everything was segregated in Livingston, but you never saw those signs, 'White Only' or 'Colored Only,' in Leggett. In fact, there was a little drugstore, and a place where you could get a malt, a burger, and you sat down next to each other, and nobody said nothing about it. But dad always said if you can't go through the front door, don't go at all.

"It was amazing. Nobody wanted integration anyway. Black teachers had their jobs, and black people didn't want to go to Livingston High School, because we knew some white guy would call someone the N-word and there'd be a fight. So we were all happy in Livingston with the way things were.

"But everything went down the drain with integration."

There weren't a lot of places in Texas as racially easygoing as Leggett, and even in that isolated community, black and white relationships were tolerated only up to a point. For the most part in Texas, white coaches had grown up in all-white communities, attended and played at all-white colleges, and learned from lionized white coaches. What they knew about black athletes was what they had heard, so when confronted with integration, white coaches had no idea how to relate to their new players, even on what seemed the simplest of matters. Leon Bedford looked on in amazement. "When we first got integration, we were in a meeting with Bob Bledsoe, the head coach [at Galveston Ball], and he was giving us all these rules: no facial hair, no hair on shoulders. Me and Kermit Courville were looking at each other, kind of saying, 'What kind of shit is this?' When he got through, I stood up and said, 'I need to find me another job,' because those rules were for coaches too. Bledsoe said, 'What's the matter, Leon?'"

"Well, the only time I cut my mustache off was when I went to the army, and I *had* to do that. But growing a mustache is a rite of passage for black kids, and now you're telling them they can't have that. White kids have hair on their shoulders, but black kids have afros—they grow up. What are you going to do, get a ruler and say how high they can be? Listen to how crazy ya'll talking."

"Well, what's your suggestion?"

"What you need to do is get the captains of our team [who had been playing at Galveston Central] and the captain of your team, let them go behind closed doors, then bring you back a dress code."

Bledsoe agreed to that, the players huddled and produced the team's dress code, requiring only that hair be of reasonable length and clean.

## "I Got Me One!"

Black coaches have long suspected that integration was pushed along by white coaches who were salivating over the prospect of adding black talent—such speed and athleticism!—to their rosters. Yes, there would be social problems, but on the football field, black kids found not only equality, but also superiority at the skill positions, all to the coaches' delight.

It took a while before black coaches gained that kind of recognition and respect from the white coaches who called the style of play at black high schools "monkey ball." Yet the prospect of getting to coach a star black athlete made them as giddy as a bunch of schoolgirls at a Beatles concert. Conroe Washington coach Charles Brown remembered the conversations he overheard between white coaches at coaching clinics: "They'd say, 'Man, I got me one [black player].' They thought I didn't know what they were talking about, but that's the way they thought of black players. They all wanted a black running back."

The lust for black running backs and other superstar-quality black players from the new, overflowing pool of black talent from the PVIL created an odd problem that perhaps no one saw coming. Billie Matthews left Kashmere in 1970 to become an assistant on Pepper Rogers's staff at Kansas. On a recruiting trip back in Houston, he had a conversation with a coaching friend who had a "six-four, 295 lineman, quick as a cat, mean as can be. I was trying to sell Billie on him. He said, 'I can't recruit black offensive linemen. The offensive line is reserved for white kids. They tell you, don't recruit black offensive linemen, but you can recruit them on defense.' I said, man, that's the stupidest thing in the world. He said, 'Yes, it is, but that's the way it is. You got to have somewhere white boys can play.'"

Matthews's revelation was an indirect concession by white coaches of the ability of black athletes to outperform their white counterparts. As demonstrated in Ty Cashion's *Pigskin Pulpit*, white coaches could not have been clearer on the issue and its implications: "[White coaches] realized that they would be surrounded by a wealth of talent. Morris Southall [Brownwood High] stated succinctly what many of them expressed: 'They're better athletes, period.' Maurice Cook [Longview Pine Tree] elaborated: 'It changed the game; I don't think there's any question about that . . . The athletic ability of the black player made you immediately, as a coach, just try to figure out a way to utilize all that speed.' Before integration, Cook remarked, 'very few people threw the ball. . . . Oh, I guess they had a split end maybe, but you never threw to him,' he laughed. 'Everybody had seven- and eight-man fronts on defense . . . It was just a run-oriented, hard-nosed, three-or-four-yards-at-a-time game. Then, when all the good black athletes came in, you could begin to see where speed came in—reverses, a lot of option, throwing the ball . . . Therefore, defenses had to adapt. As far as the strategy, I saw a big difference on both sides of the ball.'"

———

After a wildly successful career at Conroe Washington, winning two state championships in six years, Charles Brown left for Aldine Carver in 1966, eager to line up his team in an integrated situation. His first opportunity came in the season opener of his 1967 schedule, on the road against La Porte: "I used to play Joe Washington at Port Arthur every year for my first game because it helped get my team sharp. He'd whip my butt every year, but I beat him twice at Conroe going for state championships. But in 1967, I wanted to start playing white boys to let them know we didn't have tails and for my boys to find out the good football players they [whites] were. We fought like dogs, and ran the clock down to two seconds when we scored."

That touchdown narrowed the margin to 14–13, Aldine trailing, in the fourth quarter. Brown called a time-out to discuss a two-point conversion. He asked his quarterback, Charles Womack, "What's been going good for us for two or three yards? Who's the weakest player we should go at?"

Running back Larry Hebert had heard enough. Brown wasn't surprised: "He was a hell of a back. He said, 'Coach whatcha'll trying to figure out? Just run 26 power and give me the ball.' The play was that old Missouri power sweep. So we ran that, and he leaped into the end zone! You could hear a pin fall in that stadium. The people sat there for I don't know how long. We won 15–14, and nobody left."

The stunned crowd left, but not before showering Brown and his team with racial taunts that continued away from La Porte. Postgame death threats came in late-night calls to his home. On the field, white coaches shunned the traditional postgame handshake at midfield. "They were going to catch hell when they got back home for getting beat by a black man," Earvin Garnett, who coached at Wichita Falls Washington, said. "We enjoyed it to a certain extent, because we could play possum. I always said that I integrated San Angelo. We whipped them 60–0 in 1954, and they integrated the next year."

Being on the field and orchestrating games became a sanctuary for black coaches. It compensated some for the lack of civility shown them at coaching clinics and from hateful, distraught fans. But managing games could also be tricky because of all-white officiating crews. Black coaches lobbied vigorously for the teams calling games to be integrated. Washington, at Port Arthur Lincoln, and others "raised hell" about the lack of black officials and at least the appearance of not getting a fair shake. He recalled the negotiations to try to remedy the problem: "That first year, all they had was white officials. We wanted to get the best officials, but I had no voice. They said there were no qualified blacks to choose from. One night, the district coaches met at a restaurant in Nederland, and I got them to go with two black officials so that I had two and they had two. They didn't like that. When we went to five officials, we agreed that when they came to my place, we'd have three white officials of the five, and when I played at their place, we'd have three blacks. They scratched their heads, but agreed. The word was 'Joe is a racist' because of the officials, but it made sense."

The minutiae of jostling to find a racial comfort zone did not stop there. Washington noted that not everyone came around: "There were some diehards, like the guys at Vidor. That first year, we were supposed to go to there, but they said no, we'll play you away. We couldn't go to Vidor. Plus, we had to have somewhere to feed those kids. In the PVIL, we fed our kids after games in the home economic rooms, and teachers would prepare the meals. Vidor wasn't having that, either. The other schools, Port Neches and Nederland, were right down the street, so we could eat in Port Arthur—same with Orange, Jasper, and Silsbee."

Back on the field, where it really mattered, the theory was that black coaches won games only because their players had great talent, but that white coaches won because they had coaching skills. Reportedly, during one early integration season, Houston coaches were informed at a school district meeting, "We know you black coaches don't have the background of these white coaches, so we're going to tell them to take it easy on y'all until you learn how to coach." At a meeting later in the season, black coaches including Kashmere Gardens coach Billie Matthews and Yates's John Tankersley were asked to "take it easy on them white boys, 'cause they were putting fifty and sixty points on the best white teams."

The PVIL teams that did not immediately close with the merger were able to keep their footing for a while. Tradition-rich Yates continued to hold high the PVIL banner. From 1978 to 1996, the Lions had seven undefeated regular seasons; the 1985 squad finished undefeated with a UIL-first sixteen wins, and cruised by favored Odessa Permian (of *Friday Night Lights* fame) 37–0 for the 5A state title. No Houston ISD football team had won a state championship since 1953 (Houston Lamar). Coach Luther Booker's team scored at will, 659 points for the season, and held opposing offenses at bay (77 points, eight shutouts). It featured two future NFL players, running back Johnny Bailey (Chicago Bears) and defensive lineman Santana Dotson (Green Bay Packers). A media vote declared the 1985 Lions the Texas high school "Team of the Decade." The other former PVIL school to win a UIL state championship came when 3A Beaumont Hebert trounced Gainesville 35–7 in 1976.

In North Texas, Walter Day's Fort Worth Terrell Panthers were predicted to finish at the bottom of the district in their first UIL season, 1967, but won. Lufkin Dunbar was the first former PVIL team to play for the UIL state championship, in 1968, led by quarterback D. C. Nobles, who in 1971 became the first black quarterback at the University of Houston. In what has been called a classic thriller, Lufkin lost to Daingerfield 7–6 in the 1968 2A title game.

## Bellaire and Kashmere: Fights, Slights, Football

The visions came as surreal apparitions. Delvin Williams startled awake, sitting bolt upright, his heart rapidly thump-thump-thumping in the dark of his bedroom. Again. The recurring dream's unscheduled visits at first gave him a murky sense that something was wrong, but then a pleasant clarity: he had just scored the winning touchdown in a professional football game. He would stare into the darkness and see the vision playing on an undefined screen with crystal clear reception. There he was, the large stadium crowd roaring its approval, his teammates slapping his pads and his helmet, congratulating him. Then a scary but pleasant chill would ripple through his body at the thought of playing professional football. The picture faded in a blink, yet half awake he thought, "That would be great!"

Then, as suddenly as he had awakened, he fell back onto the bed fast asleep. But subconsciously, an unlikely seed of hope was being fertilized in the mind of a black kid living in an environment where hope was in short supply and dreams routinely died hard. He had no reason to believe his would be any different.

His hopes and dreams first took shape on the football practice field at Kashmere Gardens High School. Blessed with a sprinter's speed and a running back's intrinsic vision, Williams left Kashmere in 1970 as the most celebrated football player in the school's brief, thirteen-year history, and one of the most sought-after prep running backs in the country. Recruited by every major college football program, he chose the University of Kansas. Four years later he became a second-round pick of the San Francisco 49ers. He thrived in the National Football League for eight rugged seasons, becoming the first player in NFL history to rush for 1,000 yards in a season for two different teams (the 49ers and the Miami Dolphins).

All of that was down the road, a dream realized. In 1967, Coach Billie Matthews tossed him headfirst into history as a sophomore on the Rams' district-contending team, the first time he had made an organized squad. Twice, he had failed to make the team at E. O. Smith Junior High School, the main feeder to Wheatley, but his best friend, William "Chucksey" Ferguson, convinced him to give it another shot at Kashmere. Matthews immediately liked what he saw. Unable to ignore Williams's speed, the coach inserted him into first-team-varsity scrimmages in the first week of spring workouts. Williams was so impressive that *Texas Football* magazine—the always-anticipated bible from the Waco publisher Dave Campbell—mentioned both Williams and Ferguson as "up and coming players to watch" at Kashmere.

Four games into the inaugural season of integrated football in the UIL, Williams was in the lineup against Houston's Sam Houston Tigers. The two undefeated teams squared off in the first high-profile contest between black and white schools, both of them still largely segregated. The levels of significance, social and athletic, had not been foretold by his dreams, but he realized them later: "Little did I know we would be pioneers, making black history in Houston. The game would become part of black folklore. There was a sense of pride within the African American community. Our parents and their parents, coaches, and civic leaders were descendants of one or the other. Families would come out to the games and tell stories from past generations, keeping the folklore alive."

Joe Tusa, HISD athletic director, was concerned more about the junior varsity games, which would be played at each school's campus, where student bodies could not be controlled and the possibility of racial clashes was threatening. Varsity games were played at neutral sites, and this one was set for Delmar Stadium, in Houston's northwestern suburbs, a ten-mile jog west for both schools only five miles apart. Houston's black schools had only recently begun playing there, after years of holding their games at inner-city Jeppesen Stadium.

Tusa has been lauded for his management of the transition to integration in the Houston ISD. He wanted to avoid mistakes made elsewhere: "I could see what was happening in other parts of the country. Some of the other sections of the country eliminated their programs for a while because they had difficulty in putting it all together. We were very fortunate. It was quite obvious this had to come together, but in a way that we would get people to cooperate and work together. It shouldn't be something forced on people."

Keith Kilgore, president of the Touchdown Club of Houston, called Tusa's work during the era "one of the more underrated moments" of Tusa's career. "He was one of the ones that pushed for it to take place in the first place, because he just saw kids. He didn't see the color. He just saw the kids, and he was proved right."

Even Tusa had to be on edge when Kashmere and Sam Houston first took the field. The stands were filling with a mostly black audience. Williams recalled the scene: "When we went on the field for warm-ups, our side of the stands was already full, and their side was nearly full, but our people were still coming in, and they began to sit on the Sam Houston side. When the game started, I looked up in the stands, and there were more of our fans on the Sam Houston side, so they were surrounded by Kashmere fans."

It didn't take long for on-field tensions to peak. "They started calling us 'niggers,' and we responded, 'Fuck you, honky!'"

Verbal exchanges escalated into shoving matches, leading to outright fisticuffs. After a fan tossed a whiskey bottle on the field, Tusa had seen enough and briefly stopped the game just before halftime. He delivered a stern address to officials and coaches. "I could see the thing was going to explode, with blacks on one side and whites on the other," Tusa said. "I just laid down the law to both of them: clean it up."

Between insults and fights, some football got played, and Kashmere was clearly in control. The Rams won 14–6, and also took the zone crown, finishing the season with an 8–1–2 record behind a defense that allowed only 59 points. Williams summed up the aftermath: "I think both teams left with a healthy dose of respect for one another, and that's the way it should have been. Leaving with, of all things, respect for one another."

D. W. Rutledge was on the field that night for Sam Houston. He went on to distinguished career as one of the most successful coaches in Texas high school football history, winning four state championships at Converse Judson, and 198 of 234 games in seventeen years. He also served as executive director of the Texas High School Coaches Association. Looking back at the Kashmere game, he was in full agreement with Williams: "We had a great ballclub, but they just blew us away. You had to respect them. They were good."

## Segregated Integration

San Antonio Wheatley and Corpus Christi Coles were two small-market PVIL schools caught in the twilight zone created, on the one hand, by *Brown v. Board of Education* striking down segregation, and on the other by the UIL clinging to its whites-only policy. Approximately twenty-eight Texas schools had announced plans for complete or partial integration by the late summer of 1955. The San Antonio and Corpus Christi school districts were among the first to desegregate. In 1960, San Antonio became the first southern city to integrate lunch counters. That same year, Corpus Christi Miller produced the UIL's first integrated state championship football team, coached by Pete Ragus and led on the field by all-state running back Johnny Roland. As mentioned above, the UIL, as a result of the El Paso inquiry, allowed the few white schools that immediately integrated to continue participating in the league, despite the official whites-only policy. The Buccaneers beat Wichita Falls 13–6 in the 4A finals. The Southwest Conference was still several years away from integrating, so Roland left for the University of Missouri, where he played both offense and defense, and was named an all-American cornerback. In Miller's championship season, Roland rushed for 1,224 yards and scored 90 points as the Bucs finished 13–1. "When you consider the atmosphere of hostility at that time, not only against blacks but Hispanics, what we accomplished was thought to be impossible," Ragus said of that team, which included eighteen Anglos, seventeen Hispanics, and six African Americans. "We never had a problem about race within the team."

That season saw three Corpus Christi teams win state championships in football. Corpus Christi Academy won the 2A Catholic state title, and Coles, coached by John Thomas, took the PVIL's 3A crown, also beating a Wichita Falls team. The Hornets dropped WF Washington 38–21 after trailing 21–8 at halftime, in the rain. Fullback Levis Irving, the team's most valuable player, rushed for 104 yards, scored three touchdowns, and recovered a fumble playing defensive end. Willy Everhart, quarterback for the Hornets, described what happened at halftime: "We were soaking wet, hurt, taking our pads off, when Mr. Thomas walked in and told us a story about coming through the hallway to the locker room and being told by the Wichita Falls principal, 'We got this game.' Mr. Thomas told us, 'You guys let them play the first half. You gon' play the second half.' We kicked off and stopped them on the five. They never got past the forty in the second half and didn't score again."

Despite a few black students breaking the color barrier at previously all-white high schools in San Antonio and Corpus Christi, San Antonio Wheatley and Coles had to wait until 1967 to join the UIL. Both programs remained strong PVIL members to the end, Wheatley closing in 1970, and Coles graduating its final class in 1967.

Thomas began his tenure at Coles in 1941 and guided the Hornets to four state championship games, winning in 1948 and 1960, but losing in 1947 and 1952. Everhart described the coach's method: "Mr. Thomas's motto was, if you make the team, the only way to quit was to quit the earth. We ate, drank, football every day. We had a thirty-minute 'football-ology' class every morning at seven thirty, and away from school, he would call you at random, and he'd ride through the town, checking up on his players. I don't care how good you were, if he caught you out, you didn't play, and if we were going out of town, he left you at home. But he was always the kind of coach, if you had a problem, you could talk to him.

"We had a motto, too, that no one would fail. If there was something somebody couldn't do, you helped him. We stuck together."

Most of the members of the 1960 team had grown up together. They were so tight and so sure of themselves that in seventh-grade assemblies, as each class expressed its goals, the precocious football players assured everyone that by their senior season, they would win a state championship. And they did, with a swagger and a wide-open offensive attack from the shotgun, single wing, Wing-T, reverses, double and triple reverses, and even the "lonesome end" made famous by Army. According to Willy

Everhart, "We did a lot of everything, and we weren't afraid of anybody. We'd come to the line and tell the guy on the other side where the play was going and you couldn't stop it. It was cocky or whatever, but that's just how we were."

Yet the fiercest player out of Coles was the World War II hero Warren G. H. Crecy, a 150-pound "blood and guts" football player. Thomas called him the greatest player he had ever coached. That was a sign of things to come for the otherwise quiet, unassuming Crecy who joined the army and was assigned to the 761st Tank Battalion, the first group of black tankers in US Army history. Fighting in Patton's Third Army, the 761st entered combat in November 1944, and Crecy became a "killing machine." In one battlefield sequence, according to his unit: "Sergeant Warren G. H. Crecy fought through enemy positions to aid his men until his tank was destroyed. He immediately took command of another vehicle, armed with only a .30-caliber machine gun, and liquidated the enemy position that had destroyed his tank. Still under heavy fire, he helped eliminate the enemy forward observers who were directing the artillery fire that had been pinning down the American infantry. Crecy's tank became bogged down in the mud. He dismounted and fearlessly faced anti-tank, artillery and machine-gun fire as he extricated his tank. While freeing his tank, he saw that the accompanying infantry was pinned down and that the enemy had begun a counterattack. Crecy climbed up on the rear of his immobilized tank and held off the Germans with his .50-caliber machine gun while the foot soldiers withdrew. Later that day, he again exposed himself to enemy fire as he wiped out several machine-gun nests and an anti-tank position with only his machine gun. The more fire he drew, the harder he fought. After the battle, Crecy had to be pried away from his machine gun."

Crecy's Medal of Honor recommendation was denied, but his heroism under fire could never be denied. Crecy embodied every characteristic of valor, as the *Pittsburgh Courier* war correspondent Trezzvant Anderson wrote of him: "To look at Warren G. H. Crecy (the G. H. stands for Gamaliel Harding) you'd never think that here was a 'killer,' who had slain more of the enemy than any man in the 761st. He extracted a toll of lives from the enemy that would have formed the composition of 3 or 4 companies, with his machine guns alone. And yet, he is such a quiet, easy-going, meek-looking fellow, that you'd think that the fuzz which a youngster tries to cultivate for a mustache would never grow on his baby-skinned chin. And that he'd never use a word stronger than 'damn.' But here was a youth who went so primitively savage on the battle field that his only thought was to 'kill, kill, kill,' and he poured his rain of death pellets into German bodies with so much reckless abandon and joy that he was the nemesis of all the foes of the 761st. And other men craved to ride with Crecy and share the reckless thrill of killing the hated enemy that had killed their comrades. And he is now living on borrowed time. By all human equations Warren G. H. Crecy should have been dead long ago, and should have had the Congressional Medal of Honor, at least!"

Crecy's actions earned him a battlefield commission, along with the title, given by his fellow soldiers, of being "the baddest man in the 761st."

––––––

On San Antonio's east side, Coach Henry Carroll won 169 games, losing only 73 in seventeen seasons at Wheatley in a program that gave the SWAC three all-time greats—lineman Gentris Hornsby, wide receiver William "Rock" Glosson, and PVIL tennis champion Odie Posey. Hornsby was a standout at Prairie View in the late 1950s and a three-time black-college all-American. Glosson was a two-time all-American at Texas Southern, and in 1958 he caught twenty-two passes for 270 yards against Prairie View. Posey went to Southern University in Baton Rouge on a tennis scholarship, but Coach Ace Mumford diverted him to the football program as a running back. Posey went on to rack up more yards than anyone in the Jaguars' history—1,399 of them coming in 1949, when he lead the nation in rushing, a single-season best that still stands at Southern. He was a four-time all-American in a period when Southern collected three black-college national championships and in 1949 beat San Francisco State 30–0 in the Fruit Bowl, reportedly the first interracial bowl game.

The world-class sprinter Clyde Glosson was also a running back at Wheatley. He was a two-time NCAA track and field individual champion, winning the NCAA Division II 100-yard dash in 1966 and the 200-meter dash in 1968. He earned all-American honors five times at local Trinity University and was an alternate on the 1968 US Olympic team. Glosson, a seventh-round pick of the Kansas City Chiefs in 1970, played two seasons with the Buffalo Bills. He and his younger brother, Edwin, competed on Wheatley's 1965 PVIL state championship track and field team. "We had two strikes against us," Glosson said. "We were black and we were poor. Our teachers told us we had to work hard because we had to be better than everybody else, and would have to prove ourselves over and over."

Wheatley can also claim the Negro Leagues legend John "Mule" Miles, who also served during World War II as a mechanic for the Tuskegee Airmen, and the Major League Baseball slugger Cliff Johnson. Miles was with the Chicago American Giants from 1946 to 1949, and in 1947 he hit eleven home runs in eleven straight games, a feat that has never been equaled. "We had great athletes competing in a great league, but nobody knew about it," said Hensley Sapenter, a football and basketball ace at Wheatley in the 1950s who returned to the school as a coach before serving as SAISD athletic director from 1976 to 1995.

Henry Carroll ran the football show at Wheatley where home games were played on Wednesday nights at Alamo Stadium. "He was a legend," Clyde Glosson eulogized in 1989 at the funeral for his former coach. "When you left home to come to school and when you left school on your way home, he told us we belonged to him, and he didn't want us getting into trouble. And he meant it."

## Remembering the Past with Pride

*You just have to have integration. We knew it all along and we wanted it. But you miss those [PVIL] days because it was such a high. It affected the black community. It was an electrifying time. There's nothing like it now. And maybe there never will be.*

LUTHER BOOKER, Houston Yates

The PVIL made a quiet exit after the 1970 spring semester. Big-city schools had moved over to the UIL beginning with the 1967 football season, but the basketball, baseball, and track teams didn't join for another year. Smaller schools continued with the PVIL through the spring of 1970 for a final state basketball tournament. The league had peaked at about five hundred member schools in the early 1960s, but at its closing only eight historically black high schools in Texas were still standing, all in big markets: Lincoln and Madison in Dallas, Dunbar in Fort Worth, and Kashmere, Worthing, Yates, Washington, and Wheatley in Houston.

Integration rendered the PVIL and its history officially irrelevant, and immediately forgotten by most, leaving a sense that its fifty-year existence had been for naught. Intentionally or not, at most of the closing schools there were few materials left to remind younger generations of the men who had come before them and found their way through segregation to better themselves and their communities. Trophies, banners, uniforms, and other pieces of memorabilia had to be retrieved from dumpsters and cobwebbed closets for preservation by local historians and alumni associations. The few records and statistics kept by the league were ignored by the UIL for thirty-five years before their inclusion in 2005. Memories of the PVIL's gridiron feats faded with time, disappeared with mortality.

A small group of PVIL coaches, however, were well aware of the significance of their histories and the need to self-acknowledge their work. During the 1964 Prairie View Coaching Clinic, a group of seventy-five black coaches led by Don Grace of Dallas Madison formed the Lone Star Coaches Association with a goal of supporting PVIL coaches. Grace, a Livingston native, graduated from Houston Wheatley, where he was named an all-district lineman in 1947. He was an all-SWAC guard at Prairie View in 1950 and 1951. His coaching career began in 1952 at Abilene Woodson, which he guided to the state playoffs in 1953 and 1954. His 1953 team had only eighteen players, yet played for the 2A title, losing to Corsicana Jackson 19–0. At Dallas Madison, beginning in 1956, he won six city and two district titles, and twice played for the state championship, in 1963 and 1966.

To address the exclusion of black coaches from the Texas High School Coaches Association Hall of Honor, Grace met in 1980 with former PVIL coaches Billy Howard, Johnny Peoples, John Tankersley, Walter Day, Bo Humphrey, and Marion "Jap" Jones, and they set up the Prairie View Interscholastic League Coaches Association. That year in Houston, the PVILCA held its first Hall of Fame and Hall of Honor ceremonies to acknowledge former PVIL coaches and players. Jones, who got his odd nickname because of the voracious appetite he displayed at the Jap Jones Cafe, which he and friends frequented in Tyler, was a tremendous multisport star—football, basketball, track, tennis—at Dallas Washington High School and Wiley College. He is remembered at Wiley as the school's best all-around athlete. In hospitality suites at PVILCA conferences, Jones, a community activist in Fort Worth, where he had coached at Dunbar, was known to regale young coaches with stories from the good old days of the PVIL well into the night.

In 1982, Yates coach Pat Patterson became the first black coach added to the Texas High School Coaches Association Hall of Honor.

In 2005, an energetic former coach, Robert Brown, assumed duties as the PVILCA's board chairman. Brown was a quarterback at La Marque and a safety at Texas Southern after the amazing Charles Green joined the program. Brown didn't consider himself a historian, but he certainly appreciated the PVIL's history and was driven to keep it alive. He did so by aggressively connecting with former PVIL players and coaches to collect memorabilia and celebrate their careers through the Hall of Fame inductions, which came with presentations of plaques, commemorative PVILCA rings, and the right to flash them and announce, ironically, "I got me one!"

The PVIL belongs to history, but it maintains a future through the PVILCA, whose motto is "Remembering the past with pride." Brown acknowledged a deeper satisfaction in the organization's mission: "Just seeing the smiles and tears on the inductees' faces when they receive a plaque is motivating to me. Most of them have never had recognition. They're blue-collar workers, other than the guys who went to college and then the pros, but most of these guys were talented athletes who got married, went into the army, never went to college. We have a chance to recognize them. A lot of coaches lost head-coaching jobs in small towns with integration, and that really hurt the PVIL.

"If you don't understand what happened at that time, you don't understand the black man."

# Acknowledgments

I always thought it was a good sign that whomever I told I was researching and writing this book loved the idea, and the deeper I got into the details with those who knew my writing history, it was concluded this was the book I was meant to write. No pressure there! And in the almost decade that I spent thinking about it, researching it, and writing it, I told lots of folks, in conversations over a meal, at conferences, on Facebook, while catching up with old friends, or having a "so, what do you do?" conversation with friendly people I doubt I will ever see again as we passed the time waiting in a long grocery checkout line. Because I am sure that I will forget someone, here is a blanket "thank you" to everyone who I told, "I'm working on a book about football at black high schools in Texas before integration." Let me say to you all that I really appreciated your encouragements, good wishes, and even, in some cases, curiosity.

The idea for this had been simmering since the early 1980s, when I began working on a book about football at historically black colleges, which are intrinsically linked to black high schools, and especially were so before integration, as you have seen. I committed to the task in 2007 after attending my first Prairie View Interscholastic League Coaches Association Hall of Fame and Hall of Honor Banquet in Austin and being overwhelmed by the event's spirit. None have been more encouraging and helpful to me than the men of the Houston-based PVILCA, who understand the book's importance as a collective biography for them, the league's members, and their legacies. In particular, I thank Chairman Robert Brown, Ed Roby, Leroy Bookman, Clint Williams (who was one of my PE teachers at Houston's Worthing High School!), Don James, Roland Hayes, the late Walter Day, and the other members of the board.

Their guidance and insight about the PVIL and its history, their help in connecting me with interview sources, their generosity in sharing reference material, and the tales they told about "back in the day" made invaluable contributions to the book. All of them are exceptional men and role models who were students at PVIL schools and later taught and coached in the league. Each is an inspiring historian for high school athletics and black culture in Texas. Thank you all, so much, and I hope this book represents you well.

Thanks also to others related to the league and the PVILCA: Thurman Robins, whose book *Requiem for a Classic* is a thorough and excellent reference for a history of the Yates-Wheatley Thanksgiving Day game; the super scout Charles Garcia; J. Warren Singleton, a champion for helping preserve black history in Baytown, especially as it concerns Carver High School and its athletic programs; Coach James "Bo" Humphrey, from Booker T. Washington in Houston, one of the organization's pioneers; Marion O. Johnson in San Marcos was extremely helpful in talking with me about Livingston Dunbar and East Texas; Willis Turner's Jerry Blair; Houston Wheatley's Etta Walker, for all things about her alma mater; John Codwell Jr., also from Houston Wheatley and a pioneer in basketball at the University of Michigan; David O'Neal, from Galveston Central (great stories, Dave!); Mike Marzett and James Harris, from Wichita Falls Washington; George Wooldridge, from the Texarkana Dunbar Alumni Association, who shared a CD of the school's yearbooks, including the 1942 edition, which has a photo of a cute, junior music prodigy—the earliest photo I have of my mother!—and a note in the book that states, "Emily Baxter is outstanding in the field of music." She was a pianist who became a noted gospel choir musical director in Houston.

Both Greg Vincent, vice president for diversity and community engagement at the University of Texas, and Charles Breithaupt, executive director of the UIL, were enthusiastic supporters from the outset. Thank you, sirs.

I have known Brad Buchholz since the 1980s, when we worked at the *Austin American-Statesman* and were softball teammates with the "Media Mallards." Brad is an excellent writer and editor, and a good friend. Thanks for lifting my spirits when I hit a writing slump and for brainstorming directions for the book and reading one my early pieces.

Professor Frank Guridy, black history and sports kindred, gave the manuscript a good read and offered insightful suggestions for improvements.

Bertram Allen's book *Texas Black High School Sports, before 1967* was a treasure of information about the PVIL and Austin Anderson history. Well done, Bertram.

Also, I am grateful to Eugene Williams (*Forever Legends*) for his support, knowledge of PVIL football, and spreading the word to acknowledge the great athletes groomed in the league.

Troy Reeves, University of Wisconsin Archives, kindly provided oral history interviews with Coach Lewis Ritcherson and Lewis Ritcherson Jr.

At Prairie View, the special collections archivists Phyllis Earles and Lisa Stafford helped me uncover documents detailing the origins of the Texas Interscholastic League of Colored Schools; Professor Ron Goodwin, my black history partner; Texas A&M System vice chancellor Frank Jackson, a fountain of knowledge and the best black-history storyteller ever (!); and Ikhlas Sabouni, the School of Architecture dean—thanks for bringing me to "The Hill."

I thoroughly enjoyed working with Robert Devens at the University of Texas Press. He and Dave Hamrick have been wonderful throughout this process—and very patient! Many thanks, guys, for an awesome publishing experience.

I am blessed to have many good friends who offered their unfailing support. To name a few: "TB" (Thomas Bonk), yet another chapter in our voluminous brotherhood—you are the best; Roxanne Evans, my colleague in the Texas black history project; the award-winning writer and Longhorn football fan Tom Zigal—who was just as excited about this book as I was (now we can get on to our writing project); Bobby Hawthorne, the "Radical Writer," who shared much information about the UIL; Chris Barton, who has probably finished two or three more books as I write this; Delvin Williams, great guy and PVIL/NFL legend; Becka Oliver and my fellow board members at the Writer's League of Texas—especially Evelyn Palfrey, the brilliant romance novelist and my "home girl" from Texarkana (thanks for the Dunbar introductions); and the always-inspiring Sam Freedman at the *New York Times*.

Viviane Tondeur and I have been friends for thirty-four years, and we have built a loving partnership over the last ten. "Team CinnaMan!" She is my most ardent supporter and somehow still puts up with and believes in me. Thank you. Love ya, Viviane.

# Appendixes

PVIL FOOTBALL STATE CHAMPIONS

The PVIL was formed in 1920, and though a few black high schools were fielding teams at the time, there was no organized process for determining state champions until the 1940 season. The teams never received extensive media coverage, but many hometown newspapers covered playoff games, especially state championship contests. Brief accounts of the coverage, where available, are in the samples included in this listing of PVIL champions.

| Year | Class | Teams and scores | Coaches |
|------|-------|-----------------|---------|
| 1940 | 2A | Fort Worth Terrell 26<br>Austin Anderson 0 | Marion Bates<br>William Pigford |

*San Antonio Register*, **December 27, 1940**
"Fort Worth High Trounces Austin, 26–0, for State Prep School Grid Title"
By Roby Hilliard

Fort Worth, Texas—The mighty Fort Worth Cats opened an attack against the Austin Yellowjackets, Tuesday, December 17, that gave "Cow Town" the honor of being the first to hold the undisputed state AA high school championship in football. The score was 26–0.

The Anderson high team, of Austin, coached by William Pigford, F. E. Garrett, R. B. Timmons and Hearne, arrived in grand style, accompanied by their famous state champion band and two other bus loads of students and friends. The famous James Valentine, who was injured several weeks ago, saw some service in the game and demonstrated why no high school all star team could afford to leave him off.

Marion "Bull" Bates, the former Prairie View Panther all-American four-letter man, was all smiles as his proteges proceeded to hand a team coached by another Prairie Viewite—William Pigford a defeat.

It was I. M. Terrell all the way.

| Year | Class | Teams and scores | Coaches |
|------|-------|------------------|---------|
| 1941 | 2A | Dallas Washington 12<br>Houston Wheatley 0 | R. Fields<br>John Codwell |

*San Antonio Register*, **December 19**
"B. T. Washington, Dallas, Wins State Hi School Football Championship"
By R. E. Dixon

Dallas, Texas—The undefeated, untied Booker T. Washington High School Bulldogs of Dallas clinched the AA Interscholastic football championship of Texas, Thursday night, when they measured off John Codwell's Phyllis Wheatley Wildcats of Houston by a 12–0 score in Dal Hi stadium before some 4,000 spectators.

The excellent passing and punting of Sammy Briscoe, and the pass snagging of Woody Culton packed the offensive wallop that gave the local team the edge in this title tilt. Although the visitors controlled the ball for longer periods than the Bulldogs, they couldn't negotiate yardage as rapidly and as deftly as the Dallas lads, nor could they ever penetrate the Dallas 20-yard stripe.

Culton, Briscoe, Lloyd, Raney Smith, and E. J. Williams were Dallas outstanding performers. Coffey, Houston right guard, was the best defensive man on the field with Captain McCullough not far behind the agile and aggressive Coffey.

| Year | Class | Teams and scores | Coaches |
|------|-------|------------------|---------|
| 1942 | 2A | Austin Anderson 40<br>Paris Gibbons 0 | William Pigford<br>J. M. Milligan |

*Austin American-Statesman* **(reprinted on December 17, 2014)**

The Yellow Jackets rolled past Paris Gibbons 40–0 in a PVIL championship game that was played Dec. 11 [1942] at Anderson's home stadium on East 12th Street.

Coach William E. Pigford's Yellow Jackets were 11–0 in 1942. Anderson scored 248 points, and three of its seven shutouts were recorded over the season's final three weeks.

Led by players with nicknames of "Zipper," "Big Barnes" and "Big Head," Anderson only played three games that were decided by fewer than 14 points.

| Year | Class | Teams and scores | Coaches |
|------|-------|------------------|---------|
| 1943 | 2A | Houston Yates 7 | Develous Johnson, Roger Lights |
| | | Wichita Falls Washington 7 | Tennyson Miller |

### Houston Informer
"Yates, Wichita Falls, 7–7 Deadlock, Both Teams to Share State Prep Crown"

Houston—The state championship prep football was divided between two schools when the undefeated Jack Yates Lions and the undefeated Wichita Falls Leopards fought to a 7–7 deadlock on a rain soaked field Friday night at the high school stadium.

One of the smallest crowds of the season turned out to see the greatest game of the season. Both teams, with eyes on the coveted state crown, played their hearts out but could not put across the point needed to win.

Gamble, in center, played one of the best games of the season commanding his spot with deadly precision. Captain Moses was tough going as Wichita found out. Keyes, Haller, and the mighty Jennings paced the other Yates' linemen in the stiff resistance. The backfield was spotlighted by Davis and Peoples with Ross, Lawson and Daniels making good showing.

Clarence Slaughter stood out as the best that Wichita Falls had and that stood for plenty, for Herron, Smith, Nelson, and Devaugh were brilliant.

| Year | Class | Teams and scores | Coaches |
|------|-------|------------------|---------|
| 1944 | 2A | Houston Wheatley 7 | R. A. Countee |
| | | Fort Worth Terrell 6 | Marion Bates |

### Houston Chronicle, December 22
"State Negro Title Is Won by Wheatley: Hunter Sparks Drive That Brings Wildcats from Behind in 7–6 Game; McCauley Kicks Extra Point"

The Wheatley Wildcats won the state negro high school football championship by topping I. M. Terrell of Fort Worth, 7 to 6, Thursday night at the Public School Stadium.

James Hunter, sparkling back, was the difference between the two teams. After Terrell had taken a 6–0 lead in the first period Hunter sparked a 37-yard drive that carried to the 1-yard stripe where a fumble stopped the Wildcats.

Then a few minutes later Hunter took charge again, climaxing a 34-yard drive by plunging over from the 2-yard stripe. Ben McCauley booted the extra point that gave Wheatley the win.

Terrell counted its touchdown via the overhead route. Irving Garnett tossing a 32-yard pass to Percy Robinson who hauled the aerial in on the town and went over standing. Garnett was stopped as he tried to run for the extra point.

| Year | Class | Teams and scores | Coaches |
|------|-------|------------------|---------|
| 1945 | 2A | Wichita Falls Washington 12 Austin Anderson 2 | Tennyson Miller William Pigford |

*Austin American*, **December 15, 1945**
"Wichita Falls Negro Gridders Beat Anderson for State Title"

Washington high school's Leopards of Wichita Falls won the negro state football championship here Friday night by defeating the Anderson high school Yellow Jackets, 12–2.

Ballage and Crayton stood out in the Anderson line, while Bookman, Byars and Hygh led the attack. Christian, Carter, DeVaughn and Anderson led the invaders.

| Year | Class | Teams and scores | Coaches |
|------|-------|------------------|---------|
| 1946 | 2A | Dallas Washington 19 Galveston Central 19 | R. Fields Ray Sheppard |

*Dallas Morning News*, **December 15, 1946**
"Washington Ties for State Crown"

Booker T. Washington High of Dallas had a half interest in the Texas Negro High School Football Championship Saturday when the Bulldogs returned from Galveston where Friday night they battled Central High of the Island City to a 19-to-19 tie.

Since the coaches agreed prior to the game to let the outcome hinge entirely on the score and not count penetrations or first downs, they will rule as cochampions.

| Year | Class | Teams and scores | Coaches |
|------|-------|------------------|---------|
| 1947 | 2A | Fort Worth Terrell 13 | Marion Bates |
| | | Corpus Christi Coles 6 | John Thomas |

***Corpus Christi Times*, December 19, 1947**
"Hornets Edged 13–6 in Negro Grid Title Tilt"

Solomon M. Coles High School's Green Hornets bowed to an efficient I. M. Terrell High School team from Fort Worth, 13–6, in the Negro schoolboy football championship game last night in Buccaneer Stadium.

Upwards of 5,000 fans were on hand as the Hornets made a valiant, but futile, effort to gain the throne room in the first state championship football game played in the city.

Robert Meeks, 175-pound fullback, was the offensive star for the Fort Worth machine. Outstanding performers for the Hornets were Shelton and Ervin in the backfield and Bell and White in the line.

| Year | Class | Teams and scores | Coaches |
|------|-------|------------------|---------|
| 1947 | 1A | Denison Terrell 6 | E. T. Hardiman |
| | | Taylor Blackshear 6 | Vernon Anthony |

***Taylor Daily Press* December 21, 1947**
"Blackshear Wins State Grid Title: Football-Toting Panthers Tie
Terrell Dragons in Score but Take Game on First Downs"

The Blackshear Panthers of Taylor are the Class A high school football champions of the state.

Amidst the roars of the Dragons and the snarls of the Panthers, Taylor's Blackshear tied 6–6 in score with Denison's Terrell, tied 1–1 in penetrations, but won the state championship of Class A high school football on a total of 11 first downs over Denison's two in the final game played on the Duck Pond Friday night.

J. B. Scott paced the Taylor backfield and earned the sobriquet of the night's outstanding player. Starring on both offense and defense, Scott played a great game.

| Year | Class | Teams and scores | Coaches |
|------|-------|------------------|---------|
| 1948 | 2A | Corpus Christi Coles 6 | John Thomas |
| | | Dallas Washington 0 | Raymond Hollie |

**Dallas Morning News, December 12, 1948**
"Coles Beats Washington"

Solomon Coles High School of Corpus Christi took advantage of a fumble to win the state Negro schoolboy football championship with a 6-to-0 victory over Booker T. Washington Saturday night at Dal-Hi Stadium.

Approximately 4,000 fans saw Tommy Brewer set up the lone touchdown by pouncing on a James Harrison fumble on the Washington 4. Three plays later, Willie Shelton busted off right tackle from the 1 for the marker.

Carl Williams, the 135-pound Washington quarterback, was the outstanding player. Along with James Harrison, he led the ground game and did all of the punting and passing. His favorite receiver was Jimmy Banks.

| Year | Class | Teams and scores | Coaches |
|------|-------|------------------|---------|
| 1948 | 1A | Denison Terrell 13 | E. T. Hardiman |
| | | Orange Wallace 0 | Willie Ray Smith Sr. |

**Abilene Reporter-News, December 26, 1948**
"Dragons Win 13–0"

Denison, Dec. 25—The Terrell Dragons of Denison defeated Wallace High School of Orange 13–0 here Christmas Day afternoon to gain the Class A Negro high school grid crown.

| Year | Class | Teams and scores | Coaches |
|------|-------|------------------|---------|
| 1949 | 2A | Port Arthur Lincoln 13 | J. R. Edmonds |
| | | Dallas Lincoln 13 | R.E. Posey |

*Dallas Morning News*, **December 18**
"Dallas, Port Arthur Lincoln Tie, 13–13"

The Lincoln Tigers roared from behind in the last three minutes of play Saturday night at Dal-Hi Stadium to gain a 13-to-13 tie with the Lincoln High School Bumblebees of Port Arthur, to gain a share of the Negro high school, state football championship.

The two teams showed an explosive brand of football, Port Arthur's explosions coming on the ground and the Tigers' eruptions in the air.

| Year | Class | Teams and scores | Coaches |
|------|-------|------------------|---------|
| 1949 | 1A | Orange Wallace 34 | Willie Ray Smith Sr. |
|      |    | Victoria Gross 13 | J. E. Bias |

*Corsicana Daily Sun*, **December 23, 1949**
"Dragon Win"

Orange, Dec. 23—The Wallace High School Dragons of Orange defeated the Gross High Bumblebees of Victoria 34–13 for the state class A negro football championship here last night.

The Dragons previously had beaten the Lincoln High School of Port Arthur which last Saturday tied Lincoln of Dallas for the AA negro title.

| Year | Class | Teams and scores | Coaches |
|------|-------|------------------|---------|
| 1950 | 2A | Dallas Washington 24 | Raymond Hollie |
|      |    | Houston Yates 21 | Pat Patterson |

*Dallas Morning News*, **December 15, 1950**
"Washington Nips Yates, 24–21, for Title"
By John Trowbridge

A 10-yard field goal from the 15-yard inbounds marker by James Harrison with a little more than four minutes to go gave Booker T. Washington the Negro state high school football championship over Yates High of Houston at Dal-Hi Stadium Thursday night. The score was 24 to 21.

Three quick jabs that came as swiftly as a boxer's left staggered Yates and gave Washington its three touchdowns in the tingling contest.

| Year | Class | Teams and scores | Coaches |
|------|-------|------------------|---------|
| 1950 | 1A | San Angelo Blackshear 32<br>Huntsville Sam Houston | Allie Blackshear<br>Johnny Roberts |

No other information available.

| Year | Class | Teams and scores | Coaches |
|------|-------|------------------|---------|
| 1951 | 2A | Houston Yates 6<br>Waco Moore 6 | Pat Patterson<br>Les Ritcherson |

**Houston Chronicle, December 15, 1951**
"Gray Is Jekyll-Hyde In Yates' 6–6 Tie"
By Zarko Franks, Sports Staff

George Gray was both hero and fall guy in Jack Yates' 6–6 tie with Moore High of Waco in the Texas high school Negro football championship game.

It was Gray, six-seven Yates' quarterback who refused to take an ambulance ride when hurt late in the second quarter and returned to throw an 18-yard touchdown pass to Robert Scroggins Friday night at High School Stadium.

| Year | Class | Teams and scores | Coaches |
|------|-------|------------------|---------|
| 1951 | 1A | Huntsville Sam Houston 7<br>Hillsboro Peabody 6 | Johnny Roberts<br>Ben Young |

No other information available.

| Year | Class | Teams and scores | Coaches |
|------|-------|------------------|---------|
| 1952 | 3A | Waco Moore 14<br>Corpus Christi Coles 0 | Les Ritcherson<br>John Thomas |

**Waco Tribune, December 20, 1952**
"Moore High Nabs State Crown With 14–0 Win over Hornets"

Dazzling speed, and assortment of trick plays that kept the crowd of 4,000 fans gasping, and an inspired defense that attacked the massive Green Hornets carried Moore High's determined Lions to a 14–0 victory over Solomon Coles of Corpus Christi and their first full-fledged state championship in 30 years Friday night at Municipal Stadium.

Outweighed some 15 pounds per man and hampered by the heavy football, Coach Les Ritcherson's superbly-tutored squad outsmarted and outfought the hitherto undefeated, untied Gulf Coast eleven to climax a brilliant season and a marvelous comeback.

Hard-running Ray Jackson, who gained 111 yards on 21 carries and backed up the Moore forward wall with bruising effectiveness, was the ringleader—but every Lion played great ball. Finis was written to the schoolboy careers of four seniors—ends Noah Jackson and Ike Hawthorne, tackle Tampa Smith, and back Alvin Jackson—and all of them ended in a blaze of glory.

| Year | Class | Teams and scores | Coaches |
|------|-------|------------------|---------|
| 1952 | 2A | Amarillo Carver 7 | Johnny Allen |
|  |  | Palestine Lincoln 0 | Elzie Malloy |

***Palestine Herald Press*, December 20, 1952**
"Lincoln Drops Title Tilt With Amarillo"

The Lincoln High School Lions' victory string was finally cut Saturday afternoon as they fell to the Amarillo Dragons 7–0 in the negro AA state championship game, played in Amarillo.

The Lions' bid for the championship was just short of the goal as they drove within the Dragon 15-yard line numerous times but were unable to score.

| Year | Class | Teams and scores | Coaches |
|------|-------|------------------|---------|
| 1952 | 1A | Arp Industrial | Elmer Redd |
|  |  | Lockhart Carver | N/A |

No other information available.

| 1953 | 3A | Port Arthur Lincoln 38 | R. E. Posey |
|------|-----|------------------------|-------------|
|  |  | Dallas Washington 7 | Raymond Hollie |

***Dallas Morning News*, December 12, 1953**
"Port Arthur Romps, 38–7, Over Booker"
By Ozzie Hansen

Lincoln of Port Arthur scored on a 79-yard opening kickoff return, then steadily ground out touchdowns to smother Booker T. Washington of Dallas,

37 to 7, and annex the Negro state AAA championship at Dal-Hi Stadium Friday night.

A crowd of 3,500 sat through the rain and cold to watch the Bumblebees repeat an early season triumph over the Dallas champions.

| Year | Class | Teams and scores | Coaches |
|---|---|---|---|
| 1953 | 2A | Corsicana Jackson 19 | Walter Day |
| | | Abilene Woodson 0 | Donald Grace |

**Corsicana Sun, December 19**
"Bears Win State Football Championship: Jackson High's Ground Game Pays Off while Tight Defense Stops Best Efforts of Woodson Rams Eleven"

Jackson High School Bears Friday night won the championship of the AA Negro Interscholastic League of Texas. They defeated a stubborn, scrapping but outclassed Woodson Rams eleven from Abilene to win, 19–0.

The West Texans could not master the prowess, speed and ability of the 1953 champions of their class, although they held the winners scoreless in the last quarter as many replacements were used and contested stubbornly for all yards allowed the visitors.

| Year | Class | Teams and scores | Coaches |
|---|---|---|---|
| 1953 | 1A | Livingston Dunbar | Ross Hardin |
| | | West Columbia | Ewitt Myers |

No other information available.

| 1954 | 3A | Houston Wheatley 13 | Frank Walker |
| | | Waco Moore 0 | Les Ritcherson |

**Houston Chronicle, December 11, 1954**
"Wheatley Wins State after 10-Year Lapse"
By Don De Pugh

Wheatley's Wildcats finishing in the runner-up spot for city honors, went on to win the state crown here at Public School Stadium Friday night. The Wildcats, grabbing their eleventh win in 12 games, stopped Moore's Lions of Waco, 13–0, for their first state championship in 10 years.

Arthur Moore, 170-pound end, on offense and defense led the Wildcats to two quick touchdowns in the final quarter to give Houston its first state champ since Yates tied Moore in 1951, 6–6. Moore, with a 9–2 record, has played in the state finals three of the last four years, winning in '51 and '52.

| Year | Class | Teams and scores | Coaches |
| --- | --- | --- | --- |
| 1954 | 2A | Orange Wallace 39 | Willie Ray Smith Sr. |
| | | Greenville Carver 0 | C. L. Davidson |

**Greenville Morning Herald, December 18, 1954**
"Carver Loses 39–0 in State Finals: Wallace of Orange Halts 11 Game Tiger Win Streak"

Orange—Carver's Golden Tigers of Greenville finally lost a football game—but they had to go all the way to the finals before suffering their first loss of the season to Wallace of Orange, 39–0.

    The formerly undefeated and untied Tigers of coach C.L. Davidson were simply outclassed in the state's class AA Negro final grid game of '54. The only threat in the game came in the third quarter when the ball was advanced to the Dragon 9-yard line before it went over on downs.

| Year | Class | Teams and scores | Coaches |
| --- | --- | --- | --- |
| 1954 | 1A | Livingston Dunbar 25 | Ross Hardin |
| | | College Station 20 | J. R. Delly |

No other information available.

| | | | |
| --- | --- | --- | --- |
| 1955 | 3A | Port Arthur Lincoln 9 | R. E. Posey |
| | | Dallas Lincoln 6 | Farley Lewis |

**Port Arthur News, December 11**
"Port Arthur Nips Lincoln in Negro Title Game, 9–6"

Port Arthur, Texas—The Lincoln Bumblebees of Port Arthur won their second Class AA Negro high school football championship in three years here Saturday night, defeating Lincoln of Dallas by 9–6 in a drizzling rain.

    The Dallas team enjoyed its best success in the air as quarterback James Smith spearheaded the Tigers their lone touchdowns and kept them in

contention throughout the contest. His 55-yard pass to Billy Wedgeworth
in the fourth period gave Dallas its only touchdown.

| Year | Class | Teams and scores | Coaches |
|------|-------|------------------|---------|
| 1955 | 2A | Baytown Carver 33<br>Gladewater Weldon 13 | Johnny Peoples<br>C. C. Cooksey |

**Baytown Sun, December 17, 1955**
"R.I.P. Gladewater, 33–13: Panthers State Champs"
By Tom Murray, *Sun* Sports Editor

Gladewater's multiple offense was melted and reduced to junk in Memo-
rial Stadium Friday night as coach Johnny Peoples' lightning fast Carver
Panthers creamed the green-shirted East Texans, 33–13, to become the 1955
Class AA Negro State Champions.

Ignited by a sleight-of-hand quarterback, Willie Jenkins, Carver's light-
horse backfield raced through the Bumble-Bee defense for 511 yards and
called on a rugged defense to stop Gladewater's many-pronged machine with
but 178.

| Year | Class | Teams and scores | Coaches |
|------|-------|------------------|---------|
| 1955 | 1A | Rockdale Aycock 21<br>West Dunbar 7 | Ralph Johnson<br>Thomas J. Bellinger |

No other information available.

| | | | |
|------|-------|------------------|---------|
| 1956 | 3A | Austin Anderson 26<br>Dallas Washington 7 | Raymond Timmons<br>Raymond Hollie |

**Dallas Morning News, December 16, 1956**
"Bulldogs Fall in Finals, 26–7"
By Walter Robertson

Anderson of Austin cut out an early pattern, found it a perfect fit and then
almost wore it out in steamrollering Washington's Bulldogs, 26–7, in the
state Negro high school football championship game Saturday at Dal-Hi
Stadium.

A crowd of 6,500 watched Anderson's unbeaten single-wing powerhouse

---

win the school's first state title and crush Washington's bid for a repeat of the title it won back in 1950.

| Year | Class | Teams and scores | Coaches |
|------|-------|------------------|---------|
| 1956 | 2A | Corsicana Jackson 18<br>Denton Moore 0 | Walter Day<br>C. H. Collins |

**Denton Record-Chronicle, December 20, 1956**
"Bears Clip Dragons 18–0 for AA Title: Corsicana Cops Crown on Rain-Soaked Bronco Field"
By Dub Brown, *Record-Chronicle* Sports Writer

Playing on a field turned into a sea of mud, the Jackson High School Bears of Corsicana emerged from the morass of Bronco Stadium Wednesday night with the Class AA Negro state championship after downing Denton's Fred Moore High School 18–0 in the finals.

The Bears, using the running of a pair of 175-pounds plus halfbacks utilized a pass interception and a blocked punt for 12 points and added a third touchdown on an 80-yard scoring march.

| Year | Class | Teams and scores | Coaches |
|------|-------|------------------|---------|
| 1956 | 1A | Sealy Austin County 19<br>Kaufman Pyle 18 | Ulysses Giles<br>Homer Norvell |

No other information available.

| | | | |
|------|-------|------------------|---------|
| 1957 | 3A | Austin Anderson 22<br>Dallas Washington 14 | Raymond Timmons<br>Raymond Hollie |

**Austin American, December 14, 1957**
"Anderson Triumphs 22–14 for the Title"

For the second straight year, Coach Raymond Timmons' Anderson Yellow Jackets are the rulers of Negro schoolboy football.

The Yellow Jackets retained their number one standing Friday night before a packed crowd of 8,000 at Anderson Stadium but not until they had been forced into their toughest football game of the season.

| Year | Class | Teams and scores | Coaches |
|------|-------|------------------|---------|
| 1957 | 2A | Corsicana Jackson 46<br>Denton Moore 0 | Walter Day<br>C. H. Collins |

### *Corsicana Daily Sun*, December 14, 1957

"Bears Defeat Denton for Second Straight Pennant 46–0: Jackson High Starts Scoring on Third Play—Local Eleven Uses Crushing Ground Attack"
By Talmadge Canant, *Sun* Sports Editor

The Jackson Bears overwhelmed Moore High's Dragons of Denton here Friday night 46–0 to win the Class AA negro schoolboy grid title for the second straight year.

As so often this season, it was the scoring duo of Billy Christe and Ossie Jackson who accounted for most of the Bear scoring. Jackson scored three touchdowns while Christe tallied two and accounted for three points-after. Willie Newsome and Morris Johnson accounted for the remaining Bear touchdowns.

| Year | Class | Teams and scores | Coaches |
|------|-------|------------------|---------|
| 1957 | 1A | Galena Park Fidelity Manor 29<br>Vernon Washington 6 | J. C. Lilly<br><br>N/A |

No other information available.

| Year | Class | Teams and scores | Coaches |
|------|-------|------------------|---------|
| 1958 | 3A | Dallas Washington 35<br>Houston Washington 0 | Raymond Hollie<br>Alvin Sims |

### *Dallas Morning News*, December 19, 1958

"Dallasites Cop Crown, 35 to 0"
By Bill Jernigan

Dallas Washington's Bulldogs coasted unchallenged to the state Class AAA Negro championship with a convincing 35–0 victory over Houston Washington Thursday night before 3,700 at Cobb Stadium.

Fullback John Harris led the Bulldog scoring parade with two touchdowns and five extra point kicks. Halfback Stanley Jones scored two, one on a pass from Quarterback Charles Biggins, who added the fifth.

| Year | Class | Teams and scores | Coaches |
|------|-------|------------------|---------|
| 1958 | 2A | Baytown Carver 17 | Johnny Peoples |
|      |    | Denton Moore 14 | C. H. Collins |

**Baytown Sun, December 22, 1958**
"Carver Fans Celebrate State Title: Bucs Beat Denton for Crown, 17–14"

There were no classes scheduled at Carver High School Monday and it was a good thing there weren't for classrooms couldn't contain jubilant Carver students who are still celebrating their Bucs' annexation of the state AA football championship.

Coach Johnny Peoples' Bucs pulled out a 17–14 victory over a tough bunch of Denton Dragons Saturday night in Memorial Stadium to win the state championship for the second time in the history of the Lee Drive school.

| Year | Class | Teams and scores | Coaches |
|------|-------|------------------|---------|
| 1958 | 1A | Livingston Dunbar 26 | James Dewalt |
|      |    | Grand Prairie Dalworth 24 | Boston Grant |

No other information available.

| | | | |
|------|-------|------------------|---------|
| 1959 | 3A | Beaumont Hebert 37 | Clifton Ozen |
|      |    | Dallas Lincoln 0 | Farley Lewis |

**Galveston News, December 20**
"Hebert Rips Lincoln, 37–0, in State Finals"

Beaumont, Texas (Special)—Hebert High of Beaumont counted in every chapter to vault into the Negro Class AAA championship by trouncing Lincoln of Dallas, 37–0, in a final showdown held this evening in Beaumont South Park Stadium before a crowd of 5,000.

Hebert's smooth-operating split-T offense moved to its first touchdown when Herman Hudson fumbled in his end zone after a 7-yard slash over left guard and teammate Anthony Guillory pounced on the fallen ball. Carl Zenn split the uprights with the first of his two conversions.

| Year | Class | Teams and scores | Coaches |
|------|-------|------------------|---------|
| 1959 | 2A | Bay City Hilliard 22<br>Fort Worth Kirkpatrick 14 | Joe Washington Sr.<br>Gerald Seal |

**Fort Worth Star-Telegram, December 20, 1959**
"Hilliard Races Past Kirkpatrick by 22–14"
By Bill Ramsey, *Star-Telegram* Sports Writer

Behind the bulldozing runs of halfback Sam Clark, Hilliard of Bay City rode to the state 2A Negro high school football championship Saturday afternoon by edging Fort Worth Kirkpatrick, 22–14, in a finals duel played at Farrington Field.

Clark, a 198-pound bundle of sheer power, scored all Hilliard's 22 points by plowing to three touchdowns on runs of 50, 53 and six yards and adding two-point conversions following two of the scores.

| Year | Class | Teams and scores | Coaches |
|------|-------|------------------|---------|
| 1959 | 1A | West Dunbar 42<br>Livingston Dunbar 12 | Otis Williams<br>James Dewalt |

No other information available.

| | | | |
|------|-------|------------------|---------|
| 1960 | 4A | Waco Moore 6<br>Houston Washington 6 | Les Ritcherson<br>Alvin Sims |

**Dallas Express, December 17, 1960**
"Washington, Waco Tie 6–6; Co-State Champs: 6,000 Brave Wet,
Cold Weather to See Lion's TD March Killed in the Final Nine Seconds"
By Lloyd C. A. Wells, *Informer* Sports Director

Houston—Coach Alvin Sims' Heights gridders grabbed off a piece of the Class AAAA football title with Moore High Lion's of Waco here last Friday night, before a shivering crowd of 6,000 fans.

Outstanding Players

For Waco, Freddy Dotson, Willie Ward, James Givins, Sims, Iglehart and Eddie Trice stood out. For Washington, McDade, Sutton, Dearborne, Smith, Damon Gatewood, Melvin Anderson, Joe Hayes, Thomas Lindley and Alonzo Wallace looked excellent.

| Year | Class | Teams and scores | Coaches |
|---|---|---|---|
| 1960 | 3A | Corpus Christi Coles 38<br>Wichita Falls Washington 21 | John Thomas<br>Ervin Garnett |

**Wichita Falls Times, December 11**
"BTW Loses Finals 38–21"

Corpus Christi, Tex. (Special)—Solomon Coles of Corpus Christi spotted the Booker T. Washington Leopards a 21–8 halftime lead then came roaring back to post a 38–21 victory for the colored class AAA state championship win here Saturday night in Buccaneer Stadium.

Coles scored first driving 45 yards on the opening series of downs as fullback Levis Irving scored from the three yard line. Levis score 18 points in the game.

| Year | Class | Teams and scores | Coaches |
|---|---|---|---|
| 1960 | 2A | Conroe Washington 16<br>Midland Carver 6 | Charles Brown<br>Johnny Williams |

**Unidentified newspaper clipping**
"Hornets Tripped By Conroe, 16–6"

Conroe—The Conroe Washington High School Bulldogs jumped to a 14–0 lead and then fended off the hopeful Midland Carver Hornets Friday night for a 16–6 win and the state negro Class AA football championship.

The title runner-up Hornets gaining their highest position in history, almost came back in the exciting fourth quarter to tie the game, but penalties helped slow a 65-yard drive to the Conroe 13.

| Year | Class | Teams and scores | Coaches |
|---|---|---|---|
| 1960 | 1A | Brazosport Lanier 28<br>West Dunbar 24 | Cottrell McGowan<br>Otis Williams |

**Brazosport Facts, December 19, 1960**
"Lanier Wins State Championship"
By George Ferguson, *Facts* Sports Editor

Freeport's Lanier High School Wildcats refused to wilt, with key injuries and against an opposing team that outweighed them 20 pounds to the man, defeated the Dunbar Dragons from West 28–24, to bring to Brazoria County the first state football championship in history. The state finals in Negro Class-A football was played before 4,000 screaming fans at Brazosport's Hopper Field Saturday night.

Coach C. B. McGowan's Wildcats took an early lead in the state championship game and continued to lead on the scoreboard until four minutes deep in the fourth quarter, when Dunbar went out from 24–22; however, three minutes later, with five minutes remaining in the game, Lanier scored the winning touchdown, and held until the game ended. The Lanier win over the Dunbar Dragons set their 1960 record at 14–0.

| Year | Class | Teams and scores | Coaches |
|------|-------|------------------|---------|
| 1961 | 4A | Austin Anderson 20 | Raymond Timmons |
| | | Houston Yates 13 | Pat Patterson |

**Austin American, December 9, 1961**
"Anderson Claims State Title, 20–13"
Special to *The American*

Houston—Like bookends. Anderson High held up the first half of the state Negro 4A championship football tilt and Yates of Houston the second half, but six key pass interceptions gave Anderson the crown, 20–13.

Though Anderson controlled the ball most of the half, the Lions were able to gain five first downs, but lost possible driving opportunities in two more interceptions, both by the nimble hands of Orsby Crenshaw.

| Year | Class | Teams and scores | Coaches |
|------|-------|------------------|---------|
| 1961 | 3A | Baytown Carver 21 | Johnny Peoples |
| | | Fort Worth Kirkpatrick 6 | Gerald Seal |

*Fort Worth Star-Telegram*, December 3, 1961
"Carver Trims Wildcats for Crown, 21–6"

Quick-striking Baytown Carver won the state Negro 3A football championship with a 21–6 victory over the Kirkpatrick Wildcats at Farrington Field
Saturday night.

The Buccaneers scored twice in the first quarter for a 13–0 lead and the
Wildcats could never catch up.

| Year | Class | Teams and scores | Coaches |
|------|-------|------------------|---------|
| 1961 | 2A | Midland Carver 44 | Johnny Williams |
| | | Conroe Washington 16 | Charles Brown |

**Unidentified newspaper, December 17, 1961**
"Carver Nabs Title: Hornets Strike Back to Win, 44–16, after Trailing, 16–6"

With the weatherman co-operating to his fullest, a crowd estimated at 6,000
turned out in 60-degree weather to cheer the charges of Coach Johnny Williams to the pinnacle of success.

The visiting Bulldogs had the Hornets down and ready for the knockout
punch at halftime, but the hosts stormed back in the second half to turn a
close game into a one-sided rout.

| Year | Class | Teams and scores | Coaches |
|------|-------|------------------|---------|
| 1961 | 1A | Richardson Hamilton | James Griffin |
| | | Park 24 | |
| | | Sweeny Carver 0 | Elijah Childers |

*Brazosport Facts*, December 17, 1961
"Hamilton Park Bobcats Chill Sweeny's Carver, 24–0"
By Phil Ferguson, *Facts* Sports Staff

Sweeny (Special)—The All-District backfield of the Hamilton Park Bobcats
of Richardson (a Dallas suburb) proved their worth at Buck Manley Field
here Saturday night before about 2,000 fans by moving the football to a
24–0 victory over the George Washington Carver High School Wildcats of
Sweeny. The victory gave Hamilton Park the Negro Class A state football
championship.

The fans watched the Bobcats move as well through the air as they did on the ground despite the slippery ball and the light-misty rain that fell during the entire contest. Leroy Brewster, the Bobcat all-district quarterback, threw bullet passes for long yardage throughout the contest with perfection.

| Year | Class | Teams and scores | Coaches |
|------|-------|------------------|---------|
| 1962 | 4A | Houston Yates 18 | Pat Patterson |
| | | Fort Worth Dunbar 15 | Clifford Spates |

**Houston Chronicle, December 15, 1962**
"Yates Takes State Crown: Lions Beat Dunbar, 18–15, for First Title in 23 Years"
By Ellis Johnson, *Chronicle* Correspondent

It's a mighty long road that never turns and for coach Andrew L. (Pat) Patterson and the Jack Yates Lions, it turned out to be 23 years but they finally brought the state AAAA football championship home by downing Dunbar High of Ft. Worth, 18–15, Friday night at Jeppesen Stadium.

It was the sixth time Yates had made it to the finals in the school's history but only the second time for Yates to win the title and the first under coach Patterson who lost in 1961 to Austin 20–14.

Coach Patterson said, "This was the greatest Christmas present that I could get. It's my first championship and it was a long time coming. It has been a hard grind but we won . . . the defense did the job. They held them and that is where we won the game."

| Year | Class | Teams and scores | Coaches |
|------|-------|------------------|---------|
| 1962 | 3A | Fort Worth Kirkpatrick 6 | Gerald Seal |
| | | Galena Park Fidelity Manor 0 | Lester Eaton |

**Fort Worth Star-Telegram, December 16, 1962**
"Kirkpatrick Raps Fidelity for 3A Crown"

An 18-yard pass from Quarterback James Milliard to End Ronald Bailey in the first quarter were the only points as Kirkpatrick stopped Fidelity Manor of Galena Park, 6–0, in the Negro high school Class 3A state championship football game at Farrington Field Saturday.

The touchdown aerial capped a 65-yard drive that was sped along by halfback Johnny Jones' scampers of 23 and 15 yards. A running try for extra points failed and the rest of the game was a defensive battle that saw both teams thwarted on several deep thrusts.

| Year | Class | Teams and scores | Coaches |
|------|-------|------------------|---------|
| 1962 | 2A | Wharton Training 40<br>Lubbock Dunbar 6 | James Wanza<br>Jim Hillard |

### *Denton Record-Chronicle*, December 16, 1962
"Wharton AA Negro Champs"

Brownwood (AP)—Wharton Training High School Wolves amassed 433 yards, scored six touchdowns and had three others called back here Saturday en route to a 40–6 victory over Lubbock Dunbar for the Texas Class AA Negro schoolboy football title.

| Year | Class | Teams and scores | Coaches |
|------|-------|------------------|---------|
| 1962 | 1A | Taylor Price 42<br>Dayton Colbert 6 | Bud Elder<br>Duriel Harris Sr. |

No other information available.

| | | | |
|------|-------|------------------|---------|
| 1963 | 4A | Galveston Central 34<br>Dallas Madison 14 | Ed Mitchell<br>Don Grace |

### *Dallas Morning News*, December 14, 1963
"Galveston Central Jolts Madison, 34–14"

Galveston Central rook advantage of a fumble and a blocked punt to build up a 17-point halftime lead and went on to upset top-ranked Madison of Dallas, 34–14, in the state AAAA Negro championship high school football game at P. C. Cobb Stadium.

It was the first loss in 12 games for Madison, which had held the No. 1 state rank for the past six weeks.

| Year | Class | Teams and scores | Coaches |
|------|-------|------------------|---------|
| 1963 | 3A | Fort Worth Kirkpatrick 46<br>Gladewater Weldon 14 | Gerald Seal<br>C. C. Cooksey |

*Fort Worth Star-Telegram,* **December 7, 1963**
"Kirkpatrick Captures 3A Grid Title, 46–14"

Kirkpatrick's Wildcats marched to their second straight Class 3A Negro high school grid championship by routing Weldon of Gladewater, 46–14, before 3,969 at Farrington Field Friday night.

The Wildcats rolled to a comfortable 30–0 lead before they allowed Weldon to cross the goal line late in the first half.

| Year | Class | Teams and scores | Coaches |
| --- | --- | --- | --- |
| 1963 | 2A | Lubbock Dunbar 19 | Jim Hillard |
| | | Conroe Washington 14 | Charles Brown |

*Conroe Courier,* **December 18, 1963**
"Washington Bulldogs End Season in Finals"

With a state AA football championship at stake, the Booker T. Washington Bulldogs from Conroe trotted onto snow-covered Lowry Field, faced into an icy 18-degree wind and lost the biggest game of their 1963 season.

The Dunbar Panthers of Lubbock rolled over Conroe and into the state championship with a frazzled 19–14 victory on their frigid home field. The Bulldogs, with just three hours sleep after a 16-hour bus trip, lost to the heavier Panther team after enduring an immobile first half.

| Year | Class | Teams and scores | Coaches |
| --- | --- | --- | --- |
| 1963 | 1A | Smithville Brown 38 | Gene Sampson |
| | | Mineola McFarland 6 | I. C. Gregory |

No other information available.

| | | | |
| --- | --- | --- | --- |
| 1964 | 4A | Waco Moore 16 | Les Ritcherson |
| | | Houston Yates 14 | Pat Patterson |

*Houston Chronicle,* **December 12, 1964**
"Nip Yates, 16–14: Lions Capture State Crown"

James Jones kicked a 22-yard field goal in the fourth quarter Friday night to boost the Moore High Lions to the top in the Negro Class AAAA state championship showdown in Houston.

The Lions edged Houston Yates, 16–14, in a cliffhanger.

The action started early with Yates drawing first blood. Four plays after the kickoff Yates quarterback Lionel Williams rolled out for 14 yards and a touchdown. Grady Cavness kicked the extra point.

| Year | Class | Teams and scores | Coaches |
|------|-------|------------------|---------|
| 1964 | 3A | Lufkin Dunbar 20 | Elmer Redd |
| | | Marlin Washington 7 | Ras Dansby |

**Lufkin News, December 13, 1964**
"Dunbar Defeats Marlin for State Championship, 20–7"
By John Ellis, *News* Area Sports Editor

Marlin—The Dunbar Tigers proved that you don't have to run from scrimmage to score touchdowns. Coach Elmer Redd's charges did it twice here Saturday afternoon as they roared from behind with a third quarter rally to defeat the Marlin Wildcats, 20–7, and win the Class AAA Negro State Championship.

Dunbar was trailing, 7–0, in the third quarter. But, it took only six minutes and one second to score three touchdowns to make the comeback.

| Year | Class | Teams and scores | Coaches |
|------|-------|------------------|---------|
| 1964 | 2A | Sherman Douglass 32 | Ed Hunt |
| | | Conroe Washington 18 | Charles Brown |

**Sherman Democrat, December 13, 1964**
"Fred Douglass Panthers Blast Conroe 32–18"

Conroe—If there is a better Class AA Negro team in Texas the Fred Douglass Panthers must have bypassed it on their climb to their first state football championship in the history of the high school.

The Conroe Bulldogs became bridesmaids for the second straight year here Friday night, as the big, fast, and well-polished Panthers broke the championship clash wide open midway of the final quarter, scoring two quick TD's to salt away a 32–18 victory.

| Year | Class | Teams and scores | Coaches |
|------|-------|------------------|---------|
| 1964 | 1A | Bartlett Washington 8 | A. A. Powell |
| | | Garland Carver 6 | Curtis Davidson |

No other information available.

| 1965 | 4A | Houston Yates 18 | Pat Patterson |
|------|-----|-------------------|----------------|
|      |    | Fort Worth Terrell 0 | Walter Day |

**Houston Chronicle, December 11, 1965**
"Yates Pops Terrell for Title"
By Ellis Johnson, *Chronicle* Correspondent

Fort Worth—The Jack Yates Lions of Houston won their second state Class AAAA Negro schoolboy football championship in the past five years here Friday night with an 18–0 decision over favored I. M. Terrell of Fort Worth.

Yates scored once each in the second, third, and fourth quarters for the victory before 8,000 rain-soaked fans at muddy Farrington Field.

Yates locked it up in the fourth quarter when speedy halfback Otis Pointer sloshed 76 yards with 6:50 remaining in the game.

| Year | Class | Teams and scores | Coaches |
|------|-------|-------------------|----------|
| 1965 | 3A | Wichita Falls Washington 31 | Ervin Garnett |
|      |    | Nacogdoches Campbell 0 | Bo Michaels |

**Wichita Falls Times, December 12, 1965**
"Leopards Take State Crown, 31–0: Defense Keys Weird Victory"
By Ted Leach

Booker T. Washington blocked two punts, intercepted three passes, returned a fumble for a 23-yard touchdown and otherwise gave Nacogdoches a lesson in defense as it ripped the Dragons 31–0 to capture the Negro Class AAA state championship here Saturday afternoon.

It was the climax of the school's greatest season, the Leopards producing 12 victories without defeat. It also extended a 13-game winning streak that began with a victory in the season finale of 1964.

Paced by the brilliant play of Bertram Allen, Ronald Donaldson, George Flenoy, Reginald Booker, Robert Childs and James Harris, the Leopards stymied Nacogdoches to but 91 yards total offense and didn't yield a penetration.

| Year | Class | Teams and scores | Coaches |
|------|-------|------------------|---------|
| 1965 | 2A | Conroe Washington 33<br>Sherman Douglass 12 | Charles Brown<br>Ed Hunt |

***Sherman Democrat*, December 19, 1965**
"Bid For Second State Crown: Conroe Wins 33–12"
By Ed Boatman

The Fred Douglass Panthers saw their 17-game winning streak come to a screeching halt here Saturday night and at the same time their bid for a second straight Class AA Negro state championship go down the drain as Conroe overpowered the Panthers 33–12.

A bevy of swift and talented backs rolled up 365 yards on the ground while a stout forward wall put pressure on Douglass quarterback Don Campbell most of the night. The senior signal-caller did connect 14 times in 30 tries for 161 yards, but Conroe stiffened up when the Panthers crossed midfield each time.

| Year | Class | Teams and scores | Coaches |
|------|-------|------------------|---------|
| 1965 | 1A | Sweeny Carver 21<br>Cameron Price 14 | Elijah Childers<br>N/A |

***Brazosport Facts*, December 26, 1965**
"Childers Didn't Expect a State Title"

Sweeny—State championships are hard to come by these days, but coach Elijah Childers and his band of Carver Wildcats have avoided that challenge and breezed to the Class A Negro state championship in the school's final year of existence.

They move on to Sweeny High School next fall.

Childers said that it was hard to compare this championship team with the state finalist club of 1961. But as the coach put it: "The team that wins the championship is the best."

| Year | Class | Teams and scores | Coaches |
|------|-------|------------------|---------|
| 1966 | 4A | Beaumont Hebert 14<br>Dallas Madison 3 | Clifton Ozen<br>Donald Grace |

*Dallas Morning News*, **December 11, 1966**
"Madison Bows, 14–3: Hebert Defense Halts Trojans"
Staff Special to *The News*

Beaumont, Texas—Beaumont Hebert reigns as the Class AAAA state Negro
football champion, after putting up a mighty defense to stop the Trojans of
Dallas Madison here Saturday night, 14–3, before 12,000 fans.

Madison almost started the fireworks early, as Allen Thompson sped 75
yards to the Hebert 11 on the first play from scrimmage. Three plays netted
eight yards, and there the winners set the pace for the game by stopping the
Trojan attack and taking over on downs.

| Year | Class | Teams and scores | Coaches |
|------|-------|------------------|---------|
| 1966 | 3A | Lufkin Dunbar 14 | Elmer Redd |
|      |    | Wichita Falls Washington 7 | Ervin Garnett |

*Wichita Falls Times*, **December 11**
"Washington Falls in State Finale, 14–7: Lufkin's Goal-Line Stand
Halts 23-Game Win Streak"
By Ted Leach

Lufkin Dunbar hurled back Washington at its two-yard line with a tremendous defensive stand and brought to an end the state's longest winning
streak with a 14–7 victory over the Leopards in the class AAA Negro state
championship game here Saturday.

Washington's demise came with 6:32 remaining in the fourth quarter when Lufkin sophomore Willie Walker strode through the Leopards'
pass pocket to dump quarterback James Colbert for a seven-yard loss on
fourth-and-goal.

| Year | Class | Teams and scores | Coaches |
|------|-------|------------------|---------|
| 1966 | 2A | Bay City Hilliard 42 | Harry Neal |
|      |    | Denton Moore 0 | C. H. Collins |

**Denton Record-Chronicle, December 18**
"Fred Moore Loses in Bid for State AA Title, 42–0: Bay City's Hilliard
Is Too Powerful"
By Bill Rainbolt, Staff Writer

Bay City—All-State candidate Wesley Davidson led Bay City Hilliard's
unstoppable ground attack to the Class AA state title here Saturday night as
Hilliard beat Denton's Fred Moore, 42–0.

The game, close until after halftime, was played before 3,000 including a
handful of Fred Moore backers. But the Panther fans did most of the yelling
as their favorites took the Prairie View Interscholastic League title.

Davidson, a blue-chip college prospect, ran for 117 yards on 14 carries and
scored four touchdowns.

| Year | Class | Teams and scores | Coaches |
|------|-------|------------------|---------|
| 1967 | 3A | Lufkin Dunbar 44 | Elmer Redd |
|      |    | Texarkana Dunbar 24 | Dan Haskins |

**Lufkin News**
"Tigers Capture Second Consecutive: Redd's Crew Rips Texarkana, 44–24"
By David Widener, *News* Sports Editor

Lufkin Dunbar, ignited by a touchdown scored when recovering the second
half kickoff in the Texarkana end zone that overcame a 16–13 lead the Buffaloes had at intermission, smashed the visitors from the border city 44–24
Saturday night to win the State Class AAA Negro football championship for
the second straight year and third time in the last four years.

A standing room only crowd of some 6,000 witnessed the game at Panther Stadium. The victory was the 25th straight for Coach Elmer Redd's
Tigers, who will move into the AA ranks of the UIL next season.

| Year | Class | Teams and scores | Coaches |
|------|-------|------------------|---------|
| 1967 | 2A | Jasper Rowe 55 | Cliff Williams |
|      |    | Hallsville Galilee 12 | Bobby Nevels |

No other information available.

| Year | Class | Teams and scores | Coaches |
|------|-------|------------------|---------|
| 1967 | 1A | Willis 30 | Julius Shanklin |
|      |    | Trinity 10 | Mack Collier |

No other information available.

| 1968 | 3A | Corsicana Jackson 31 | Alex Williams |
|------|-----|----------------------|---------------|
|      |     | Gladewater Weldon 6  | Walter Derrick |

***Corsicana Sun*, December 1**
"Finish 10–0: Jackson State PVL Champ"

Gladewater, Tex.—The Jackson Bears are Texas State champions in Class 3-A of the Prairie View League for 1968. Jackson earned the distinction by finishing a perfect football season with a 10–0 season and a final 31–6 victory Friday night here before a huge crowd over Gladewater.

Jackson High turned in a special effort against a big and rugged Gladewater team to become the state champs in the final season of the Prairie View League. Next season the Bears will join the ranks of the UIL in District 12-AA, but they went out in '68 in a blaze of glory.

As was the case all season the Bears were led by the likes of Robert Mitchell, Bobby Sanford, Ricky Sutton, Raymond Bell, Bobby Hudson, Leroy Johnson, Vernal Brandon, Marlon Gooden, Floyd Ballard and others.

| Year | Class | Teams and scores | Coaches |
|------|-------|------------------|---------|
| 1969 | 3A    | Weirgate         | Edward Ross |
|      |       | Calvert Spigner  | Frank Fryer |

No other information available.

## PVIL MILESTONES

Nov. 1920—As a result of a meeting between members of the Colored Teachers State Association of Texas and L. W. Rogers, first assistant state superintendent of education, the Texas Interscholastic League of Colored Schools (TILCS) was organized to form a league to govern athletic and academic competition for black high schools. The league comprised forty schools.

Apr. 1921—The first TILCS track and academic state competitions were held at Prairie View A&M College.

1923—The TILCS came under the authority of Prairie View A&M College, thereby becoming the PVIL.

Apr. 1927—League membership was more than 300 schools, supervised by W. R. Banks, Prairie View principal.

Oct. 29, 1927—Houston Yates and Houston Wheatley met for the first time. Yates won 19–6.

Nov. 28, 1935—Before six thousand fans, Yates and Wheatley met for the first time on Thanksgiving Day. Yates won 20–14.

1937—The Lone Star Interscholastic and Athletic Coaches Association was formed at Bishop College in Marshall.

Spring 1939—The PVIL was formally divided into four districts statewide. For the first time, state champions would be determined by a playoff system. Schools were classified (AA, A, or B) by the size of their enrollments.

Fall 1939—Yates won the last mythical state championship, beating Dallas Lincoln 13–6.

Dec. 25, 1939—The Chocolate Bowl Classic was held at Houston's Buffalo Stadium. The Texas state champion, Temple Dunbar, met Bogalusa, the Louisiana black state champion.

Mar. 2, 1940—Yates beat Houston Wheatley 33–19 for the first PVIL basketball state title.

Apr. 13, 1940—At Prairie View, Dallas Lincoln won the first PVIL track and field state title.

Dec. 24, 1940—Fort Worth Terrell, coached by Marion "Bull" Bates, won the first PVIL state title in football by defeating Austin Anderson 26–0.

Dec. 1951—San Francisco University's Ollie Matson, a Yates grad, became the first black Texan to receive votes for the Heisman Trophy, finishing ninth with ninety-five votes.

1955—Charlie "Choo-Choo" Brackins (Dallas Lincoln and Prairie View) became the first black quarterback drafted by the NFL when he was taken in the sixteenth round by the Green Bay Packers.

1955—Houston Wheatley won its sixth straight basketball state championship.

1956—Yates won the first PVIL state championship in baseball.

June 30, 1961—The first PVIL-sponsored East-West all-star football game was held in Beaumont.

Nov. 23, 1961—Yates defeated Houston Wheatley 21–15 before forty thousand fans in the teams' annual Thanksgiving Day game.

1964—The Texas African American Coaches Association, forerunner of the PVILCA, was created, with Don Grace as executive director.

1965—The University Interscholastic League's Legislative Council voted to remove the stipulation that its member schools must be "white," paving the way for a merger with the PVIL.

Apr. 30, 1966—An overflow crowd of more than seven thousand fans watched Reginald Robinson of Wichita Falls Washington run a wind-aided 9.1 100-yard dash at the PVIL state track meet at Prairie View.

Fall 1966—San Antonio Wheatley became the first former PVIL school to play football in the UIL.

1967—The UIL integrated, allowing black public schools to compete against their white counterparts for district honors.

Spring 1967—Five NFL teams chose former PVIL players as their first draft picks. Ironically, this year was the first since 1940 that the PVIL would not have a football season. The drafted players were:

- Bubba Smith (Beaumont Hebert, Michigan State), taken as the first overall choice in the draft, by the Baltimore Colts.
- Mel Farr (Beaumont Hebert, UCLA), chosen seventh overall, by the Detroit Lions.
- Gene Washington (Baytown Carver, Michigan State), chosen eighth overall, by the Minnesota Vikings.
- Gene Upshaw (Robstown, Texas A&I), chosen seventeenth overall, by the Oakland Raiders.
- Willie Ellison (Lockhart Carver, Texas Southern), chosen thirty-third overall, in the second round by the Los Angeles Rams, who did not have a first-round pick.

Spring 1967—San Antonio Wheatley became the first former PVIL school to compete at the UIL state track meet. Wheatley scored 44 points and finished second to Odessa Ector (54 points).

Jan. 30, 1968—The first black college quarterback to be drafted in the NFL's first round was Tennessee State's Eldridge Dickey, who had played at Houston Washington. The Oakland Raiders took Dickey ahead of Alabama's Ken Stabler, Oakland's second-round pick.

Mar. 8, 1968—Lubbock Dunbar became the first all-black team to play in the UIL state basketball tournament. Dunbar defeated Seguin 89–72 in the semifinals, but lost in the 3A title game to Richardson Lake Highlands 51–49.

Mar. 10, 1968—In its first year in the UIL state basketball tournament, Houston Wheatley beat Dallas Jefferson 85–80 for the Class 4A state championship. It was Wheatley's thirteenth state basketball championship.

1968—Quarterback Dwain Frazier (Houston Elmore) threw for 588 yards against Aldine Carver. His performance remained a state record for eighteen years.

1970—The PVIL closed.

Dec. 1976—Beaumont Hebert defeated Gainesville 35–7, becoming the first historically black school to win a UIL 3A state football championship.

Feb. 29, 1980—A "roast and toast" banquet was held in honor of Coach Ben Young at Bill Howard's club in Waco.

July 23, 1980—The first PVIL Hall of Fame and Hall of Honor banquet was held in Houston.

July 1982—Andrew "Pat" Patterson (Yates) became the first coach from the PVIL elected to the Texas High School Coaches Association Hall of Honor.

Dec. 1985—Yates defeated Odessa Permian 37–0 to become the first historically black high school to win the UIL Class 5A state championship in football.

Dec. 12, 2001—The UIL honored the PVIL in Austin.

2005—The Texas African American Coaches Association became the PVIL Coaches Association (PVILCA), with Robert Brown assuming duties as the organization's chairman.

May 9, 2005—The PVILCA met with Prairie View A&M president George Wright to discuss full recognition of all PVIL records.

May 13, 2005—The PVILCA met with UIL athletic director Charles Breithaupt and University of Texas vice president James L. Hill to discuss full recognition of all PVIL records. Later that year, the UIL began recognizing PVIL state championship records alongside all UIL records.

# Select Bibliography

## BOOKS

Allen, Bertram Leon. *The History and Memory of Old Anderson High School, 1907–1970*. Bertram L. Allen, 1988.
———. *Texas Black High School Sports, before 1967*. Bertram L. Allen, 1991.
Boudreaux, Tommie D., and Alice M. Gatson. *African Americans of Galveston*. Arcadia, 2013.
Cashion, Ty. *Pigskin Pulpit: A Social History of Texas High School Football Coaches*. Texas State Historical Association, 1998.
Day, Walter. *Remembering the Past with Pride: Organized High School Football for Blacks in Texas*. Walter Day, 1993.
Dent, Jim. *The Kids Got It Right*. Thomas Dunne, 2013.
Garrison, Rita. *Big Bubba: The Life of Charles "Bubba" Smith*. Rita Garrison, 2012.
Hawthorne, Bobby. *University Interscholastic League: An Illustrated History of 100 Years of Service*. University Interscholastic League.
Hudson, Frankie. *Where R All My Fans?* Frankie Hudson, 2012.
Lattin, David. *Slam Dunk to Glory*. White Stone Books, 2006.
Lewis, Dwight, and Susan Thomas. *A Will to Win*. Cumberland, 1983.
Luke, Bob. *Willie Wells: "El Diablo" of the Negro Leagues*. University of Texas Press, 2007.
McMurray, Bill. *Texas High School Football*. Icarus.
Norwood, Stephen H. *Real Football: Conversations on America's Game*. University Press of Mississippi, 2004.
Patoski, Joe Nick. *Texas High School Football: More Than the Game*. Bob Bullock Texas State History Museum, 2011.
Robins, Thurman W. *Requiem For a Classic: Thanksgiving Turkey Day Classic*. AuthorHouse, 2015.

Shabazz, Amilcar. *Advancing Democracy: African Americans and the Struggle for Access and Equity in Higher Education in Texas.* University of North Carolina Press, 2004.

Sherrod, Rick. *Texas High School Football Dynasties.* History Press, 2013.

Stratton, Florence. *The Story of Beaumont.* Hercules Publishing and Printing, 1925.

Taylor, Otis. *Otis Taylor: The Need to Win.* Sports Publishing, 2003.

Texas Education Agency. *Texas Public Schools Sesquicentennial Handbook, 1854–2004.* tea.texas.gov/index4.aspx?id=6499.

Woolfolk, George Ruble. *Prairie View: A Study in Public Conscience, 1878–1946.* Pageant, 1962.


ARTICLES, PERIODICALS, AND OTHER SOURCES

Anderson Alumni Association. "Seven Years of Yellow Jackets Greatness, 1955–1961." Unpublished manuscript; copy in author's possession.

Brooks, Gabriel. "Why the Region Has Won 46 State Championships since 1964 after Winning Only Two before Then." *Marshall News Messenger,* December 18, 2011.

Coleman, Adam. "Historical Houston High School Athletics Programs Have Roots in PVIL." *Houston Chronicle,* August 12, 2016.

Complete All-Time Playoff Brackets. Pigskinprep.com.

*Fred Moore High School: It's More than Just a Game.* DVD, Denton Public Library.

Harwell, Debbie Z. "William S. Holland: A Mighty Lion at Yates High School." *Houston History,* December 2010.

History of the City of Orange. orangetexas.net/about-orange/orange-history.

Hornsby, Alton. "Negro Education in Texas, 1865–1917." Master's thesis, University of Texas, 1962.

Humphrey, James "Bo." Oral history interview by Adrienne Cain, February 8, 2013. Houston Public Library Digital Archives, Gregory School. digital.houstonlibrary.net/oral-history/james-humphrey_OHGS0057.php.

Lone Star Football Network. lsfn.net/index.asp.

Lopez, John P. "A League of Their Own." Houston Chronicle, September 27, 1992.

Luberto, D. Keith. "The Integration Movement: Texas High School Athletic and Academic Contests." *Journal of Sport and Social Issues,* May 1994.

Lufkin Panther Sports. lufkinpanthersports.invisionzone.com/index.php?/topic/4476-lufkin-dunbar.

Montgomery County, Texas, Schools. countygenweb.com/txmontgomery /schools.htm.

*Negro Education in Texas, 1934–1935.* Bulletin of the State Department of Education, no. 343, March 1935.

Newspapers.com.

*Orange Leader.* "Wallace High School Mentor Has Built Up Remarkable Record with His Teams." February 13, 1949. Available at texashistory .unt.edu/ark:/67531/metapth308796/m1/7/zoom/print/?resolution=3& lat=5993&lon=2061.

Portal to Texas History. texashistory.unt.edu.

Sawyer, Amanda. "A. J. Moore High School." Waco History, wacohistory.org /items/show/22.

Texarkana Dunbar, Class of 1959. dunbartexarkana.org/index.html.

Texas High School Football History. texashighschoolfootballhistory.com /won-loss_records.html.

*Texas Standard.* Texas State Teachers Association.

Texas State Historical Association. tshaonline.org.

Texas State Historical Association. "Education for African Americans." tshaonline.org/handbook/online/articles/kde02.

Texas Tech University. Southwest Collections/Special Collections Library. Oral History Collection, *Damon Hill.*

Waits, Tim. "Temple Dunbar's PVIL Championships Shouldn't Be Forgotten." *Temple Daily Telegram,* February 8, 2009. tdtnews.com/archive /article_f006bda3-e88f-5905-a895-71d97cdaf1b4.html?mode=jqm.

Wilbanks, Billy. "Texas High School Football Hall of Fame." March 27, 2013. drbillywilbanks.com/txfootball/football-hall-of-fame.pdf.

# Index

Harvey, John, 59
Haskins, Dan, *photo*, 197–183, 228
Hayes, Bob "Bullet", 67, 69, 71
Hayes, Joe, 217
Hayes, Lester, 44, 158
Haynes, Abner, 51
Hebert, Larry, 187
Hebert, Usan, 119
Hebert High School (Beaumont),
    3, 37–38, 46, 51–52, 55, 66, 114–
    115, 119–120, 122–123, 125–132,
    134, 142–143, 168, 189, 216,
    226–227, 232
Heisman Trophy, 41, 87, 169, 175, 230
Henderson, Arthur Ray, 51
Henderson, Thomas "Hollywood," 59
Henderson, Tillman, 166
Herskowitz, Mickey, 2
Hickey, Red, 43
Hicks, Roy, 135
Hicks, Vernon, 99
Hicks, W. K., 51
Hill, Damon, 51, 88–91
Hill, James, 93, 232
Hill, Jimmy, 44
Hill, Lovette, 137
Hill, Winston, 51, 66, 69
Hillard, Jim, 222, 223
Hilliard High School (Bay City), 68,
    85–86, 88, 183, 217, 227
Hillsboro Peabody. *See* Peabody High
    School (Hillsboro)
historically black colleges, 6, 31–32,
    41–42, 54, 98, 129
Holland, Ed, 51
Holland, Herman, 34
Holland, William, 143–144, 148, 156
Hollie, Raymond, 81, 207, 208, 210,
    213, 214, 215
Hood, John Bell, 15
Horton, Roy, 59, *photo*
Houston, Ken, 21, 38, 40, 42, 51

Houston Independent School
    District, 3, 72, 140, 189, 191
Houston Oilers, 66–67, 69–72,
    76–77, 82
Houston riot of 1917, 5, 173–174
Houston's Sam Houston. *See* Sam
    Houston High School (Houston)
Houston Washington. *See* Booker
    T. Washington High School
    (Houston)
Houston Wheatley. *See* Phillis
    Wheatley High School (Houston)
Houston Yates. *See* Jack Yates High
    School (Houston)
Hubbard, Ellis, 11, 12–14, 19, 22
Hughes, Eddie, 151
Hughes, Langston, 26
Humphrey, Bo, 55, 113, 122, 142, 150,
    197
Hunt, Ed, 224, 226
Hunt, Lamar, 47
Hunter, James, 204–205
Huntsville Sam Houston. *See* Sam
    Houston High School (Huntsville)
Huston-Tillotson College, 8, 34,
    *photo*, 180
Hutchins, Roy, 133

I. M. Terrell High School (Fort
    Worth), 8, 32, 34, 51, 92, 143, 173,
    189, 202–207, 224–225, 230
Iglehart, Floyd, 78, 137–138, 217
Irving, Levis, 193, 218

Jackson, Aaron, 158
Jackson, Alvin, 210
Jackson, Andrew Webster, 84. *See
    also* A. W. Jackson High School
    (Rosenberg)
Jackson, Frank, 31
Jackson, Lonnie, 58
Jackson, Noah, 210